GEORGE SAVAGE

FRENCH DECORATIVE ART
1638–1793

Allen Lane The Penguin Press

Copyright © George Savage, 1969

First published in 1969

Allen Lane The Penguin Press
Vigo Street, London W1

SBN 7139 0054 7

Designed by John Douet

Printed in Great Britain by
W. & J. Mackay & Co. Ltd, Chatham

Frontispiece:

Part of a room at Osterley Park decorated with fitted
Gobelins tapestry, designed by Boucher in 1775.
The *canapé* and *fauteuils* are covered with tapestry woven
en suite. The carpet is by Moore of London.

Contents

List of Plates

The illustrations are reproduced by courtesy of the following owners to whom my grateful thanks are due.

British Museum 88, 98 Charlottenburg, Berlin 9 Christie, Manson & Woods Ltd 20–22, 28, 29, 39, 63, 68, 85 Dorotheum, Vienna 7 Paul Getty, Esq. 30 Mrs Diana Imber 95, 96 Metropolitan Museum, New York 24 Musée de la Ferronerie, Rouen 87 Musée du Louvre 93 The National Trust 52 Parke-Bernet Galleries, New York 26, 64, 77, 78, 84, 110 Smithsonian Institute, Washington 94 Sotheby & Co. 19, 40, 48, 49, 61, 62, 82, 90, 91 Victoria and Albert Museum 3, 12–18, 41–7, 50, 51, 53–5, 59, 60, 75, 76, 92, 97, 100–9, 111, 112 Wallace Collection 1, 2, 4, 10, 11, 23, 25, 27, 31–8, 56–8, 65, 66, 69–74, 79–81, 83, 86, 89.

Preface

Those of us whose acquaintance with modern French taste in interior decoration is limited to hotels (using the word in its modern sense), or to a casual inspection of the stock of a provincial *palais d'ameublement*, could be forgiven for concluding that French genius in this field was a thing of the past. The truth is that modern French taste is certainly no worse than popular taste in England; it is merely bad in a different way. Mercifully we cease to react to our day-to-day surroundings, but new horrors still have power to shock.

However, the French genius which manifested itself between the building of Versailles and the Revolution influenced the whole of Europe in its day, and it still dominates the great sale-rooms of the world. Wherever a sumptuous interior is commissioned regardless of expense, either for private pleasure or national prestige, the decorator nearly always turns to eighteenth-century France. This was a unique phase in the history of the decorative arts, and the essential collaboration between patrons, dealers, and craftsmen is hardly likely to recur in the foreseeable future. It was a period when taste was almost instinctively of an elegance which hardly had a parallel in former times, and certainly not since then. It was an age when men spent as they had rarely spent before on the manifold arts of display, often ruining themselves to surpass their neighbours.

Unfortunately there is little left in France, apart from museum collections and a few *châteaux*, to serve as a guide to French interiors of earlier times. The palace of Versailles would surely have been the most splendid of European showpieces had it survived intact, but it was largely stripped of its movables by the Revolutionaries, and, in consequence, American and English collections are in some ways richer than those of France. What remains, however, is still an unsurpassed essay in the Grand Manner, even though it lacks those things which formerly gave it life.

It is not easy to find accurate equivalents for many (perhaps most) of the French terms used in describing the decorative arts. The student of the language soon discovers the existence of a category of words termed 'false friends' because, despite their resemblance to English words, the meaning is different. The dictionary will also prove to be a false friend. For instance, it defines a *commode* as a chest of drawers, which it is, but only in a very limited sense; an *armoire* cannot be accurately translated by 'wardrobe'; *ébéniste* does not mean precisely a cabinet-maker; nor is a *menuisier* solely a carpenter. The imprecision arises principally from differences of origin and evolution, and it is important to make the distinction. In describing English furniture of the eighteenth century there is a point at which the chest of drawers becomes a *commode*, and it is often thus described because there is no adequate English word. For this reason, therefore, French terms have been employed here rather than approximate English ones, although each has been explained for the benefit of the reader to whom the subject is new.

The book is intended to be an introduction to a field in which information in English designed for the general reader and the collector is conspicuously absent. Its purpose is to help the reader who is not well-acquainted with the subject to derive enjoyment from visits to French museums and *châteaux*, and to make the acquisition of greater knowledge easier. There are a number of scholarly works available in English, notably those of Pierre Verlet and Francis Watson, which are essential to those who wish to pursue the subject in more detail. These are listed in the Bibliography.

It has been said, with truth, that every man has two countries – his own and France – which is perhaps the greatest tribute which could be paid to the pervasion of French art and culture. To those who want to study the objects discussed at first-hand without crossing the Channel, the Wallace Collection in London is perhaps the finest assemblage to be found anywhere outside the borders of France itself, and it is rarely approached in that country. The Jones Bequest at the Victoria and Albert Museum, and the *boudoir* of Mme de Sérilly, are essential to the study of the subject. Outside London, Waddesdon Manor (now belonging to the National Trust and open to the public) houses the Rothschild Collection, of which a catalogue in ten volumes is in course of preparation. Many English country houses contain fine examples of the objects described in this book, often acquired by purchase or royal gift in the eighteenth century. Two of them are Goodwood House and Woburn Abbey.

In the United States, the Wrightsman Collection of the Metropolitan Museum of Art, New York, and the collections of the Boston Museum of Fine Arts and the Philadelphia Museum of Art are notable. There are also objects worth studying in Detroit, Cleveland, Chicago, and San Francisco. The Henry E. Huntington Library and Art Gallery, San Marino, and the J. Paul Getty Museum, Malibu, both in southern California, have important material.

London/Lodève, 1968   G.S.

Versailles and the French Court Style

It is essential to begin by outlining the social climate in which the French Court style in the decorative arts developed. Unlike England, where royal influence was rarely of much importance, the course of art in France after the Renaissance owes so much to royal patronage that it cannot be separated from the fortunes of the royal house. In these pages we shall discuss a span of nearly one hundred and fifty years – the reigns of three kings and a regency. It will be an account of the rise of French decorative art to an eminence never since seriously challenged.

During the period mentioned we can recognize four principal styles, three of which are usually designated by the names of the kings in whose reigns they developed – Louis Quatorze (1638–1715, acceded 1643), Louis Quinze (1710–74), and Louis Seize (1754–93). The Regency of the duc d'Orléans occupied the years between the accession of Louis Quinze and his majority in 1723.

These broad classifications are useful, but not entirely accurate. We can, for instance, trace three fairly distinct phases of the Louis Quatorze style. The style of the Regency was largely one of transition between a movement which had already begun in the later years of the reign of Louis Quatorze and the development of the rococo style during the first part of the reign of Louis Quinze. The style often called 'Louis Seize' began about fifteen years before his accession to the throne and is itself divisible into two fairly distinct parts, the second of which began about 1780 and continued until the Revolution, the later phase being more the product of the influence of Marie-Antoinette and the King's two brothers, the comte d'Artois and the comte de Provence (later Charles X and Louis XVIII respectively) than of the King himself.

The styles of France during this period may be divided into two well-marked and fairly distinctive categories. The first of these is best called the 'French Court style' in recognition of the decisive part played in its evolution by Versailles. The second is usually termed 'Provincial' to denote the fact that the style associated with it developed outside Paris, although it was influenced to a varying degree by the capital – an influence which fluctuated according to local connexions with the Court, the distance from Paris, and the state of communications at the time. Southern France, for instance, separated from the North by the Massif Central which was relatively difficult to traverse, was far less affected by metropolitan styles than Normandy or the Loire.

For the most part Provincial furniture often retained elements of the Louis Treize period (1601–43) and tended to be the work of the *menuisier* rather than the *ébéniste*.★ Paris fashions were adopted tardily, but they persisted in the provinces beyond their metropolitan currency, giving rise to often complex problems of dating. Generally, however, it is reasonably safe to assume that very little Provincial furniture is as early as the style of ornament appears to suggest.

The French Court style began with the building of Versailles by Louis Quatorze. The King's accession came at a time of greatly increasing prosperity and of rapid growth in expenditure on the arts generally. This had, by the end of the century, assumed unprecedented proportions, and Dr Martin Lister – later physician to Queen Anne – who was in Paris in 1698, wrote in his *Journal*:

As the Houses are magnificent without, so the Finishing within side and Furniture answer in Riches and Neatness, as with Hangings of Rich Tapestry raised with Gold and Silver Threads, Crimson Damask, and Velvet Beds, or of Gold and Silver Tissue. Cabinets and Bureaus of Ivory inlaid with Tortoiseshell, and Gold and Silver plates in a 100 different manners [a reference to the cabinets of André-Charles Boulle and his followers]: Branches and Candlesticks of Crystal [i.e. rock-crystal]; but above all most rare Pictures. The Gildings, Carvings, and Paintings of the Roof [i.e. ceiling] are admirable. . . . You can come into no private house of any Man of Substance but you see something of them: and they are frequently observed to ruine themselves in these Expenses. Here as soon as ever a Man gets anything by Fortune or Inheritance he lays it out in some such way as now named.

Two especially noteworthy art-collectors of the early years of the new reign were the Finance Minister, Nicolas Fouquet, and Giulio Mazarini – Cardinal Mazarin. Fouquet, who died in 1680, acquired an enormous fortune largely by fraud, and he was finally arrested and imprisoned for life. Louis's Chief Minister, Mazarin, acquired his own fortune in circumstances hardly less creditable, but he did much to influence the young King's tastes in the direction of art-patronage. Mazarin was also an art-dealer on a notable scale, maintaining an ecclesiastical purchasing-agent in Italy.

Mazarin's death in 1661 may be regarded as the opening of the phase of French decorative art with which we are here principally concerned. The King announced that he would henceforward govern France in person, but the success of his policies was in great part due to the abilities of his chosen instrument, Jean-Baptiste Colbert (1619–83), Finance Minister of genius. As he lay dying Mazarin had said to the King, 'Sire, to you I owe everything, but I believe I repay part of the debt by leaving you Colbert'. But, as Voltaire remarks of Colbert's founding of the Academy of Architecture in 1671, 'A Vitruvius is not enough; one must

2   ★ These terms are more fully defined on page 59. A *menuisier* is approximately equivalent to a worker in solid wood, usually with additional carved work, and an *ébéniste* to one who employs veneers (*placage*).

have an Augustus to employ him'. This latter-day Augustus was Louis Quatorze, who was to prove not only a man of taste but a patron of the arts on an almost unprecedented scale (at least since the days of the Roman Empire), and he imposed his ideas on the art of his time.

The developments which followed the King's assumption of personal power demanded money in vast quantities. This, Colbert, who became Chief Minister in 1661, set himself to supply. Almost at once he began to re-form the financial structure, imprisoning dishonest administrators and forcing the *fermiers-généraux* (tax-farmers) to disgorge some of their immense profits. We shall return later to the *fermiers-généraux* to examine the part they played in the development of French art during the eighteenth century. They purchased from the King the right to collect certain taxes which made money immediately available to the King's Treasury without the bother of collecting it. They recouped themselves by extortions which earned them the hatred of the taxpayer, and they spent heavily in decorating their *hôtels* (i.e. town mansions), and *châteaux* (country houses).

It was to Colbert that the King turned for the vast sums necessary to finance the building and furnishing of Versailles, estimated to be in excess of one hundred and fifty million pounds of today's money, and the problem of supply was solved by organizing the arts on a national scale. Both Louis and Colbert intended that art should reflect the glory of France. Colbert founded a kind of Fine Arts Commission in 1663 and the Academy of Architecture already mentioned in 1671, but the most important development was the establishment of the *Manufacture royale des meubles* de la Couronne*, which started with the acquisition of the Gobelins tapestry-weaving enterprise for the King. To this was added the carpet-weaving factory of La Savonnerie (so called because it was housed in a disused soap-factory), which was followed by the organization of facilities for manufacturing objects of all kinds suitable for furnishing the royal palaces. Numerous subsidies were granted to existing factories for the same purpose, notably to the tapestry-looms of Beauvais and to various cloth-making enterprises.

Colbert placed the new *Manufacture* under the general direction of the painter Charles Le Brun in 1663, and the output included painting and sculpture, as well as almost every conceivable variety of decorative art. This, however, was far from an unmitigated expense to the Crown. Even as late as the period of the Revolution in 1793 exports from the royal enterprises were worth three million *livres* annually.†

---

* The word *meuble* means, literally, 'movable'. It refers to all the movable furnishings of the house. The house itself is often called an *immeuble* (i.e. immovable). This distinction is an important one. Later we shall see that some items of furniture, such as *console* tables (page 60), were in effect *immeubles*.

† Since prices in *livres* will frequently be quoted elsewhere it is desirable to make some estimate of its present-day value. From 1726 onwards (i.e. after the inflation

3

Charles Le Brun (1619–90) had been the precocious pupil of Simon Vouet who, at the age of fifteen, had painted a history picture for Cardinal Richelieu. After a visit to Italy, where he came under the influence of Poussin, he was given numerous commissions, among them the decoration of the *château* of Vaux-le-Vicomte for Nicolas Fouquet. Mazarin presented him to Anne of Austria, and Louis entrusted him with the decoration of the Galerie d'Apollon at the Louvre.★ A man of vast energies, he was given the task of painting some of the principal parts of Versailles, including the ceiling of the Galerie des Glaces, the largest painted surface existing in France, which represents allegorically the history and triumphs of Louis's reign. He was also responsible for the paintings in the adjoining Salon de la Paix and the Salon de la Guerre at either end. As the King's chief painter he worked at Saint-Germain, Sceaux, and Marly, and as director of the *Manufacture royale* he prepared cartoons for tapestries and designed furniture, goldsmiths' work, and wrought-ironwork, overseeing almost every detail of production. Le Brun in fact became virtual dictator of the arts in France, and his principal claims to fame lie in his abilities as an administrator, and as a designer and decorator. His paintings, to the taste of today, were academically conceived and pretentious in design, but this is a verdict which time may easily reverse.

In 1648 Le Brun had been concerned in the foundation of an Academy of Painting and Sculpture. Its origin was to some extent political, the intention being to free painting and sculpture from the influence of the Guilds and to raise the social status of those practising these arts. Similar Academies had already been founded in Italy, leaving the decorative arts to be organized by the Guilds. This was yet another stage in the divorce between the fine arts and the decorative arts which started in sixteenth-century Italy. Until then the artist had been a man of parts – architect, sculptor, goldsmith, designer, and painter – and painting was often the least regarded of his accomplishments. He maintained a workshop, employed assistants and took apprentices, and his signature was often little more than the trade mark of his establishment. Until the latter part of the sixteenth century the goldsmith, who was often a sculptor as well, had, after the architect, been the most highly valued artist, but the effect of the founding of Academies was to foster specialization, and to elevate the arts

---

of John Law) the rate of exchange was stabilized at 24 *livres* to the £ sterling. The *livre* was therefore worth approximately 10½d., a value quoted by Arthur Young in 1788. For a modern equivalent multiply by twelve – say approximately ten shillings. The gold *louis* after 1726 was worth approximately £1 in gold, say about £12 today.

★ Le Brun, in fact, never finished it. It was finally completed in 1851 by Félix Duban. Le Brun originally intended the figure of Apollo, from which it gets its name, to be allegorical of *le Roi Soleil* – the Sun King – but the present painting of Apollo and the Python is the work of Delacroix. The original designs for the Galerie were the work of Le Brun.

of painting and sculpture above those whose purpose was principally decorative. The evil effect of this divorce on the arts generally did not become fully apparent until the nineteenth century, when furniture, metalwork, and fabrics began to be made by machine in large quantities.

As director of the Academy of Painting Le Brun brought it into Colbert's organization, and a French Academy was founded in Rome for the training of young artists. These developments brought the arts generally almost completely under Colbert's domination, and therefore that of the King, and uniformity of taste was in great measure achieved throughout France, especially in the larger cities. Despite assertions to the contrary, however, this was by no means universal, and those unconnected with fashionable Court circles often remained largely unaffected, either from choice or necessity.

If corners of provincial France, in the South especially, resisted the new influences, they were accepted eagerly outside her borders. The princes of the German states built palaces in emulation of Versailles, French was the official language of much of Germany, and its rulers even took mistresses in emulation of the French King, apparently believing them to be an indispensable concomitant of the French Court style. In England, Charles II, at one time a fugitive in France, wanted to make Whitehall Palace another Versailles, but Parliament refused to vote the money and the plans were shelved. Had they been implemented Whitehall would have been a not unworthy rival, but the project was finally abandoned because of Dutch William's preference for Hampton Court, and the destruction of Whitehall by fire in 1698. The influence of Versailles eventually extended north to Prussia and Sweden and south to Italy. Even in the nineteenth century it was still potent. Ludwig II of Bavaria took Louis Quatorze as a model and created the Spiegelsaal at Herrenchiemsee at vast expense in imitation of the Galerie des Glaces.★

Architecture and the decorative arts during the Versailles period of the reign of Louis Quatorze, and virtually to the end of the Regency, were a French version of the Italian baroque style. The return to the classical style of Greece and Rome during the early years of the Renaissance had been accompanied by a renewal of interest in secular concerns and the progressive weakening of the power of the Roman Church, culminating in the Reformation. The development by the Jesuits of the baroque style in both architecture and interior decoration in Italy was primarily an attempt to strengthen the Church's hold on the people, and to this end the older classical styles were adapted in a manner calculated to impress the

---

★ A surprising instance of the influence of Versailles in the Far East is the Maison Carré, a pavilion in the grounds of the Yuan-ming-yuan (the Summer Palace) at Peking. This, designed by Père Castiglione, has characteristically baroque flights of steps, but the whole was incongruously decorated with a mixture of European and Chinese motifs calculated to appeal to the taste of the Emperor K'ang Hsi. A print of this subject dated 1786 is in the Bibliothèque Nationale in Paris.

5

untutored mind. In a sense, baroque is the art of the theatre back-cloth. To such distortions as the twisted column and the broken pediment were added vast flights of steps, the use of painted *stucco* to simulate marble, the representation of drapes in carved marble, the use of pillars which had no functional purpose, the apparent enlargement of interiors by *trompe l'œil* mural painting and elaborate ceiling-painting, and a profusion of rich colouring and gilding. In its secular form the richest baroque interiors are those we commonly refer to as being in the Grand Manner.

Baroque had its beginnings in Rome, and it is perhaps appropriate that its principal exponent also achieved a reputation as a theatre *impresario*. Evelyn wrote of Giovanni Lorenzo Bernini, who unsuccessfully submitted designs for extensions to the Louvre, that 'a little before my coming to the City [of Rome] he gave a public opera wherein he painted the scenes, cut the statues, invented the engines, composed the music, writ the comedy, and built the theatre'. Of Bernini's baldachin in Saint Peter's, done at the age of thirty-one, Evelyn writes that 'with the pedestal, crown, and statues above it [it forms] a thing of that art, vastness, and magnificence, as is beyond all that man's industry has produced'. Bernini often used techniques more suited to the theatre, mixing white and coloured marbles with bronze and *stucco*, and using coloured lights in the form of stained-glass windows as illumination.

The style needed to be adapted to its new purpose, but in the capable hands of Le Brun it developed into a symbol of national prestige and the absolute monarchy of Louis Quatorze. In the course of its translation from an ecclesiastical to a secular style the baroque of Italy assumed characteristics which were markedly French. The existing French tradition was mainly classical, and this tempered the excesses of the Italian style in the direction of plainer, more restrained exteriors and more dignified, slightly pompous, interiors. The strength of this tradition was probably the reason for the rejection of Bernini's designs for the Louvre in 1665, rather than the intrigues of the successful Perrault (page 151). Bernini executed a bust of the King and left Paris, remarking that if a Roman exterior had not been desired there was no reason why he should have been brought from Rome. From the time of this rejection the current of influence started to flow in the reverse direction, from Paris to Rome, culminating in Le Brun's election as President of the Academy of Saint Luke in 1675.

In any case the King was lukewarm towards the project for enlarging the Louvre, even though Colbert personally favoured it. Louis's preference for Versailles was a product of his minority when, during the insurrection of the Fronde, he had been forced several times to flee with his mother from Paris. He conceived a distaste for the capital which had treated him with such scant civility.

About 1624 Lemercier had built a hunting-lodge at Versailles for Louis Treize which forms part of the present edifice. At first the new King continued to use it as a hunting-lodge, as a venue for summer entertainments and *fêtes*, and as a place of assignation from which to conduct his liaison with Mlle de la Vallière, who was supplanted as the King's mistress by Mme de Montespan in 1667.

The first series of major additions and alterations were started in 1668 when Louis Le Vau, who died in 1670, added two wings to the original building. The architect who followed, Jules Hardouin-Mansart, added a storey to Le Vau's building and constructed the famous Galerie des Glaces in 1679, as well as the long south wing. The north wing was added in 1684. The longest façade is about 650 metres in length.

In Mansart's day as many as thirty-five thousand men, whose ranks were decimated by malaria, were employed on the work, which included elaborate water-gardens and fountains supplied by immense water-wheels on the Seine.

The completed palace was large enough for ten thousand people, and the King transferred his Court there in 1684. In 1698 Martin Lister referred to it as 'without dispute the most magnificent [palace] of any in Europe'. Adding, 'Yet what of it was first built and much admired 30 years ago is now no longer relisht. However, this the King intends to rebuild where it is faulty.'

Of the reign of Louis Quatorze, among the most illustrious of French monarchs, there is need to mention only a few events which bear upon our subject. In the fields of art and letters his reign was no less distinguished than the eighteenth century, although its greatest days had passed before the death of Colbert in 1683. Despite his own undoubted abilities as a statesman the King was severely handicapped by the loss of Colbert, and although Louis Quatorze was, perhaps, as worthy of being an absolute monarch as anyone who has ever occupied that position, his aspirations were far higher than his achievements. In his *Mémoires* he wrote:

. . . there shall be neither indigence nor beggary in my kingdom, nor anyone, however wretched, who shall not be assured of his daily bread, either through his own toil, or through the ordinary and regulated assistance of the State.

Manufacturing industry expanded enormously, and all the things once imported from Italy, Germany, Flanders, and England were now produced within the boundaries of France.★ Colbert fostered this increase in production and demanded that the quality should be good. He discontinued the collection of customs duties between the provinces and reduced the toll-houses on the roads. He improved communications, and constructed a canal through the Languedoc to join the Atlantic to the Mediterranean. The King presided over the fortnightly meetings of the

★ The last surviving factory built by Colbert, comprising factory-buildings, the director's house, and the houses of the workers, is to be found at Villeneuvette in the Languedoc.

Council of Commerce. The French mercantile fleet, as well as the navy, was greatly enlarged, and the Compagnie des Indes was established in 1654.

But the King's reign was marred by numerous wars, and by the Revocation of the Edict of Nantes in 1685. The first largely nullified the efforts of the King and his Ministers to bring prosperity to France, and the second, by driving the Huguenots abroad, deprived France of many of her best craftsmen who had been extensively employed by Colbert.

Of the King's mistresses, the two most worthy of mention are Mme de Montespan and Mme de Maintenon. The first attracted the King's attention in 1667, and bore him eight children, who were legitimized after the death of his offspring by the Queen. His natural sons, the duc de Maine and the comte de Toulouse, were declared heirs to the throne in default of princes of the blood. Mme de Maintenon was governess to Mme de Montespan's children. The King eventually married her morganatically in 1685 after the death of the Queen. The most surprising aspect of her character was a severely moral outlook, and she exerted considerable political influence. After the King's death she retired to a home for poor girls of good family which she had established at Saint-Cyr. Her connexion with the Jesuits has sometimes been advanced as the reason for her interest in the Revocation of the Edict of Nantes, but there is no good reason to assume that she did more than approve it.

The last years of the reign of Louis Quatorze were troubled by wars and economic difficulties which made him extremely unpopular, and his death in 1715 was little regretted. The strictness of etiquette at his Court and his unvarying insistence on protocol, had combined to produce an irksome restraint which its members were only too pleased to throw off.

II

Philippe, duc d'Orléans (1674–1723), was, according to his own statement, entrusted by the dying King with the task of ruling France as Regent. He assumed the Regency at the age of forty-one with a life of debauchery behind him. Despite this he was a kindly man of considerable personal charm, widely read and cultivated, with unusual skill as a negotiator. Although he was, like so many of his contemporaries, a willing victim of Law's wild-cat schemes (later to be discussed) he was in other ways a competent and efficient administrator, popular with the people whose interests he had at heart. Law's schemes had no historical precedent by which they could be tested, and no doubt those who resisted them did so from an innate conservatism rather than from any real insight into their ultimate effect. The new Regent had the common touch, employing the picturesque language of the people in the Council Chamber when he thought it would serve his purpose, although he could adopt a regal air when occasion demanded it. Gossip that he wanted to supplant the new

King on the throne of France seems to have been entirely without foundation, and was certainly never apparent in his actions. Suggestions that he attempted to poison the youthful Louis are equally baseless. Of his administration during a very difficult period, it may be said that it revealed a talent for statecraft which, in more favourable circumstances, might have placed him among France's more distinguished rulers. Perhaps the worst that can be said is that, unlike Louis Quatorze, he too easily trimmed his sails to the prevailing wind, and his promises were unreliable.

'The Regency', wrote Michelet, 'is a whole century compressed into eight years.' Certainly it was a period of economic and social revolution of a kind almost without precedent. Vast improvements in communications were started, free education was established, and – a more dubious benefit – the art of accountancy began to flourish.

How dubious was the last benefit may be seen from the use made of it by John Law, an expatriate Scot, whose theories, rejected in England, coloured the financial structure of the whole of the eighteenth century, although they will seem not unfamiliar today. Law first appeared in Paris towards the end of 1707, and at this time he had already closely studied the system of the Dutch bankers. Louis Quatorze, more perceptive than the Regent, instructed the police to accelerate his departure, but the duc d'Orléans was fatally attracted to his ideas, which were, fundamentally, the extension of trade by the indiscriminate creation of credit.

When the King died the Treasury was empty and Government securities discredited. The Regent was compelled to peg the value of money in circulation, but the Regency Council, with rare perceptiveness, decisively rejected the introduction of paper money on the ground that the Government would be certain to abuse it!

A number of reforms designed to stimulate trade were introduced, one of them being a reduction of the *taille*, a form of property tax, and an attempt was made to squeeze the financiers. But this proved to be a generally unpopular measure, not only with the squeezed but with the public at large, and it was soon seen to be disastrous to trade.

When the effect of these measures became apparent new expedients were tried, and Law was given an opportunity to put his theories into practice. His methods included the issue of paper money, and he undertook to redeem the securities of the previous reign at a discount of eighty per cent. Money became cheap, trade flourished, and prices actually fell.

The Bank established by Law to carry on these undertakings was not obliged to retain a fixed gold reserve to cover a percentage of its note issue, and notes were issued wildly in excess of the reserve. Spurred on by the Regent, who spent the newly-printed money lavishly, inflation flourished, and the situation became more precarious with the floating of the Mississippi Company to exploit concessions in French Louisiana. The chicanery with which the operations of financing this Company were

9

carried on does not here concern us. Suffice it to say that neither dishonest company promoters of today, nor twentieth-century governments, have much improved on the methods adopted.

The subsequent boom in the Company's stock, accelerated by fraudulent reports from America on its prospects, reached fantastic heights, and the subsequent crash was as much due to Law's Scots canniness as to any lack of confidence in the future on the part of his dupes. It was discovered that he was selling his own stock to purchase land.

By 1720 most of those who still preserved a shred of judgement were uneasy. Speculators were becoming bankrupt, and the Bank's paper was being offered at a discount for cash. Shares had been issued to a far greater value than the nebulous assets of the Company could support, and a point was eventually reached where it became an offence to hold more than a stipulated amount of coin. Ultimately, the choice was between shares which paid no dividend and paper which was worthless, and the use of gold and silver by goldsmiths had to be severely restricted because people were turning to objects made of the precious metals to preserve some of their fortune. Land and works of art rose in demand steadily and prices climbed steeply. Ultimately, even the possession of objects made by the goldsmith, and precious stones, became illegal, and the police were authorized to make house-to-house searches, seizing whatever they found.

Confidence had gone, however, and nothing could avert disaster. On 21 May 1720, Law declared himself bankrupt, and the Bank's securities and paper money were devalued by fifty per cent. The débâcle was complete, although a few of the more astute among the financiers turned it to good account and laid the foundation of large fortunes. Most people were impoverished, many were bankrupt, and on 13 December 1720, Law fled from Paris and found refuge in Venice, where he died in 1729.

The memory of Law's inflation has never been entirely erased from the minds of Frenchmen. Far more than any other European nation they prefer to trust objects of value, and gold and silver coin, rather than paper, and they have preserved a congenital distrust of banks and government financial policies. Strangely enough, however, the effects of Law's inflation were largely confined to individuals, and the country as a whole emerged stronger than before, especially in commerce, industry, and shipping.

The circumstances of the time were especially favourable to progress in the arts. Vast sums were available for spending, often among those to whom it had previously been scarce, and artists and craftsmen received their full share. The feverishness of the pursuit of wealth and pleasure brought a new and unwonted gaiety to the arts which will later be discussed, but perhaps one of the most potent influences was that inspiration no longer came from Versailles, but from Paris instead. Now the greatest spenders were not the nobility, but the financiers, the bankers, and the *fermiers-généraux* who were to become more influential as the century unfolded.

III

The auspices under which Louis Quinze began his reign were not especially favourable. As a child he was studious, and took delight in military exercises. He had many of the qualities essential to his great office, unlike his grandson who succeeded him, and he was introduced to affairs of state in 1720 when he first attended the deliberations of the Regency Council. He was crowned at Rheims when he reached his majority at the age of thirteen, and in 1725 he married Marie Leczinska, a Polish princess and daughter of Stanislas Leczinski, who had been driven out of his kingdom by Augustus the Strong, Elector of Saxony, and lived in exile at Weissenburg in Alsace. The new Queen gave birth to her first child, the Dauphin of France, in 1729.

Louis's first Minister was the licentious Cardinal Dubois, former tutor to the Regent, who aspired to be another Mazarin, and who, even in the short time he maintained himself in office, amassed a fortune of more than two million *livres*. His furniture, which was sold after his death, realized 800,000 *livres*. Of Dubois, Saint-Simon wrote:

He looked like a ferret and a prig. Duplicity was writ large on his face, and he made no attempt to cover up the looseness of his conduct. . . . He was a cringing flatterer, readily adopting any tone or playing any part to gain various ends he sought to attain.

The King was more fortunate in his second choice, his own former tutor, Cardinal Fleury, at one time Bishop of Fréjus, who was born in the small town of Lodève in the Languedoc. Fleury, appointed in 1726, had an extraordinary influence over the young King, and he was undoubtedly the most honest administrator of the reign. His policies restored credit and revived trade. The value of the *livre*, which had fluctuated wildly since the resounding crash which had followed Law's inflation, began to steady and the provinces grew richer. Soon a massive deficit had been turned into a surplus of fifteen million *livres*.

For a long time Louis continued faithful to the Queen against all temptations placed in his way by intriguing courtiers. To every attempt to awaken his interest elsewhere he would reply: 'I think the Queen more beautiful.' But Marie Leczinska was a homely girl, and no doubt he would, in the end, have tired of lack of variety, but the Queen, after bearing ten children in rapid succession, was persuaded to evade the King's attentions. According to contemporary gossip she made the excuse that it was a saint's day, and even the more prominent among the saints were sufficiently numerous to provide excuses for a good part of the year. But Marie even began to evoke minor saints whose days usually passed unnoticed, and the King turned to others more compliant, among whom the first of prominence in the social circles of the day was one of several sisters, the gawky comtesse de Mailly, affectionate and safely without ambition. She was temporarily supplanted by her sister, Mme de Vintimille, who died soon afterwards in childbirth leaving a son so much like the King that the Court called him the 'demi-Louis'. Mme de Mailly then regained her ascendancy and, with Mme de Charolais and the comtesse de Toulouse, organized the notorious supper-parties in the *petits appartements* at Versailles, to which a secret door in the wall of the King's bedroom gave access.

Meanwhile Fleury ruled France with wisdom, tolerance, and a strong desire for peace, and the King whiled away his days in the chase, for which he had conceived an obsession. Fleury's gravest fault was that he kept affairs of state in his own hands, and encouraged the King to a life of idleness and pleasure, only consulting him as a matter of form. For this reason Louis grew up with little of his great-grandfather's interest in affairs of state.

With time on his hands he turned his mind elsewhere. He bought and redecorated the *château* of Choisy, away from the prying and inquisitive eyes which surrounded him at Versailles, and here were the apartments of the reigning mistress. 'The delicate carving', wrote a contemporary, 'the gold and blue, the furniture and the wealth of beautiful mirrors, gave an atmosphere of elegant simplicity and fascination.' Another contemporary refers to the changes in architectural fashion that had taken place since the days of Louis Quatorze, of which Choisy and the *petits appartements* were early examples. Hitherto huge Salons and long galleries had been the general rule, but, starting in 1722 with the Palais-Bourbon, changes began which were to end in a fashion for smaller rooms, more specialized in their purposes. He goes on,

De Cotte, who died in 1735, was the first to put mirrors over our chimney-pieces. . . since then fireplaces turning on a pivot to heat two rooms have been in demand, and heating pipes which radiate a genial warmth have been invented [a kind of central heating], making those not in the secret think the weather has become warmer.

Of the fire-places turning on a pivot Maurepas tells of the wife of a *fermier-général*, who had one which opened into the house next door, of which she was the tenant, through which her lovers made entry and exit.

As the King's mistress the marquise de Tournelle had been preceded by the duchesse de Lauragais; both were sisters of Mme de Mailly. This curious situation attracted the attention of one contemporary versifier:

> *Amateur de la famille,*
> *Maître Louis de sa béquille*
> *Toutes les sœurs honorera.*
> *Cependant Monsieur le père*
> *Reste toujours en fourrière*
> *Avec tous ces honneurs-là.*★

12   ★ Collector of the family, Master Louis will treat all the sisters alike. But their father remains in the pound [he was being sued by his creditors] notwithstanding all these honours.

Of all the sisters, only Mme de Flavacourt resisted successfully.

The marquise de la Tournelle sought and acquired the title of duchesse de Châteauroux, and Mme de Mailly was dismissed with an annual pension of 40,000 *livres* and a mansion in the rue Saint-Thomas du Louvre, long since demolished. The new duchess was ambitious and interfered in affairs of state. She urged the King to place himself at the head of his troops during the War of the Austrian Succession, and wrote: 'The King is delighted, and I am almost wild with joy. I feel it is I who have won these battles.' Louis, however, became seriously ill at Metz, and although the duchess was in daily attendance at his bedside, the Bishop of Soissons found time to persuade the King, who thought his death to be imminent, to dismiss her. In fear for her life she took a coach for Paris, arriving after many dangers.

Public grief and apprehension were very real. Spontaneously the King was called Louis the Well-Beloved, and profound relief and rejoicing greeted the news of his convalescence.

In 1744 he made a triumphal entry into Paris, staying for several days to show himself to the people. Soon he was reconciled with the duchess, but before she could return to Court she died suddenly of fever, although rumour had it that she had been poisoned.

Now the stage was set for the entry of Mme de Pompadour (1721–64). After the death of the duchess the Court buzzed with speculation. Who, everyone was asking, would be her successor? Candidates were numerous. Court beauties busied themselves decking their charms, bathing and perfuming, lest opportunity catch them unaware. They swarmed to Versailles and scrambled to attract the attention of the King. Dignity was thrown to the winds, and each was the enemy of the other.

Among those who frequented the Court at this time was Jeanne-Antoinette Poisson, daughter of François Poisson of unsavoury reputation and Louise-Madeleine de la Motte. Her godfather was Paris de Montmartel, a financier, who was one of her father's employers. Her mother is reputed to have been one of the loveliest women in Paris, and rumours that Jeanne was really the daughter of Montmartel were not wanting, and were perhaps not without foundation. Another of Mme Poisson's lovers was the *fermier-général*, Le Normant de Tournhem, a director of the Compagnie des Indes, and this association seems to have been a lasting one. Eventually, at nineteen, the young Jeanne was married to his nephew Le Normant d'Etiolles, Director of Public Works, with a dowry amounting to 120,000 *livres* and a large house in Paris. To her husband, with whom she was much in love, she once remarked, 'I shall never leave you', adding, 'except, of course, for the King'.

The future Mme de Pompadour was educated at the Ursuline Convent at Poissy, where she was extremely popular, and when she was nine years old a fortune-teller predicted that she would become the King's mistress. This she did not forget in later years. In her account book she made the

13

entry: 'To Mme Lebon, who told me when I was nine that I should become the King's mistress, 600 *livres*.'

It was not long before Jeanne had succeeded in entering the circle which met in the *salon* of Mme Geoffrin, widow of a director of the Saint-Gobain glass factory. This was among the most civilized of the age, where writers and artists of distinction foregathered. She entertained at the *château* of Etiolles, to which many distinguished people came, among them Voltaire who was particularly charmed by her wit, grace, and good sense. It was not far from Etiolles to Versailles, and when a ball was held at Versailles on 24 February 1745, to celebrate the marriage of the Dauphin to the Infanta of Spain, the future marquise de Pompadour was among the company. Here she met the King who was disguised as a yew-tree, while Jeanne was a lovely Diana. Louis had acquired his new mistress.

The financiers in particular were delighted, for the aristocracy persisted in treating them as *parvenus*. The old nobility would have allowed to pass unnoticed a liaison with a girl from the labouring classes, but this was worse. Jeanne was a *bourgeoise*, and Louis met the first difficulty when, in due time, he wanted his new mistress to be presented at Court. The task was finally undertaken, ungraciously enough, by the Princesse de Conti in return for the King's promise to pay the old lady's gambling debts.

The Queen was not unfriendly. Jeanne expressed a sincere desire to please her, and Marie Leczinska remarked to one of her circle, 'Since there must be someone like her, I prefer her to another.'

Jeanne's dignity in a situation fraught with pitfalls on every side, which would have taxed the ingenuity of someone much more experienced, was at first commended. The Court did not begin to turn against her until she made her first mistake by procuring the dismissal of the Comptroller-General of Finance, Orry de Vignory. Orry was honest and capable but inflexible, and Jeanne yielded to pressure from her friends, the *fermiers-généraux*, who found him a nuisance. But the new Comptroller, Machault d'Arnouville, did not please them any better for much the same reasons, and Jeanne was eventually persuaded to procure his dismissal also.

The marquise was not above begging places for her friends, but rarely for those who were unworthy. Her most successful excursion into nepotism was the appointment she secured for her brother, Abel François Poisson, who became Directeur des Bâtiments in succession to Le Normant de Tournhem, and subsequently marquis de Marigny. He was efficient and extremely popular, and the most eminent artists of the day praised his enlightened patronage. The King himself invited the marquis to dine at a private dinner-party, with his sister as the only other guest, a rare honour, and soon Marigny was not undeservedly recognized as an arbiter of elegance who exercised great influence on the arts of his day.

Mme de Pompadour's new position was far from easy. Louis was prey to fits of depression. He detested etiquette and ceremony, and since the death of Fleury he had taken to spending hours on affairs of state.

To escape he climbed a secret stairway to Jeanne's apartment at Versailles where he could sit gazing over the lawns.

Jeanne acted in a small theatre with only fifteen seats which the King built for her, and here she displayed exceptional talent as an actress, singer and dancer. Later a larger theatre was built, where more ambitious productions were staged, the scenery and properties coming from the Menus-Plaisirs where everything necessary for royal *fêtes* and ceremonies was stored.

Jeanne's role as a patroness of the arts is what chiefly concerns us here. This has been disputed, but there seems little doubt that it was very great. In evidence we may adduce the fact that the style which predominated in the first part of the King's reign is often known in France as '*le style Pompadour*', which is perhaps an exaggeration, but entries in Duvaux's account-books referring to certain pieces of furniture as '*à la Pompadour*' cannot so easily be dismissed. The influential role she played in establishing the royal porcelain factory at Sèvres is equally certain, and she bought numerous houses, spending largely on remodelling and redecorating them. The first was at Crécy, where she founded a hospital and paid for its upkeep. The Hermitage at Versailles was a small house designed by Lassurance, her favourite architect, and decorated internally by Jacques Verberckt. She had a *château* at Versailles, and the *hôtel* d'Evreux in Paris, in the Elysée, the former designed by Lassurance and decorated by Verberckt. Both reverted to the King when she died. Of her other houses La Celle, Saint-Ouen, Bellevue, and Menars are the best known. Bellevue was near to the site of the porcelain factory at Sèvres, built on a height with magnificent views over Saint-Cloud and Paris.

Bellevue was the marquise's most important achievement, and she paid for it from her own purse. Those who contributed to its decoration included Oudry, Caffiéri, Boucher, Van Loo, Coustou, and Verberckt, with furniture supplied by the Court dealer, Lazare Duvaux. While at Bellevue she persuaded the King to transfer the porcelain factory from the fortress of Vincennes to the new site at Sèvres and to subsidize it. The marquise was the factory's best saleswoman, and the King himself took part, unpacking new production in the library at Versailles and selling it to members of the Court at enormous prices. The marquise persuaded Boucher to provide designs and models, and she plagued Machault for money to extend its activities. Much of its success was due to her interest and intervention.

Intimate relations with the King ended in 1751. For a long time Jeanne had contended with a temperament by nature frigid and this was worsened by the failing health which was to end in her premature death. But she and Louis remained close friends, and her influence actually strengthened with the passing of the years. She became increasingly involved in affairs of state, and the lampoons with which her enemies persecuted her multiplied. Soon the Court was divided into the party of

15

the Queen and the party of the marquise. Maurepas, whose dismissal she had secured, was especially scurrilous, alluding to her *bourgeois* origin, which was never forgotten, in obscene verses. '*Catin subalterne*' (subordinate prostitute) was one of the least of his insults. But her influence was widely recognized, and in the sphere of the arts we first hear the description '*à la Pompadour*', which occurs in Duvaux's account-books.

The charge that she found new partners for the King is probably false, and the suggestion that she helped to organize the notorious Parc-aux-Cerfs without foundation. This – the Deer Park – was, according to popular rumour, where girls of plebeian origin were taken to be prepared for the King's bed. They were, it was said, dressed, perfumed, and taught how to behave and what would be expected from them. The Deer Park, however, has been the subject of much exaggeration, both as to the number of girls who passed through it, and the orgies said to have taken place there. It probably existed as a small *maison de convenance* where the King entertained mistresses of a day who were well rewarded for their services.

In 1757 the comte de Stainville, created duc de Choiseul, took office as the King's Chief Minister. Choiseul, one of the marquise's *protégés*, was immensely rich in consequence of a marriage to one of her friends, the daughter of the banker Crozat, but, despite an exceptionally acute intellect, he was unwise enough to quarrel with the Dauphin, which led to his downfall. Choiseul was a patron of the arts on a large scale, and a record survives of the appearance of his house in the decoration of the well-known '*boîte Choiseul*' which shows his bedroom. Another snuff-box in the Louvre shows the same room at a later date.

The marquise's health began seriously to decline during the last years of her life. Always frail, she had become progressively weaker with the passing years. To her life was always a struggle, and she rouged and powdered to cover the wasting effects of her illness. She spent long hours lying on a *chaise-longue* at the foot of her bed, and at Versailles a chair-lift was installed to take her to the upper floor when she was no longer strong enough to climb the stairs.

After a severe haemorrhage from the lungs in February 1764 the King showed great anxiety and solicitude, visiting her almost daily. On 7 April in the same year she collapsed. She knew that the end was near. On 15 April, in the afternoon, she received Choiseul and Soubise, and then asked to be left alone with her women and the *curé*. Later in the afternoon the *curé* prepared to leave. 'One moment, Monsieur *le curé*,' she called, 'and we will leave together.'

A last flash of wit, and the most cultivated woman of the day was dead. Gossip tried to suggest that the King was unmoved, but it seems that he watched the melancholy funeral procession leave Versailles for Paris from a balcony. Tears rolled down his cheeks. 'That', he said to the valet who was with him, 'is the only respect I can pay her.'

Louis was left to the bosom of his family – to a wife of whom he had tired although affection still remained, to a straitlaced son and his wife, and to Mesdames, his elderly aunts, who led lives of irreproachable virtue. Mme de Pompadour was the only one of his mistresses who had not sought personal advantage, and who had loved the King as a man. Of her Voltaire wrote: 'Her lively gait became a regal carriage, her roguish glance became majestic, her voice acquired royal dignity, and her mind rose with her rank.' She could hardly have asked for more.

The Dauphin died soon afterwards, in 1765, of pulmonary tuberculosis. King Stanislas died in 1766. The Queen succumbed in the same year, and the King was profoundly shocked and moved by her death. He thought of remarrying but consoled himself with Mlle de Romans and a succession of unsatisfactory adventures. Then his valet met with the comte du Barry, who offered him a certain Mlle Lange, a former mistress. This was Jeanne Becu, whose putative father was a monk called Frère Ange.

Often underestimated is the part played by Jeanne Becu who, like Marie-Antoinette, influenced the course of the Court style during the latter part of the eighteenth century. She had become the mistress of the comte du Barry at the age of fifteen, and her origins made her presentation at Court a matter of difficulty. The King solved the problem by marrying her to the comte's brother, Guillaume, by which she became Marie-Jeanne Gomart de Vaubernier, the comtesse du Barry. Even then her début at Versailles in 1769 met with a great deal of opposition.

The King gave her the *château* of Louveciennes, near Marly and not far from Paris, which was reconstructed in the most fashionable style. Both Louveciennes and her apartment at Versailles were conspicuous for splendour in an age of magnificence. Her expenditure with the *ciseleur-fondeur* Pierre Gouthière (page 100) must alone have exceeded a million *livres*.

That Mme du Barry had the taste for ostentation which sometimes goes with a plebeian origin cannot be disputed, but, like the *fermiers-généraux*, who often came from the same social class, she had the wit to turn to the most fashionable artists of the day who were already working in the style associated with Louis Seize, employing Gouthière as her adviser. How well he performed what must, at the time, have been a congenial task may be deduced from the inventory of 1794, made after her execution for the heinous crime of 'having worn black for the death of the tyrant', which lists paintings by Watteau, Van Loo, Fragonard, Boucher, and Greuze, and sculptures by Pajou, Falconet, and Coysevox, as well as many pieces of furniture almost equalling in richness some of the finest of those which had graced the seventeenth century. Among the few things she had in common with Marie-Antoinette was a taste for furniture ornamented with plaques of Sèvres porcelain.

IV

The marriage between the new Dauphin, the King's grandson, and

Marie-Antoinette, daughter of Maria-Theresa, was intended to cement a *rapprochement* between the Houses of Habsburg and Bourbon. The ceremony took place at Versailles on 16 May 1770, the celebrations marred by a prodigious rainstorm. Her nuptial bed was sprinkled with holy water by the Archbishop of Rheims, but this does not seem to have been particularly efficacious, for the future Louis Seize wrote in his diary the next morning the single word, *Rien* – Nothing. Seven years were to pass before the Queen could, in a letter to her mother, announce a pregnancy. The Dauphin's impotence was an open secret, known alike to the Court and to the streets of Paris, and it was no doubt responsible for the defects of character which he displayed in later life, even when his disability had been overcome. Louis Seize did not share a taste for art-patronage with his illustrious predecessors. He was passionately fond of hunting, and spent a great deal of his leisure time practising the craft of the locksmith in which he acquired considerable proficiency.

Marie-Antoinette was more socially inclined. Except for a somewhat perversely exercised strength of will akin to obstinacy she might almost have been termed flighty. She enjoyed an endless round of pleasure-seeking, and she had her lovers, among them, it was rumoured, the English Ambassador, John Frederick Sackville, the third Duke of Dorset, who referred to her in his letters to England as 'Mrs B'.

After her placid existence at Schönbrunn, life at Versailles was not easy for Marie-Antoinette. The Court buzzed and hummed with intrigue confusing to a newcomer. There was, for instance, the comtesse du Barry, mistress of the aging Louis Quinze. Good-natured and well-meaning, Mme du Barry still found it difficult to tolerate the insult offered by the new Dauphine, who persistently and publicly ignored her. The King was compelled to intervene, and with great difficulty arranged an armed truce between the two women, but not before the quarrel had led to the brink of open rupture between Paris and Vienna, and had even threatened to degenerate into open war. Mme du Barry's triumph, a pyrrhic victory, was short-lived. It did not survive the King's death. Louis Quinze succumbed to smallpox in 1774, and the dying King sent his mistress to the nearby *château* of Rueil to await the end. On 10 May 1774, Marie-Antoinette became Queen of France.

Estrangement between the new King and his Queen was soon evident to the Court. Louis retired early to bed; the Queen followed her inclinations to the gaming-table or the ball. 'My tastes do not accord with those of the King', she wrote to a friend. 'He is only interested in hunting and mechanical things. . . .' But the King was tolerant and good-humoured, and he interfered little with his wife's pleasure-seeking. An open breach was avoided, and each went their own ways.

If the King went early to bed, his brother, the comte d'Artois, did not, and he accompanied the Queen on her nocturnal excursions and gambling frolics. His extravagances and hers titillated a public over-ready to be scandalized. Especially after the affair of the Queen's necklace, a *cause célèbre* which led to the imprisonment of the unfortunate Cardinal de Rohan in 1785, lampoons became more scurrilous, one naming thirty-four persons of both sexes with whom the Queen was alleged to have had improper relations, among them the comte d'Artois, and the ill-fated Princesse de Lamballe whose body was destined to be desecrated by the Paris mob, and whose head was triumphantly carried through the streets on a pike. Actors and lackeys were also named, and many of the lampoons were obscenely illustrated. No doubt the fact that the authors went unpunished tempted the sculptor Pajou to model thinly-disguised portraits of the Queen in a state of partial nudity (plate 78), and there can be little doubt that Marie-Antoinette had her lovers, among whom may be named the Swedish count, Axel von Fersen. Equally it is certain that, as in the case of Mme de Pompadour, much of the malicious gossip of the time was grossly exaggerated and without foundation, the product of overheated imaginations. In what scurrilous directions they led may be seen from one of the charges preferred against the Queen during the Revolution, when she was accused of incest with her son, the Dauphin who became Louis XVII, who was then aged nine!

The influence of the Queen on the decorative arts was very great. Verlet refers to the 'Louis Seize or Marie-Antoinette' style, suggesting that the latter could well be regarded as more appropriate. The influence of the Queen and the Court style was especially to be seen in the Petit Trianon, a summer pavilion built in 1764 where Louis Quinze had dallied with Mme du Barry. Here a ready-laid table rose into the private dining-chamber through the floor – a convenience which the King had learned from his father-in-law, Stanislas Leczinski.

The Petit Trianon had cost Louis Quinze three-quarters of a million *livres*. The alterations and redecorations undertaken by the Queen cost another two million. Small, but sumptuously furnished, it had an Anglo-Chinese garden of the kind to be seen in England, designed by 'Capability' Brown. Within its boundaries also was an *hameau* with thatched cottages, barns, chicken-runs, and haystacks, which was artificially aged and inhabited by real peasants and real cows which were milked by the Queen, when the spirit moved her, into vessels of Sèvres porcelain in a spotless dairy, while the sheep were led by silken ribbons tied around their necks. Arthur Young saw the Queen's '*jardin anglois*' (*sic*) in 1788, and wrote: 'It contains about 100 acres, disposed in the taste of what we read of in books of Chinese gardening, whence it is supposed the English style was taken. There is more of Sir William Chambers [who wrote a *Dissertation on Chinese Gardening*] here than Mr Brown – more effort than nature – and more expense than taste.'

The return to a simple and primitive life – a notion propounded by Rousseau – was fashionable, and the Queen sought the peace of Petit Trianon as a relaxation from an endless round of more hectic pleasures.

19

Its atmosphere was that of a pleasure-house. A grotto in the garden provided opportunities for amorous dalliance, artificial ruins such as Robert loved to paint were concealed among the trees, swings like the one in Fragonard's famous painting were hung from the branches, and the Queen and her friends danced on the lawns. Swans serenely floated on an artificial lake which was fed by a brook supplied with water from Marly. Arthur Young wrote:

It is not easy to conceive anything which art can introduce into a garden which is not here; woods, rocks, lawns, rivers, islands, cascades, grottos, walks, temples, and even villages. There are parts of the design very pretty and well executed. The only fault is too much crowding. . . . But the glory of Le Petite Trianon [*sic*] is the exotic trees and shrubs. The world has been successfully rifled to decorate it. . . . Of the buildings, the temple of love is truly elegant.

The Queen built a small private theatre and appeared on its stage with members of her intimate circle, and many were the *fêtes* of which it was the centre, the guests being fed in marquees.

But while the King neglected his duties in hunting and playing the locksmith, and Marie-Antoinette absented herself from Court, in the corridors of Versailles the numerous lackeys and underlings tore the Queen's reputation to shreds with imagined obscenities, while the nobility mourned the *Grand Siècle*. Marie-Antoinette recklessly disregarded the gossip which surrounded her on every side. She was everywhere escorted by the comte d'Artois and encircled by favourites from whom she demanded nothing except that they should not bore her. A habit of walking hand-in-hand or with her arm round the waist of a woman friend provoked the most malicious speculations. An example survives in a crudely delineated illustration to a contemporary play called *La Destruction de l'aristocratisme*, which shows the Queen in an obviously erotic embrace with the duchesse de Polignac. These libels and slanders soon became widely known to the Paris mob as well as to the Court at Vienna. Many were the letters sent by the Austrian Ambassador to Schönbrunn complaining of Marie-Antoinette's indiscretions until Joseph II thought it essential to journey to Paris. The birth of the Dauphin brought some alleviation. It was a subject of universal rejoicing and the King and Queen regained much of their lost popularity. But this was short-lived, and Marie-Antoinette returned once more to the seclusion and luxury of the Petit Trianon.

Disapproval now began to assume the proportions of a conspiracy, which was joined by dismissed ministers of state, women of irreproachable virtue soured by a failure to attract temptation, disappointed place-hunters, and those whom the Queen neglected. Increasingly their resentment was directed against the Queen, and to this conspiracy, as yet unorganized, belonged the King's brother, the comte de Provence, who followed Napoleon I as Louis XVIII. The sinister part he played in the downfall of his brother, and of the Dauphin (Louis XVII) can only be guessed at, but he had, without doubt, set his ambition on the crown of France. The duc d'Orléans, the egregious Philippe Egalité, whose donning of the Phrygian cap did not save him from the guillotine, was probably at the hub of the conspiracy, and the Palais-Royal was the centre of a Revolutionary cabal. A printing-press housed there produced some of the scurrilous verses and engravings which were circulating, and, since they sold for a high price, the trade brought no small profit to those responsible. The Queen suffered the indignities already endured by Mme de Pompadour and Mme du Barry and, like them, could only reply by ignoring her persecutors.

The storm broke in earnest in 1789. In September a Flemish regiment was moved to Versailles because the French guards were no longer to be trusted, and on 5 October a monstrous army of women converged on Versailles, ostensibly to demand bread but in reality to bring the King to Paris in accordance with a plot hatched by Choderlos de Laclos to whom this task had been entrusted by the duc d'Orléans. Louis at first pacified the women, but this was no part of the plot. On the day following agitators inflamed the crowd to attack the Queen's apartments. The guards died at their posts, and Marie-Antoinette barely escaped with her life to the apartments of the King. Soon afterwards they both left Versailles for the last time, escorted to Paris as prisoners of the mob. The King was executed on 21 January 1793, and the Queen on 16 October of the same year.*

V

One's first impression of Versailles is of a group of buildings rather than of a single palace because of the piecemeal way in which it was enlarged. It was based on a series of plans, each developing from the other, and the old hunting-lodge survives as the nucleus of the vast aggregate which grew up around it.

The interior, even bereft of its more spectacular furnishings, is on a massive scale unmatched elsewhere. The salons on the first floor which comprise the Grands Appartements were dedicated to the planets, with the King's as the sun (Apollo). They are entered through the Salon d'Hercule which, despite its earlier appearance, was redecorated by Louis Quinze, the bronzework dating from about 1730. The ceiling painting, the *Apotheosis of Hercules*, is the work of Lemoyne. Here the guards used to be stationed to turn back those of whom they disapproved, although entry to the King's presence was usually easy enough for anyone well

---

* For a picture of Paris during the years immediately preceding the Revolution, Louis-Sebastien Mercer's *Tableau de Paris* should be consulted. An abridged translation by Helen Simpson was published in 1933. Arthur Young is also worth consulting. An abridged version of his *Travels in France* is published in the Everyman Library.

dressed and of good appearance. The Salon de l'Abondance which follows was decorated under the general superintendence of Le Brun with battle-scenes by Van Meulen. Here the King kept his collection of medals and antique gems. The Salon de Venus, the ceiling painted with the *Triumph of Venus*, has doors flanked by pillars with bronze capitals and bases, with bronze bas-reliefs above, and walls panelled with marble. The Salon de Diane, at one time the billiard-room, has a ceiling painting of the *Huntress* by Blanchard, and here may be found Bernini's bust of Louis Quatorze. It was furnished with crystal chandeliers and orange trees in silver tubs. The Salon de Mars, once the ballroom and concert-room, is devoted to the art of war. The walls were hung with crimson velvet with *passementeries* (or fringes) of gold in winter, while the summer furnishing (*meuble d'été*) was of gold and silver brocade. Here were seventeen pieces of silver furniture, as well as two silver chandeliers and seventeen of crystal. The Salon de Mercure was the State bedroom, divided by a silver balustrade. It housed a magnificent State bed with a canopy suspended from the ceiling where Louis Quatorze lay in state in 1715. It was once remarkable for a *meuble brodé*★ of great magnificence. It was also a card-room, and the place where the royal family foregathered. The Salon d'Apollon was, as might be anticipated from its name, the throne room, with crimson velvet hangings and pilasters of gold thread which, according to a contemporary, simulated goldsmiths' work. The summer furnishings included *meubles brodés* of which nothing survives. Added to the silver furniture these made an *ensemble* without parallel in Europe, lit by a thousand candles in the evening. The ceiling painting is upheld by *stucco* nymphs of almost life-size.

From here the visitor entered the Salon de la Guerre which, with the Salon de la Paix at the other end, formed part of Mansart's Galerie des Glaces. The ceiling paintings were designed by Le Brun, and the subjects are continued in the Galerie and in the Salon at the other end. The Salon de la Guerre, with walls panelled with pale green marble veined with white, was completed in 1678. The Galerie des Glaces is where the Court foregathered, and for which no special *entrée* was necessary. It is the largest Salon in the palace, 235 feet long and 30 feet wide, with a height of 43 feet. It was started by Mansart in 1679 and completed three years later. Separating the mirrors are pilasters with bronze capitals of the new French Order invented by Le Brun, with cocks' heads, fleur-de-lys, and sun-faces. Among the artists employed, apart from Le Brun, may be numbered Caffiéri, Coysevox, Tuby, Cucci, and Ladoiseau. One wall is lined with mirrors, and the other with windows which open on to a magnificent prospect of the gardens. The Salon de la Paix beyond is decorated with emblems of peace, and with trophies representing Music and the Arts. This was the Queen's card-room, and it formed the entry

★ This term, hardly translatable, refers to embroidered panels in high relief which are discussed on page 131.

to the Queen's state apartments, the first of which is the Chambre de la Reine, redecorated by Louis Quinze and by Louis Seize, where the confinements of the Queens of France took place. The private apartments of Marie-Antoinette are reached from this room, and the decorations are largely in the Louis Seize style as the Queen left them. Here she received her intimate friends. The Salle du Grand Couvert de la Reine was where both Marie Leczinska and Marie-Antoinette dined in public. The Salon de la Reine was the Queen's Presence Chamber, hung with Gobelins tapestries representing the Coronation of Louis Quatorze and his visit to the Gobelins workshops. Beyond this is the Salle des Gardes de la Reine where the Swiss guards defended the Queen to the death on 6 October 1789, and this leads to the Escalier de Marbre, sometimes called the Escalier de la Reine. Across the landing is the door leading to the apartments of Mme de Maintenon, furnished by Louis Quatorze in 1682 but redecorated in the nineteenth century by Louis-Philippe. Nearby is the Salle de 1792, once called the Salon des Marchands, where dealers were admitted to the palace for the purpose of interviewing royal and aristocratic clients.

Returning to the Galerie des Glaces we see two doors panelled with mirrors, through one of which the visitor entered the Oeil de Boeuf, so called from its 'bull's eye' window. This is decorated in the later style of Louis Quatorze, and here members of the Court used to wait for admission to the Chambre du Roi, the bed-chamber of Louis Quatorze where he died in 1715, and where the daily ceremonies of the *lever* and the *coucher* took place. The King lunched daily at a small table placed in the window, and from the balcony Louis Seize and Marie-Antoinette confronted the mob on 6 October 1789. The *boiseries* (panelling) and the balustrade belong to the reign of Louis Quatorze, but much of the room was redecorated later, the chimney-pieces for instance dating from the reign of Louis Quinze. The Salon du Conseil, redecorated in 1775, was the centre of government in France in the seventeenth century, although the King gave audiences and received ambassadors in his Chamber. The Cabinets du Roi, the *petits appartements* of Louis Quinze, open from here, the Chambre de Louis Quinze being decorated with *boiseries* by Verberckt and Gobelins tapestries belonging to the 'Don Quixote' series. It was in this room that the King died in 1774. The Cabinet de la Pendule, also with magnificent *boiseries* by Verberckt, is the site of a remarkable astronomical clock by Passement and Caffiéri which shows the phases of the sun, moon, and planets. The Cabinet des Chiens was reserved for the King's favourite dogs and the servants who looked after them, and his Salle à Manger was the King's private dining-room, from which he could reach the apartments of Mme de Pompadour and those of Mme du Barry. He watched the funeral procession of Mme de Pompadour from the Cabinet d'Angle. The Salon de Musique belonged to the King's favourite daughter, Mme Adelaide, and here Mozart played as a child in 1763.

This is a brief description of the first floor (the *piano nobile*) of the part of the *château* which surrounds on three sides the Cour Royale and Cour de Marbre. It would be tedious to pursue the subject into the south and north wings, which are now art-galleries. We must also pass over the gardens of Versailles, however reluctantly. Designed by André Le Nôtre, they influenced garden-design throughout Europe until they were superseded, in their turn, by the *goût anglo-chinois* in the eighteenth century (page 31). The fountains, for which the most elaborate hydraulic machinery was constructed, were the work of Mansart and Francine, and sculpture by the best masters was under the direction of Le Brun and Mignard.

We must also at this point pass over the numerous buildings which centred around the palace. Some, like Marly and the Trianon de Porcelaine, no longer exist. The Grand Trianon was built by Louis Quatorze for himself. '*Versailles pour la cour*', he said, '*Marly pour mes amis, et Trianon pour moi*'.★ The architect was Mansart, and it was started in 1687. The decoration was similar in many ways to that of the palace itself, and it is especially noted for superb marble decoration. It has a small Galerie des Glaces. The apartments of Mme de Maintenon were occupied in turn by Louis Quinze, Stanislas Leczinski, Mme de Pompadour, and Napoleon and Marie-Louise, but Trianon was little used after the death of Louis Quatorze, and it was, in fact, far more occupied in the nineteenth century than in the eighteenth, when it was used both by Louis-Philippe, who largely spoiled it, and Napoleon III. Gabriel's Petit Trianon is later discussed. This, built for Louis Quinze in 1764, was occupied by Mme du Barry for a short period, but it is especially associated with Marie-Antoinette.

A collection of exotic animals was kept at La Ménagerie – an elephant and some camels, but principally exotic birds of all kinds, storks, flamingos, pelicans, parrots, toucans, and so forth – the latter a fashion perhaps started by Diane de Poitiers with the aviaries at Anet. These inspired some contemporary decoration.

Marly, started in 1680 with Mansart as architect, was built amid woods at enormous expense. It was the summer residence where the King entertained his friends. Louis Quinze seldom visited it, and during the Revolution it was first looted and then turned into a textile factory. The factory-owner demolished the building piecemeal and sold the materials. Saint-Cloud, too, has gone, like so many others. It survived until 1870, and was then destroyed during the Franco-Prussian War. Clagny, built for Mme de Montespan and the King's natural children, did not survive the eighteenth century. It was demolished in 1775. This once had the distinction of being one of the most beautiful houses in France, and the later additions to Versailles were largely based on its design.

★ 'Versailles for the Court, Marly for my friends, and Trianon for me.' An invitation to Marly was much sought as a mark of royal favour.

This book is largely devoted to the influence of Versailles on the decorative art of France. Versailles was the creation of kings, and in its turn it influenced the taste of kings. Only during the Regency was Paris the focal point. One would have thought it likely that so puissant a symbol of royalty and the *ancien régime* would have been destroyed during the Revolution, but strangely enough, apart from much of its furniture, it survived almost intact.

Louis XVIII toyed with the idea of reviving its former glories and made a few additions, but he abandoned the project. Louis-Philippe, a descendant of the Regent, damaged it with pointless demolitions and alterations, doing far more injury to the interior than the Revolutionaries. Its adaptation as a museum did even more damage.

Enough still remained, however, adequately to testify to former glories, and under a succession of custodians of taste, beginning with Pierre de Nolhac in 1887, much has been done to restore it. It would hardly have been possible to refurnish it, except partially, because the original pieces had been scattered to the four winds of heaven during the Revolution and the First Empire, and a large number of identifiable royal pieces are now in foreign museums and private collections.

The work of restoration goes on, however, done with a care and skill which is testimony to the survival of the French genius in the decorative arts, and we can now gain a truer impression of Versailles as it once was than at any time during the last one hundred and fifty years.

VI

Apart from the continuing influence of Versailles the course of the arts in the eighteenth century was much affected by the extremely fashionable *salons* presided over by cultured and intelligent women. These were the resort of artists, men of letters, philosophers, hawkers of utopias, and even financiers. They had their origin in the small and intimate groups which foregathered in the *ruelles* of the seventeenth century discussed on page 153.

The most influential were *salons* such as that of the Prince de Conti at the Temple, of which the painter Ollivier has left two representations. His *Thé à l'anglaise*, painted in 1773 and now in the Louvre, shows the young Mozart playing to a distinguished company. But these were minor Courts rather than *salons*, like that of Stanislas Leczinski in Lorraine, and *salons* proper were on a somewhat lower plane.

In the early part of the eighteenth century there were four which were more than ordinarily influential. The earliest was that of Mme de Lambert, which was followed by that of Mme de Tencin who frequented her rival's *salon* to seduce its *habitués* – a plan later followed by Mme Geoffrin. 'Do you know why La Geoffrin comes here?' remarked Mme de Tencin to a friend. 'She comes to see what she can pick up from my stock-in-trade.'

In turn Suzanne Necker attended Mme Geoffrin's *salon* for the same purpose.

The *salons* of Mme de Lambert were held on Tuesdays and Wednesdays in the part of the Palais Mazarin (now the Bibliothèque Nationale) which she rented from the duc de Nevers. After her death at the age of eighty-six D'Argenson wrote: 'To be received at her house was thought to be an honour by those on whom it was conferred.' He goes on to say that the popular passion for card-playing was only rarely in evidence.

Mme de Tencin was a *protégée* of Cardinal Dubois, the minister during the Regency and one-time tutor to the Regent, and she made a fortune by speculation during Law's inflation which she was wise enough to retain. Her *salon* became fashionable about 1733 when Mme de Lambert died. Mme du Deffand's *salon* was attended by the young Voltaire and Montesquieu. Towards the end of her life she corresponded with Horace Walpole, and from 1753 she struggled with the handicap of blindness.

Mme Geoffrin married, at fourteen, a director of the Saint-Gobain glass factory and a prominent business man, who was thirty-four years her senior. As a widow she established her *salon* in a large house in the rue Saint-Honoré – artists on Mondays and men of letters on Wednesdays. To help a friend she sold three superb paintings by Van Loo (who attended on Mondays) which went to Catherine the Great, and the blank spaces on the walls were filled with landscapes by Hubert Robert. This resulted in a close friendship between Robert and Mme Geoffrin, and he later painted a series of intimate domestic pictures of the Geoffrin household which give us a glimpse of the contemporary scene.

In the reign of Louis Seize, Suzanne Necker, whose daughter was to become Mme de Staël, entertained on Tuesdays and Fridays. Her husband, a banker and a syndic of the Compagnie des Indes, became Director-General of Finance in 1777. Mme Necker's *salon* was predominantly literary, and here Diderot and D'Alembert held forth. Her daughter, an *émigrée* in England during the Revolution, held a *salon* which was especially an avenue for advanced political ideas.

The *salon* as a medium for the interchange of ideas was principally a product of the eighteenth century and, as an institution, it became more purely social and less influential during the nineteenth century.

Hardly of special importance to our present subject, but perhaps deserving mention, were the coffee-houses which, as in England, emerged as a serious rival to the tavern as a place of public resort during the latter part of the seventeenth century. The first *café* seems to have been opened in Marseille, centre of the Near Eastern trade, in 1671, and the drinking of coffee became fashionable with the arrival of an ambassador from Turkey in 1668. The large *cafés* became a favourite resort for those who wanted to exchange news and gossip. Arthur Young dined at one in Paris about which he wrote:

. . . well-dressed people; everything clean, good, and well served; but here, as everywhere else, you pay a good price for good things; we ought never to forget that a low price for bad things is not cheapness.

Nor should we forget the stage as a vehicle for the propagation of ideas and as a source of inspiration for the decorative arts. It was extremely influential at a time when other media were scanty, and it was said of one play, *Turcaret* by Le Sage, produced in 1709, which exposed the extortions of the *fermiers-généraux*, that sixty thousand *livres* were offered to suppress it.

When the reign of Louis Seize was drawing to its tragic close the supremacy of French art and decoration, and the French way of life, was acknowledged throughout Europe. French artists were commissioned by almost every European prince, from Sweden and Russia in the north to Italy in the south. French architecture was everywhere imitated and French was the language of most European Courts. All kinds of people, from princes to the agriculturist, Arthur Young, made the journey to France to see Paris, the semi-public Court life at Versailles, and even the provinces. Young's travels are quoted by French writers on the period, and he left a mass of detailed general information on eighteenth-century French trade and industry, as well as on the social life of the time. He gives a picture of Paris just before the Revolution which in many ways ranks with that of Martin Lister written almost a century earlier.

The policy laid down by Louis Quatorze in matters of the arts had been completely justified.

2

The Progression of Styles

To arrive at a viable picture of the French interior of former times it will be necessary to describe and trace the evolution of a large number of diverse objects which will be grouped under the principal chapter headings of furniture, metalwork, ceramics (*faïence*, porcelain, and glass) and *tapisserie* (tapestries and soft furnishings generally).

Since they all conform to the fashions of their period, it is desirable to clear the ground by discussing styles generally, tracing the manner in which these styles affected the various objects which went to make up the interior scene. Style is also the key to dating, and once the salient features of each new development have been mastered it will be found possible to assign a period to most objects without difficulty.

It is a very common form of classification to divide French decorative art of the period in question into relatively self-contained compartments corresponding to the reigns of the three kings of Versailles – Louis Quatorze, Louis Quinze, and Louis Seize, with the addition of a fourth termed the Regency. This classification is useful, but only in a very broad sense, and if we examine it closely we find that it does not entirely accord with observations.

The style termed 'Louis Quatorze' may be divided into three fairly distinct parts. The earliest, in which the styles of the preceding reign of Louis Treize were largely followed, begins in 1640 and ends about 1655 or a little later. The middle period lasts almost to the end of the century, and the final period, beginning about 1700, foreshadows developments which were much more marked during the Regency, and which came to fruition in the early years of the reign of Louis Quinze. Strictly, the Regency is a period during which the late Louis Quatorze style begins to merge with the earliest manifestations of that associated with Louis Quinze. It is late baroque turning into rococo – a process which was a continuous evolution without any clear lines of demarcation.

The Regency period marks a stage in the struggle between two opposing schools in European art which had been going on since the early years of the sixteenth century; between the followers of Vitruvius and Palladio on the one hand, and those who were carried along by the stream of which Michelangelo was the source on the other. One of the reasons why rococo never secured a foothold in England to the extent that it did in France (where for more than two decades classical disciplines were largely discarded, inside if not out) was the strength of the hold which, following Wren's fall from favour, the adherents of Palladio (led by the Earl of Burlington) secured on architectural design. But even William Kent, an uncompromising Palladian in his architectural and furniture designs, turned to rococo when he functioned as a landscape gardener, an aspect of his work too often neglected. The French were convinced classicists by tradition, but we observe a gradual weakening of classical disciplines after 1700, and the main-stream of classical tradition was not rejoined until after 1750 with the beginning of the neo-classical style.*

Louis Quatorze had a passion for symmetry which amounted almost to an obsession. He loved, above all, long symmetrical lines and receding vistas, and he could not bear them to be interrupted by so much as a draught-screen (*paravent*). Mme de Maintenon, however, had no strong convictions on the necessity for symmetry, but she detested draughts. When the King was present she had to dispense even with the comfort of a screen, and, shivering with cold, she protested that she would 'die from symmetry'.

The idea of symmetry is, in fact, so important to our subject that it is appropriate to discuss it at this point before proceeding to consider the styles associated with Louis Quatorze in more detail.

Symmetry in ornament, the notion that one half of an object, or even of a decorative scheme, should be the mirror-image of the other half, is a well-established phenomenon. It is also world-wide, and lack of symmetry has always been unusual in the past. But its opposite notion, that of asymmetry, prevailed in French interior decoration and ornament for about a quarter of a century, beginning about 1730. Curiously enough, at a time when symmetry had become unfashionable in ornament especially, we find a particular insistence on the agreement of the various components making up the interior scene. The woodwork of chairs and sofas, for instance, was curved and carved to match the ornament of the panelling, and the soft furnishings – curtains, *portières* (door curtains), seat covers, bedspreads, and so forth – were selected to match each other. To some extent, therefore, the idea of symmetry emerged, even in an age of asymmetry, but in a different form.

Asymmetry is the principal determining feature of the Louis Quinze style, which is usually called rococo or *rocaille*, and is also known, in France especially, as '*le style Pompadour*' or even '*le style Boucher*', neither of which is accurate, although, of the two, the latter has more to commend it. Rococo was also termed, at the time, the 'new taste' (*goût nouveau*) and the *genre pittoresque* (literally, the 'picturesque style'), and the latter concept requires closer examination.

Chinese porcelain, then extremely popular, was generally symmetrical in its ornament, and the making of vases in matching and symmetrical garnitures was no mere European innovation. Altar vases were being made in sets almost as far back as our knowledge takes us, the earliest in bronze. Japanese porcelain, on the other hand, especially the varieties

<hr />

* Strictly, the term *neo-classicism* can hardly be applied to English art, because there never was a serious break in the English classical tradition. Palladianism merged into the style of the Adam Brothers almost imperceptibly, and with little more than a comparatively mild protest from Sir William Chambers.

from Arita (Hizen Province) which were painted by the decorator Sakaida Kakiemon and his followers, was noted for asymmetricality in the disposition of much of the ornament, and it is worth recalling that, although it was imported into Europe in smaller quantities than porcelain from China, it was undoubtedly more highly valued, perhaps for this reason. It is the *première qualité du japon* of eighteenth-century French inventories and sale catalogues.

A few seventeenth-century design-books had occasionally included more or less isolated examples of asymmetrical ornament, principally cartouches, and designs of this kind came from the Dutch silversmith Adam van Vianen, as well as the Nürnberger, Christoph Jamnitzer. Design-books of the end of the seventeenth century, notably those of Paul Decker and Jean I Bérain, had made use of a space-saving device whereby two halves of a design were printed side by side, either side needing its mirror-image to complete it. As they appeared on the page, however, neither side matched the other, giving an impression of asymmetricality if the design were regarded as complete – which may have influenced rococo designers.

The term *genre pittoresque* cannot today be translated by the English 'picturesque', although the two concepts were at first related. It is usual now to regard a picturesque scene as one suggesting a subject for a painting, but in eighteenth-century England (the hey-day of the landscape gardener) it meant the imitation of a painting, the creation of a landscape in the manner of Claude Lorraine or Salvator Rosa for example, both among the most admired of painters at the time. This is confirmed by Uvedale Price (*Essays on the Picturesque*), who wrote in 1794 'that the chief object in view was to recommend the study of pictures, and the principles of painting, as the best guide . . . to the improvement of real landscape', and Dallaway mentions that Salvator Rosa and Claude Lorraine were generally regarded as being the most infallible guides to the picturesque.

It is not, perhaps, an entirely unwarranted digression to turn for a moment to garden design, because this art had a much greater impact on the course of art in the eighteenth century than is generally supposed. André Le Nôtre had laid out the magnificent formal gardens at Versailles, the 'green geometries' that inspired those of Hampton Court accompanying Wren's additions. The asymmetrical and informal garden – the 'studied disorder' which is a feature of French rococo – began early in the eighteenth century with such designs as that of the Serpentine as part of the gardens of Kensington Palace by Bridgman, and by the creation of an informal garden at Twickenham by Alexander Pope. These two inspired William Kent, who, in turn, influenced 'Capability' Brown. That English gardens such as these owe something to the peculiar genius of the Chinese as landscape gardeners is certain. Much had been sent back to Europe on this and kindred subjects by the Jesuit

31

missionaries,★ and Walpole wrote in his *Essay on Modern Gardening* that they are 'as whimsically irregular as European gardens are formal and unvaried'. Eighteenth-century England even borrowed a word from the Far East for this irregularity – Sharawadgi – although it seems to be neither Chinese nor Japanese. The English picturesque garden, fashionable in France before mid century, came to be called the '*jardin chinois*' there, and the English taste in garden design '*le goût anglo-chinois*'.

In a climate of this kind the growth of rococo is less surprising. The beginning of asymmetry in French interior decoration – the *genre pittoresque* – may be dated fairly precisely to about 1725, although the word itself was not admitted by the French Academy until 1732. It can be seen, for instance, in the bronze mounts of *commodes* of the period. The one by Cressent (plate 1) belongs to the Regency of the duc d'Orléans, and although the mounts exhibit the kind of lively curves first to be seen towards the end of the reign of Louis Quatorze they are still symmetrical. The one shown on plate 2, however, is only a few years later, but the mounts are decidedly asymmetrical.

In its broadest aspects the style of Louis Quatorze is notable for symmetry and spaciousness. The eighteenth century saw a reduction in scale in the size of rooms, which became smaller and more intimate, the *salon* being increasingly reserved for State occasions. With this reduction in scale came the multiplication in the number of rooms set apart for specific purposes, so that the whole air of the century changes from that of the preceding one. The predominant architectural style of the seventeenth century is a classicism not as uncompromising as that of Palladio, Inigo Jones, and the disciples of Vitruvius, but nevertheless based fairly rigidly on the Five Orders, and on the proportional system laid down by the most respected authorities with suitable modifications.† Externally the lines of great buildings were inclined to be simple, and integrally sculptured ornament was reduced almost to a minimum.

The period of decoration of Versailles is the point at which this book begins, and it also marks the introduction of the Grand Manner in French interior decoration. Ornament was extremely diverse in subject and treatment and based on the great classical repertory inherited from Imperial Rome. It had a richness of quality rare at any period, sumptuous in its effect and masculine in its strength. The salons of Versailles with their profusion of marbles and gilded bronze, their silver furniture and tapestries, attained a perfection never since equalled. If, today, it is sometimes considered

★ For instance, *A particular account of the Emperor of China's Gardens near Pekin. A letter from F. Attiret, a French missionary, to his friend at Paris*, 1743. In England, Sir William Chambers published his influential *Dissertation on Oriental Gardening* in 1772, but the whole subject had been discussed long before this.

† The mathematical relationship of the parts to the whole in architecture was based on theories elaborated by the Greeks and recorded by Vitruvius. It influenced Renaissance art from the sixteenth century onwards, and was the subject of numerous treatises.

pompous this is, perhaps, because in the intervening three centuries we have lowered our sights.

Among the *motifs* of the period we recognize easily the mask surrounded by radiating shafts of light – the symbol of *le roi soleil* (the Sun King), and the intertwined Ls, the King's monogram, both to be seen again in the eighteenth century. Trophies of arms, often in the form of *chutes*,* were also popular as a decorative *motif*, frequently in bronze with added acanthus foliage and that of the laurel and the oak, as well as garlands of flowers. The chimney-piece, always the principal feature of the room, was usually comparatively plain in design, the richness concentrated in the materials. It was surmounted by a painting or a bas-relief of some classical subject, the latter sometimes imitated *en grisaille*.† Painted ceilings adorned the more important rooms, and tapestries and paintings covered large areas of the walls.

Above all there was colour, rich colour of a kind which, from what few guides we have, we must assume also decorated the interior scene in Imperial Rome. The notion that Greek and Roman interiors were predominantly white, or coloured in pale pastel shades like the later neo-classical colour-schemes, did not exist before the last decades of the eighteenth century. It was, perhaps, the product of a rash assumption that because excavated antique marbles were always white when found they had always been in that state. In Greek and Roman times, however, marbles were stained and painted, and often gilded as well, not statuary only but also structural marble. The kind of statuary the Greeks valued most was not white marble but chryselephantine work, such as the Olympian Zeus, one of the wonders of the ancient world, made of gold and ivory with eyes inlaid with semi-precious stones or enamel. In Roman times bronze, most of it gilded, decorated interiors, forming the capitals of columns and pilasters, and gilded copper was often used for roofing. Bernini looted the Pantheon to make his baldachin for Saint Peter's, the surplus metal going to the cannon-founders. The practice of covering structural timbers with copper, often gilded, is mentioned by Homer in the *Odyssey*:

> The walls plated bright with brass, on either side
> Stretched from the portal to th' interior house,
> With azure cornice crowned; the doors were gold
> Which shut the palace fast; silver the posts
> Rear'd on a brazen threshold, and above,
> The lintels, silver, architraved with gold.

and Nero sheathed the interior of a theatre with gold, although only for a

---

* *Chutes* (literally, *falling*) are a type of ornament long and narrow applied to wall-panels. The term is also used in reference to the applied bronze decoration of such things as table-legs.

† Painting *en grisaille*, that is to say, in shades of grey, imitated relief sculpture and had been fashionable since the sixteenth century.

single day. The name given to his palace – the Domus Aurea or Golden House – refers to the profusion of gold and silver which ornamented it. Whiteness, in fact, belongs not to the classical age but to the neo-classical.

Among the classical forms taken over by the sculptors of the seventeenth century may be numbered the term or *gaîne*, the head and torso of a figure ending in a tapering pedestal. Statues and busts decorated exteriors as they had done in Imperial Rome, and Le Nôtre's splendid formal gardens laid out at Versailles needed figures and groups to decorate them. The water-gardens, especially elaborate, called for vast fountains of bronze, lead, and marble. Fountains are a sure touchstone to the splendour of a city or a palace.

The changes which characterize the next period were partly a natural response to the social and economic evolution of the century, and partly a product of the financial difficulties of the time. Gilded wood and bronze began to replace silver and silver-gilt for the larger objects, and we are inclined to overlook the fact that style is always, to some extent, dictated by the available materials as well as by their connotation. A lavish display of the precious metals inevitably sets the scale for the rest of the decorative scheme, because their intrinsic worth is recognized and accepted. The popularity of gilding was not merely because those who commissioned such work liked the colour, or appreciated the fact that gold lent an untarnishable surface to the underlying material, but because work of this kind looked opulent. But gilded wood especially cannot be made to simulate cast and chiselled metal and its employment led to subtle changes in style because of its different texture and the difference in the tools needed to shape it.

Particularly after 1700, the last years of the King's reign, we begin to notice a fresh grace and lightness in the ornamental *motifs* and the introduction of new kinds of decoration which developed at an increasing pace during the Regency, eventually to culminate in the *genre pittoresque* of Louis Quinze.

If the political events of Louis' reign were unpleasant realities, at least one's surroundings could express the gaiety it was difficult to feel otherwise. But in this new development we find several elements which are complete novelties. Far Eastern art had been particularly sought in Northern Europe since the beginning of the seventeenth century, when the Dutch looted Spanish and Portuguese ships returning from the Far East. Mazarin had a not inconsiderable collection, principally silks, porcelain, and lacquer, and both Louis Treize and James I of England bought porcelain from the Dutch. When Evelyn was in Paris in 1644 he visited, in the Isle du Palais, a shop called

34

Noah's Ark, where are sold all curiosities, natural or artificial, Indian or European, for luxury or use, as cabinets [of lacquer], shells, ivory, porcelain [from China], dried fishes, insects, birds, pictures, and a thousand exotic extravagances.

In both seventeenth- and eighteenth-century records it is sometimes difficult to separate, from their description, objects imported from China, Japan, Siam, and Persia. These things were brought to Europe in the ships of the various East India Companies, often trans-shipped in Indian *entrepôts*, or at Batavia in the Dutch East Indies. Thus we sometimes find mention of 'Indian' porcelain, although it was never made in India, and Chinese silks are often called 'Indian'. The Coromandel screen (so-called) was made from incised and coloured Chinese lacquer panels, which received the name from the fact that they were trans-shipped on India's Coromandel coast. On the other hand eighteenth-century records are sometimes specific. The best Japanese porcelain for instance was clearly described as *première qualité du japon*, from which we may deduce the fact that the origin was important in this case.

Louis Quatorze was very fond of these exotic extravagances, and porcelain vases, lacquer, and other objects from the Far East decorated the salons of Versailles. Especially popular were vases made in the last years of the Ming dynasty and the first part of the reign of the Ch'ing Emperor K'ang Hsi (1666–1726). These, in sets of three, five, or seven, formed the *garniture de cheminée*, placed on the mantelshelf, which continued to be popular throughout the first quarter of the eighteenth century. At first in the Chinese taste, these were later decorated, usually at Canton, with designs which included armorial bearings specially commissioned by European purchasers. They are today classified as Chinese export porcelain, and are considered in more detail later.

But the demand for Chinese porcelain, with its novel decoration, far outran the supply, even though a fairly usual cargo amounted to a hundred thousand pieces of all kinds, and European craftsmen and designers imitated Chinese decoration without understanding, sometimes blending it with European *motifs* often of unbroken classical descent. These mixtures are termed *chinoiseries*. They first appeared in the second half of the seventeenth century, the product of numerous travel-books, and continued to be popular until well beyond the middle of the eighteenth century. One of the first designers to adopt the *chinoiserie* in France was Jean I Bérain (1640–1711), who was succeeded as '*dessinateur du cabinet du Roi*' by his son, Jean II Bérain. A page from the elder Bérain's design-book is illustrated on plate 6. Bérain's subject-matter included Far Eastern *motifs* of all kinds in association with typically baroque strapwork, and baldachins, masks, and *motifs* derived from the old Roman grotesque ornament which Raphael took from the excavated Golden House of Nero. Monkeys (*singes*) were a frequent addition, a subject developed later in an amusing fashion in the *singeries* of Christoph Huet at Chantilly.* At first

35

* These decorations were executed before 1741, in which year Huet rendered more or less confined to tapestries, *faïence*, and sometimes the typical marquetry of Boulle (page 61) based on the designs of Bérain, the fashion for *chinoiseries* began to sweep Europe, forming perhaps the most out-standing decorative theme of the early years of the great Meissen porcelain factory of Augustus the Strong, inspiring such painters as Boucher, and, with the invention of a varnish suitable for imitating Chinese lacquer by the Brothers Martin (*vernis Martin*), providing the means for decorating some of the most colourful furniture of the reign of Louis Quinze.

An important influence on this emerging style was the establishment of a factory for the manufacturing of mirror-glass at Saint-Gobain in Picardy (discussed on page 129). Until this time mirrors, apart from such exceptions as those to be found in the Galerie des Glaces (which were imported at enormous cost from Venice), had often been extremely small in size. The cost was high, and it was to remain high for a good many years, but the large scale of the new manufactory brought the price down to a point where at least most of the wealthier people could afford them. Large mirrors were still usually made in sections, but they began to decorate the space above the chimney-piece and the piers between windows (pier-glasses or *trumeaux*), and even above the door (the over-door mirror – *dessus de porte*). The multiple reflections of several such mirrors more or less opposite to each other influenced the decoration of the room itself, as well as adding to its brightness, and they took the place of the carvings and paintings which had formerly been fashionable. The elaborately carved frames provided a new element in room-decoration of which craftsmen took full advantage.

The distinction often drawn between the final years of Louis Quatorze and the period of the Regency is largely artificial, and the term 'Regency' cannot, for the most part, be regarded as much more than an indication of date. One or two characteristics which place an object in this period rather than in that of the former King include the smiling female mask and the occurrence of such fabulous animals as the chimera or griffin, and the dragon. Furniture-mounts were used in a manner not be seen earlier, especially those of the *ébéniste* Charles Cressent (1685–1768) who was also a skilled bronzeworker. They anticipate in their variety and position the dispositions to become popular under Louis Quinze, but they lack the rococo asymmetry. The voluminous skirts of the period (*à paniers*, i.e. hooped) demanded, and got, the accommodation of an armchair (*fauteuil*) with a wider seat and, for the same reason, the front supports carrying the arm-rests (*accotoirs*) were set back by about one-third of the depth of the seat instead of continuing the line of the front legs.

---

his account. Hunting-scenes, tea-parties, and so on were designed in 'the Chinese taste' with amusing apes wearing the Condé livery attending mandarins. Apart from the famous Salon des Singes there is also a Petite Singerie similarly painted. Until the discovery of the account mentioned these *singeries* were attributed to Watteau, and even to Oudry.

Rococo, it has been said, began when the scrolls stopped being symmetrical, and for practical purposes this definition, despite its superficiality, could hardly be bettered. It is impossible, in a general work such as this, to discuss the subject adequately. It is a far more important phase in the development of art generally than is often supposed. It swept Europe in a manner which had few precedents. We are here only concerned with its manifestations in France, but Bavarian rococo for instance is an important aspect of the whole subject, and only in Palladian England did the fashion fail to take a firm hold.

Among the earliest instances of the use of asymmetry may be cited the designs of Juste-Aurèle Meissonnier (1695–1750), a goldsmith and *ornemaniste* who succeeded Jean II Bérain as designer to the King. A page from one of his design-books appears on plate 67. The first of his designs to reveal the new tendencies, which became well marked soon afterwards, was a weather-vane for the duc de Mortemart done in 1724, which had as part of its decoration a shell and a jet of water. Water and attendant rockwork (*rocaille*) was a principal keynote of the new style, especially in its early stages. Numerous suggestions have been advanced to account for the emphasis on rockwork, which is thought to have been inspired by that decorating the grottos and gardens of Versailles (the Grotte d' Apollon, for instance), but remembering the close association of rococo with the fashion for Chinese art one speculates on the possibility of inspiration from the fantastic and distorted rocks so much sought by the Chinese for the decoration of their own gardens, and so often depicted in porcelain painting especially. *Rocaille* is a customary French term for the style as a whole.

The addition of shell-work is a natural extension of the subject of rocks and water, but it must be remembered that almost throughout the eighteenth century shells of all kinds were a passion among collectors, and large quantities of exotic shells were assembled and displayed in cabinets. Shells formed part of the stock of the shop called Noah's Ark seen by Evelyn in 1644, and they were certainly as avidly collected in eighteenth-century England. Plate 5 shows a tureen from the famous 'Swan' service made at the Meissen factory for Augustus III for presentation to the factory's director, the Count von Brühl, in 1737. The service has water for its theme, and it is the first instance of rococo porcelain-designing from the Saxon factory, no doubt based on engravings from Paris then being imported as models.

Another feature of the rococo style is the numerous graceful curves of the ornament, to be seen in decorative carvings such as those adorning the *boiseries*, as part of table-supports and chairs, and in the outlines of chimney-pieces and table-tops of marble. Mouldings in the case of door-panels were often given a double curve at the top which rose to a high point at the centre of the door with two leaves, and these replaced earlier rectangular panels. Arches of all kinds rose from their springers to

37

a central point embellished with carved ornament, known as an *agrafe* (literally, a clasp), which was framed with asymmetrical scrollwork, and the outlines of *chenets* (andirons) were contained within a scalene triangle. The cartouche was also used as a point of emphasis to which mouldings tended, and this was framed in similar style with asymmetrical scrolls. The acanthus leaf continued to be widely employed, but, unlike that of earlier periods, its tip was often twisted to one side.

Nevertheless we find, here and there, decoration undoubtedly belonging to this period which is far more restrained in its use of curves, and not every designer of the period was seduced by the new asymmetry – although they did not reject the other elements of the style. But these were exceptional, and pronounced asymmetry in ornament was the rule.

At first the reaction from asymmetry which began during the reign of Louis Quinze soon after mid century, with which the name of Louis Seize is associated, represented to some extent a return to the classicism of Louis Quatorze, and some of the decoration of this time is almost perplexing in its resemblance to the older period. But the new classicism was fundamentally different, with characteristics which were the product of the events which had intervened between the two versions.

In 1719 the town of Herculaneum, buried by the same eruption of Vesuvius in A.D. 79 as the one which overwhelmed Pompeii, was found accidentally by Prince Elbeuf who was looking for a source of ready-cut building stone. About the middle of the eighteenth century the first serious excavations were started at Pompeii itself, although the site had been known since 1594. In consequence of these discoveries interest in both Roman and Greek art and institutions began to make headway, especially among a section of French society which was dissatisfied with the luxury and frivolity of the Court of Louis Quinze and the intervention of Mme de Pompadour. The principal exponents of this early phase of neo-classicism were Johann Joachim Winckelmann, art-historian and one-time librarian to count von Bünau at Dresden, who was appointed librarian to Cardinal Albani in Rome, and Anne-Claude-Philippe de Tubières, comte de Caylus, a collector of antiquities whose important work on classical and Egyptian art was published in five volumes between 1752 and 1755.★ To the work of these two men must be added the slightly later catalogue of the collection of the English Ambassador at Naples, Sir William Hamilton, which was much consulted by designers in France and England.

The name of Mme de Pompadour is so firmly associated with rococo that it is easy to overlook the fact that she was one of the first to adopt the new style in her private apartments, although the King remained faithful to rococo and the marquise perforce had to do the same in public. In 1746 she secured for her brother, later the marquis de Marigny, the office of Directeur des Bâtiments, and in 1748 a mission comprising the

★ *Recueil d'Antiquitées Égyptiennes, Étrusques, Grecques, Romaines, et Gauloises.*

marquis, the architect Soufflot, and the engraver and designer Cochin, went to Italy to study antique art, called by some 'the true beauty'. To this must be added the influence of Piranesi, whose engravings depicting Roman antiquities were extremely popular.

The new classical style falls into two fairly distinct parts. The first is best termed 'transitional' because it represents the transition from rococo to the revival of classical symmetry. Work of this period sometimes contains elements of both styles, although rococo diminishes in strength and influence the more closely we approach the accession of Louis Seize in 1774. The second phase beginning a little before 1780 might well be termed the Marie-Antoinette style, since it was fostered and largely inspired by her influence.

Curves began to disappear almost at once. Chair-legs for instance became straight and tapering instead of curved, and the same kind of changes are to be observed in furniture generally. The new style at first drew more heavily on Greece than had the decoration of Louis Quatorze, for example in the employment of the Greek wave pattern as a frieze ornament, but the principal source of ornament was still largely Roman. In its general aspect revived classical ornament was lighter and with perhaps a more conscious striving after elegance than is to be seen in the seventeenth century; it is feminine rather than masculine.★

About 1770 we notice also a new kind of ornament altogether, based on rustic joys and the simple life. In the park of the Petit Trianon at Versailles Marie-Antoinette had a *hameau*, designed by Hubert Robert, of rustic houses, occupied by real peasants engaged in agricultural pursuits with the usual domestic animals. Milk from the cows was taken to the Queen's dairy, where she amused herself by making butter and cheese as a relaxation from the sophistication of Court life, and it is to this that we owe new kinds of ornament, such as beehives, baskets of osier, and agricultural implements. Another innovation was the use of sentimental attributes: hearts pierced with arrows, quivers, flaming torches, and garlands of roses. Sentiment degenerated into sentimentality, a vice, first appearing soon after the ending of the Seven Years' War, which was inherited by the nineteenth century. It was also widespread. It is as evident in the *biscuit* porcelain figures of Sèvres as in the *bourgeois* family groups of Acier at Meissen. Its appeal to the taste of the time may be deduced from the paintings of Greuze and from the fantastic success of Goethe's immature novel, *The Sorrows of Werther*, which was known and read far beyond the frontiers of Germany. The Man of Feeling emerged, and Diderot attacked the sensuality of Boucher and his followers, saying: 'To show virtue charming and vice hateful should be the aim of every honest man who employs pen, brush, and the sculptor's chisel', thus linking art and morality for the first time. Greuze enjoyed wide

39

★ A tendency perhaps well represented by Bouchardon's statue, 'Love making himself a bow out of the club of Hercules'.

popularity with paintings which foreshadowed the worst excesses of the Victorians. He was, it has been said, 'a moralist with a passion for lovely shoulders: a preacher who reveals the bosom of young girls'.*

Such affinities as the neo-classical style possessed with the classicism of Louis Quatorze are principally to be found in the design of permanent and semi-permanent interior installations, and these soon withered away as the new style took hold. Neo-classicists detested the Renaissance, and on the few occasions when Renaissance works were sold by auction prices were generally low. This is partly because Renaissance classicism, although it was much nearer to that of Greece and Rome than their own version, did not accord with the current notions of antiquity which were culled from the villas of Pompeii rather than from the great palaces of the ancient metropolis. Thus, the arabesques which were so popular a part of decoration under Louis Seize owed much more to Pompeii than to the grotesques of Nero's Golden House and Raphael's *loggie*. A curious survival, however, was the furniture of the great Boulle, more often than not indebted to Bérain's designs. It was not only avidly collected but freely imitated throughout the eighteenth century and into the nineteenth, probably reaching the height of its popularity in the 1770s. A nineteenth-century table by the Edgware Road inheritor of the Boulle tradition, Louis Le Gaigneur, is in the Queen's Presence Chamber at Windsor Castle, and a mid-seventeenth-century writing-desk with the arms of the de Retz family is in the Queen's drawing-room. At the same time there was also a demand for seventeenth-century sculpture, especially the work of Puget, Girardon, and Coysevox, although little for excavated Greek and Roman marbles.

The difference between the old classicism and the new was more than the product of a mere shift in emphasis from Imperial Rome to Pompeii. Neo-classicism, the fag-end of a long tradition, was also a deliberately contrived reaction from rococo, as much literary and political in inspiration as artistic. It was not merely a case of fashionable people seeking something new to be fashionable about.

If the promoters of the new style disliked rococo, their political bias made them almost equally antipathetic to Louis Quatorze and Louis Quinze. The intellectual climate of France had been changing steadily since the end of the seventeenth century. Then men had met injustice with a lampoon, and the enormities of the taxation system with a scurrilous epigram. 'They sing,' said Mazarin, 'and then they pay.' But in the eighteenth century they no longer sang. Instead, the foundations of the established order were brought under searching examination and criticism. Administration was not so much tyrannical as intolerably lax. The

* The Romantic movement, with its emphasis on emotion rather than reason, became so much a feature of the new classicism, especially in its later phases, that the term 'romantic classicism', despite its antithetical nature, seems not unjustified. The first instance of the word 'romantic' being used in a sense which is approximately the same as that of today does not occur before 1757.

Treasury was identified with the King's private purse, and when he needed money Louis Quinze took it from public funds, scribbling a receipt for the Treasurer. The tax-farmers reaped a rich harvest because machinery for the public collection of taxes hardly existed, and in exchange for their privileges they rewarded the members of the Court handsomely, and sometimes the King himself. 'The tax-gatherers,' writes one historian of the times, 'had at their service a code so complex that the taxpayer could not know it', which almost proves the truth of the old adage that the more things change the more they remain the same, but for the fact that in those days defaulters went to the galleys.

In this atmosphere literary talent began to flourish as never before, and writers particularly invaded the political sphere. The most influential of the thinkers of the period were perhaps Voltaire, Montesquieu, and Rousseau, and Diderot, the latter editor of the *Encyclopédie* which advanced radical views.

Neo-classicism was, to some extent at least, a product of these movements in its initial stages, but by 1780 the influence of Marie-Antoinette and Versailles had diverted the earlier simplicity into channels as luxurious and extravagant as those which had contained the rococo of Louis Quinze.

In recording the part played by the Queen, however, it is easy to overlook the earlier influence of Mme du Barry, whose purchases while Louis Quinze was still alive did much to influence the future course of the style. With the help of the dealer, Poirier, she made fashionable the decoration of furniture with Sèvres porcelain plaques – small tables, *secrétaires*, and *commodes* – paying extremely high prices. She employed the *ciseleur-fondeur*, Gouthière, to execute the gilt-bronze decorations for the Pavillon de Louveciennes, and her purchases did not end with the death of the King. After her return from exile she continued to spend heavily, and when she met her ignominious death at the hands of the executioner during the Terror she still owed Gouthière an enormous sum for work of this kind which his heirs attempted to collect from her estate after his death in 1814. A law-suit dragged on until 1836 when it was settled for a derisory fraction of the original sum.

Louis Seize and Marie-Antoinette left Versailles for the last time in 1789, driven out by the Paris mob. They returned to the capital which had been abandoned by the royal family in the days of Louis Quatorze, and soon afterwards the royal furnishings were unceremoniously dumped into carts and Versailles was bereft of much of its former glory. Some of the royal possessions disappeared across the Channel to England; others became part of the stock of the *brocanteur*, many of them to be sold for absurdly low prices in the years which followed. A few survived to be bought in the 1830s by the more discerning collectors, and by the 1870s French furniture and porcelain of a kind even remotely connected with royalty had achieved a dizzy sale-room eminence which even today is rarely approached.

41

Thus ended an almost unprecedented period in the history of the decorative arts, of which the Empire style of Napoleon was but a pompous echo. It was a period during which the emphasis had been largely on novelty and the acquisition of the latest fashion, and this had been made possible by the scale on which the arts were organized in France since the days of Colbert. If we look only at the cost to France of achieving this pre-eminence it seems high, but against it we must weigh the vast return from exports and the prestige which undoubtedly accrued and was reflected in other spheres, not the least that of foreign relations. Even in the nineteenth and twentieth centuries the position of Paris as the artistic capital of the world, a position by no means unprofitable, must eventually be traced to the decisions taken by Louis Quatorze to employ art as an outward and visible symbol of the greatness of France.

For a century and a half the outmoded had been relegated to the attics, a situation which has no parallel. Pierre Verlet has referred to gifts of unfashionable furniture to the lesser nobility belonging to the Court, and to the system of precedence whereby unwanted objects were removed from Versailles to the smaller royal *châteaux*. The same authority discusses the difference in taste and buying habits between the rich *fermiers-généraux* on the one hand, and the learned professions, represented by lawyers and members of the *Parlements*, on the other, dividing them into innovators and conservators. The economic climate of the time has been examined by Gerald Reitlinger in Volume II of the *Economics of Taste*. He points out that the aristocracy, whose wealth was largely derived from landed estates, commanded far less in liquid resources than the *fermiers-généraux*, who were also financiers. Therefore, what we see from the period of Law's inflation on, almost to the beginning of the Revolution in 1789, is the taste of Versailles supported by financiers rather than by noblemen. That these sumptuous interiors achieved so high a level of excellence was due to the example of Versailles and the patronage of artists and craftsmen of skill and taste.

In a manner not without parallel today the *fermiers-généraux*, who knew better than anyone the shaky foundation on which the value of the *livre* rested, bought works of art on an immense scale, not only as a symbol of prestige but also as an investment, and this brought in its train a rise in prices which was stimulated by the lavish expenditure of Louis Quinze and Mme de Pompadour. As Reitlinger points out, apart from Oriental lacquer furniture, the most expensive objects were those of gilt-bronze or those heavily mounted with it, which was at least to some extent the product of the cost of mercuric gilding, even though the actual gold value was negligible. Mounts lacquered and polished could be bought much more cheaply. Fine marbles for table-tops and for such decorative objects as urns and pedestals were also dear, and semi-precious stones such as jasper and chalcedony dearer still. In judging the cost of works of art at this time we must remember that materials were usually expensive and most kinds of labour cheap.

No doubt prices were enhanced by the popularity of public auctions, a common enough feature of the art-market in ancient Rome but much less in evidence thereafter as a method of dispersal. Competitive bidding pushed prices upwards, but a formidable difficulty in the way of an extension of this kind of selling was the care with which all the interior elements were made to harmonize one with the other, largely depriving them of their meaning when separated from their immediate surroundings. It was quite often essential, when buying a Paris *hôtel*, to buy the furnishing as well. Despite this contrary indication, however, auction prices had reached almost unprecedented heights before the end of the century, a rising market brought to an end only by the Revolution. The problem of what to do with the possessions of Louis Capet, the members of his Court, and of those financiers insufficiently astute to read the warning signs while there was yet time, was gravely mishandled. Much was destroyed, and much more sold in circumstances which made it impossible for a fair price to be realized. The duc d'Orléans, Philippe Egalité, attempted to sell the Regent's picture collection abroad in 1790 for 100,000 guineas, but without success, although the Dutch and Flemish paintings came to England later. The collection of Louis Seize's Finance Minister, Calonne, was sold by Christie's in 1795, but for much lower prices than those at which he had bought them.

The market for antiques, apart from old master paintings, did exist in the eighteenth century, despite the emphasis on what was new; but for the most part little was bought from the immediate past, and only a few discerning collectors ventured even as far afield as Renaissance and Roman bronzes. Much more fashionable was the collecting of curiosities of natural history, such as shells and mineralogical specimens which were often mounted in gilt-bronze. On page 34 I quote Evelyn's description of the stock of the shop called Noah's Ark. By how much taste had changed may be judged from the stock of Gersaint a century later. The following is a translation of his trade-card:

À la pagode [at the sign of the *pagode*] Gersaint, *marchant jouailler* on the Notre Dame bridge, sells all kinds of *cainquaillerie* both tasteful and new, trinkets (*bijoux*), mirrors, cabinet-pictures [i.e. pictures not intended for a fixed position as part of the permanent decoration], *pagodes*, lacquer and porcelain from Japan, shells and other natural history objects, *cailloux* [i.e. pebbles, mineralogical specimens], *agathe* [agate], and generally all merchandise both strange and curious, in Paris, 1749.

This advertisement needs elucidation at several points. A *marchand jouailler* today keeps what in England would be a jeweller's shop, selling jewellery and small silver articles, but in eighteenth-century Paris the term was much more loosely interpreted and meant a dealer in *objets*

43

d'art as well. Duvaux called himself a *marchand bijoutier* which means much the same. *Cainquaillerie* is the modern *quincaillerie*, a store dealing in iron-mongery – except that in Gersaint's case the stock was limited to decorative ironwork, wrought-iron grilles and lattices, and ornamental locks and hinges. *Pagodes* or *magots* were small seated figures of the Chinese monk Pu-t'ai, with grinning face and bare belly, who often appeared as part of early *chinoiseries* and was the subject of some of the first porcelain figures to come from the Meissen factory. It can also mean the many-storeyed Chinese pavilions known as pagodas, and the expression *à pagodes* applied to furniture appears to have meant the use of lacquer panels with Oriental pictorial subjects in the construction of various kinds of case furniture. Mme de Pompadour, for instance, had two *commodes à pagodes* of this kind.

There are a number of contemporary descriptions of collections of curiosities. An English example of what appealed to the collector of the eighteenth century may be found in the catalogue of Strawberry Hill prepared for visitors by Horace Walpole, from which it may be seen that he possessed Cardinal Wolsey's hat and John Dee's divining-stone, actually a piece of cannel coal which had formerly belonged to Lady Betty Germaine at Knole. For French collections at the turn of the century we may profitably turn to Lister:

I saw Monsieur Tournefort's collection of shells, which are well chosen and not above one or two of a sort; but very perfect and beautiful, and in good order, consisting of about 20 drawers. . . . I shall say nothing of his vast collection of seeds and fruits, and dried plants, which alone amounts to 8000, but in this he equals, if not excels, all the most curious herbalists in Europe. He also showed me ten or twelve sheets of vellom, on each of which were painted in water colours very lively, one single plant, mostly in flower, by the best artist in Paris at the King's charge. Dr Tournefort shewed me a present which was made him by his countryman of Provence, Monsieur Boyeur d'Aguilles, of a large book in folio of curious stamps [i.e. engravings] . . . I saw the apartment of Monsieur Viviers in the arsenal; it consists in seven or eight ground [floor] rooms looking into the great garden; these rooms are small, but most curiously furnished, and have in them the greatest variety and best sorted China ware I ever saw, besides Pagods and China pictures; also elegant rich bureaus, book-cases, and some paintings of the best masters.

He visited the aged André le Nôtre (Monsieur le Nostre), who he found, at eighty-nine years of age, very quick and lively. There was

a great collection of choice pictures, porcellans, some of which were jars of a most extraordinary size, some old Roman heads and bustos, and intire statues; a great collection of stamps [prints] very richly bound up in books [but] . . . there was not anything of natural history in his cabinet.

In the 'workhouse' of Monsieur Gerradon (Girardon) in the Louvre he

44

was shown many ancient marble statues, and brass (bronze) statues and 'Vasa' (vases or urns), 'and a hundred other things relating to antiquity'. Girardon also possessed the mummy of 'a woman intire. The scent of her hand was to me not unpleasant, but I could not liken it to any perfume now in use with us.' In the collection of 'M. Buco', Keeper of the Archives to the *Parlement*, he found books in cases with brass trellisage covering the doors, and the 'famous enammel vessels, formerly made in Poitu which are not now to be had'. The same man had a 'hippocampus', about four inches long, which from Lister's description was a sea-horse, given to him by Lady Portsmouth and perhaps from King Charles's collection. At the house of Monsieur Morin, 'one of the Académie des Sciences', he was shown minerals – jaspers, onyxes, agates, and lodestones from Siam, as well as a great block of amethyst 'two or three hundred weight' from France 'designed for a pavement in Marchetterie (marquetry) of which he showed me a Cartoon drawn in natural colours'.

Lister, however, was a man of scientific curiosity and his visits seem to have been confined to those who shared his tastes. He did not go into the fashionable houses, or, if he did, he left no record behind of what he saw.

3
Designers and *Ornemanistes*

Throughout the period discussed the course taken by the decorative arts in France was strongly influenced by designers of ornament who were usually appointed by the King and employed by the royal manufactories. Few of them were solely *ornemanistes*; most were celebrated in other branches of the arts. Not a few published books or sheets of designs for the use of other craftsmen.

At the beginning of the seventeenth century the most outstanding of the early baroque designers was the painter Simon Vouet (1590–1649), who spent fifteen years in Italy and was influenced by Veronese, Raphael, and Caravaggio. Vouet helped to decorate the Palais du Luxembourg, and he provided numerous cartoons for the tapestry-workers of the Louvre, where he was given apartments. He completed a vast amount of work, much of it with the help of his pupils, among whom Le Brun was the most outstanding. Vouet it was, perhaps, who was responsible for the fashion for floral decoration which is always greatly in evidence thereafter. He appears to have influenced the sculptor and designer Jean Le Pautre (d. 1695), who worked at Versailles during the time of Le Vau. Le Pautre's designs are those of a sculptor, richly charged – 'overcharged' might be a better description – with classical figures, usually in high relief, and nude or almost so, in conjunction with scrolling acanthus, and floral and foliate garlands. These can be well seen in his designs for chimney-pieces. One is described as '*à l'italienne*, invented and engraved by I. Le Paultre, 1665', and another, even richer, flanked by Corinthian columns and surmounted by an allegorical group and a centrally disposed painting, as '*à la romaine*'. These, sold in Paris by Mariette, a print-dealer of the rue Saint-Jacques, testify to the continuing Italian influence inherited from the sixteenth century. Le Pautre's designs for *stucco* ceilings were no less elaborate, and those of complete rooms might almost be described as the apotheosis of the Grand Manner. Those for cabinets on ornately carved gilt stands match his more permanent architectural work, and he is generally notable for an air of massiveness and height. Although it is impossible to relate any existing interiors to his actual published designs, his influence must have made a very considerable contribution to the middle Louis Quatorze style. Other members of the same family also functioned as designers, notably the architect Pierre Le Pautre, whose designs, far less ornate, foreshadowed the style of the Regency.

Charles Le Brun has already been mentioned. In his day Le Brun dominated the whole field of decorative art in France, and he continued to do so until the death of Colbert in 1683. Colbert's successor, Louvois, replaced Le Brun by Mignard, but because of the difficulties of the time the royal manufactories were already in decline. To the foundations laid by Le Brun much of the pre-eminence of French art throughout the succeeding centuries is due.

Daniel Marot (1650–c. 1712), son of Jean Marot, was a Huguenot who left France after the Revocation of the Edict of Nantes to become architect to William III of England. Both father and son were prolific designers, but Daniel is by far the better known. He seems to have specialized in the design of beds, the most important item of household furniture in the seventeenth century. Either with posts (*lit à la française*) surmounted by a canopy, or with a canopy supported only at the back (*lit à la duchesse*), his designs called for tasselled drapes and valances of the utmost richness which inspired the ornament known as *lambrequins*, much used as a painted *motif* on *faïence* during the last years of the seventeenth century. His canopies were surmounted at each corner by plumes. Some of Marot's chimney-piece designs for the first time provided space for the display of porcelain and *faïence* vases, which he may have done for the English Queen Mary. Chimney-pieces very similar in design are to be found at Hampton Court, where the Queen had introduced the fashion for Oriental porcelain and European tin-enamelled ware (delft) into England. In his designs for panels Marot made use of strapwork in conjunction with foliage, especially acanthus scrolls, floral garlands, and foliate swags, as well as *grotesques*, some with popular allegorical subjects. Apart from interior fittings, he designed *console* tables, cabinets, mirror-frames, lighting appliances, and even such small items as snuff-boxes. He also specialized in the design of elaborately ornamented cases for long-case clocks, termed *régulateurs* in France.

The final period of the Louis Quatorze style is perhaps best represented by Jean I Bérain (1640–1711), who worked with his brother Claude (d. 1726) now rarely mentioned. He attracted the attention of Le Brun by whom he was trained, working on the Galerie d'Apollon at the Louvre, and he was appointed *dessinateur de la chambre et du cabinet du Roi* in 1674, with an apartment in the Louvre. Bérain designed not only interiors but settings for all kinds of royal functions, especially *fêtes* and theatrical performances. He is notable for a kind of *grotesque* ornament (plate 6) especially characteristic of the last decades of the King's reign, which influenced the course taken by later rococo designers.

The sheet from one of his design-books illustrated here is typical of much of his work. If we analyse it we shall find a great deal in common with the decoration of Urbino *maiolica* after the middle of the sixteenth century. It is, in fact, a development of late sixteenth-century Renaissance *grotesque* ornament, although still in a direct line of descent from that decorating Nero's Golden House.

In the centre we notice cupids hammering a flaming heart on an anvil, reminiscent of those to be found at Pompeii in the House of the Vettii (before A.D. 79). Below, supporting the anvil, is a term, and on either side what are actually tripods, although only two of the legs are visible,

48

ornamented with rams' heads which are characteristically Roman in origin. The hoof-feet (*pied de biche*), occur on furniture of the period, particularly that of A.-C. Boulle. On either side are figures with wings instead of arms, terminating in *consoles*, and at the bottom crouching sphinxes back-to-back are posed on pedestals of typically late baroque form. Between them are squatting long-horned rams in a pose characteristic of *grotesque* figures decorating Urbino *maiolica*. Masks (*mascarons*) are a typically Renaissance kind of ornament inherited from Rome which continued in favour throughout much of the eighteenth century in one form or another. The angular strapwork came originally from the Netherlands, probably arriving in Holland from Spain where it was inspired originally by Islamic metalwork. Nevertheless, some of the *motifs* are new, especially the monkeys (*singes*) which are manipulating floral swings on either side of the central panel.

Sphinxes, incidentally, were an especially popular kind of ornament during the early years of the eighteenth century, appearing in a variety of forms, including the decorative *chenets* (andirons). Many were recognizable portraits of Court beauties. I recall two in bronze, for instance, now in a private collection and divorced from the remainder, and without their original gilding, which are excellent likenesses of Mme de Parabère, mistress of the Regent. Portrait sphinxes, no doubt derived from this source, became a favourite with the English porcelain factories of Bow and Chelsea especially at mid century, Kitty Clive and Peg Woffington, the English actresses, being among those represented.

If we now look at this sheet as a whole and draw a vertical line down the centre we find that in almost every case the elements of design on one side are repeated on the other. There are, however, a few minor exceptions, such as the monkeys, the position of the figures in the swings, a snail on the strapwork beneath one monkey which is absent from beneath the other, and an alteration in the pose of the male figures of the groups below the panels framing the cupids. These divergences create an air of lively fantasy, and they are also steps in the direction of asymmetry. In other Bérain designs more or less contemporary we find Chinese figures in tall conical hats beneath a scrolled canopy with a distinctly Chinese flavour, the curving eaves taken from the Chinese pagoda. These Chinese *motifs* were a consequence of the King's interest in Chinese art, evinced in the Trianon de Porcelaine at Versailles (page 111), and the Oriental decoration of the *château* of Meudon belonging to the Dauphin who died in 1711. The fashion received notable impetus from an embassy from the King of Siam in 1688.

Bérain made a great many engraved designs of chimney-pieces in which he used the space-saving device referred to in the preceding chapter, resulting, in one case at least, in the juxtaposition of the scrolls of two distinct cartouches in a manner which makes the whole almost indistinguishable from the characteristic rococo cartouche of twenty-five years

49

or so later. Like those of Marot, Bérain's chimney-piece designs are lower than those of Le Pautre, with a mantelshelf for the display of a clock and the popular porcelain garnitures instead of the elaborate sculptured ornament preferred by the latter. Another marked difference is that Le Pautre's chimney-pieces were designed for a painting above the fireplace, whereas those of Bérain provided space for a mirror.

Bérain's designs were widely employed by craftsmen of all kinds. Much of the decoration of Boulle's typical brass and tortoiseshell marquetry is fairly obviously inspired by this source, and the *faïence* of Moustiers employed Bérain's *grotesques* for a notable series of dishes. Boulle, whose career as an *ébéniste* is discussed on page 61, was also a designer in his own right who worked not only for the King but for the more prominent of the financiers at the end of the seventeenth century, such as Crozat and Samuel Bernard. His skill as a bronzeworker and designer is especially notable in his chandeliers and sconces, some of which foreshadow rococo asymmetry. His private collection included drawings by Raphael, wax maquettes, engravings, and many other works of art.

Robert de Cotte (1656–1735), pupil and brother-in-law of Hardouin-Mansart, was an *ornemaniste* as well as an architect who eventually became *premier architecte du Roi* and director of the *manufactures du Roi* about 1699. He exerted considerable influence on the development of the Regency style, and probably collaborated with Bérain and Boulle.

Belonging to the same period was a skilled designer, Claude Gillot (1673–1721), noted for theatrical decoration and his scenes from the Italian Comedy,★ who employed the popular satyrs, *grotesques*, and monkeys. Claude III Audran (1658–1734), *conservateur* at the Luxembourg, was a painter who decorated many *châteaux* and designed tapestries with the *motifs* which Bérain had made familiar. He also designed the noted Gobelins tapestry series of the 'History of Don Quixote' (page 142) and the 'History of Jason' (after De Troy), both in collaboration with Pierre François Cozette, later director of the most important department of the Gobelins tapestry manufacture.

Gillot and Audran are joined by their connexion with Antoine Watteau (1684–1721), son of a master-tiler of Valenciennes, who was both a painter and an influential designer. He was a pupil of Gillot's in

★ The theatre has been a favourite source of inspiration for the decorative arts since the seventeenth century. From 1700 to about 1770 the Italian Comedy was especially popular. This was staged by troupes of strolling players, not only at country fairs but in the sophisticated cities. It was in the form of a *scenario*, the actors improvising the dialogue and the action. The principal characters were Harlequin, Pantaloon, Pedrolino or Pierrot, the Doctor, the Lawyer, Mezzetino, the Captain, and Scaramouche. A popular company played in Paris in 1687 where they were seen by Augustus the Strong and invited to Dresden. The Comedy (called in Italian the *Commedia dell'arte*) certainly existed in its later form as early as the beginning of the sixteenth century, and it probably had its origins in the Roman theatre.

1704, attracting the notice of Audran a little later, in 1709. Watteau's painting has today tended to overshadow his work and influence as a designer, but his *arabesques* (the common term for the form taken by *grotesques* in the eighteenth century) inspired the *ébéniste* and sculptor Cressent, and he also developed the popular monkeys. Indeed, Huet's *singeries* at Chantilly were at one time attributed to the hand of Watteau. His characteristic subjects of gallantry were widely popular, being copied on to the porcelain of Meissen in the 1740s. In the *Anecdotes of Painting* Horace Walpole comments on Watteau's painting:

His nymphs are as much below the forbidding majesty of goddesses as they are above the hoyden awkwardness of country girls. In his halts and marches of armies [the Flemish military scenes], the careless slouch of his soldiers still retains the air of a nation which aspires to be agreeable as well as victorious.

Walpole goes on to say that he had lately realized, after a journey to Paris, that Watteau's trees were copied from those of the Tuileries and the villas near Paris.

Watteau later gained the patronage of Antoine Crozat, the financier, and his reputation at the time was so high that seven hundred of his paintings were engraved on the initiative of Jean de Jullienne, one of his friends, as the *Recueil Jullienne*. He died in the arms of his friend, Gersaint, the art-dealer. Watteau's designs have an air of fantasy almost without parallel at that time, considerably influencing the course of design throughout the first half of the eighteenth century, and although his early work as a designer faintly echoes that of Bérain, it is an obvious and important source of the rococo phase. The designs of Gillot on the other hand have greater affinities with the seventeenth century.

The painter Jean-Baptiste Oudry (1689–1755) was perhaps most influential in the field of the decorative arts as director first of the Beauvais tapestry-looms and then of the Gobelins manufactory, a position which he held during the reign of Louis Quinze (page 139). His death almost marked the end of Colbert's organization of the arts, although royal patronage continued virtually undiminished. As a painter Oudry was especially attracted to animals and the chase, and his work was an extremely popular source for decoration of all kinds. His style is not unlike that of Desportes with whom he is sometimes confused. Desportes was a slightly earlier painter of similar subjects who helped to decorate many of the principal *châteaux* of the time, including Versailles and Marly, and Chantilly which belonged to the Prince de Condé.

François Lemoyne (1688–1737) also inspired some of the decorative art of his day. One of his principal works was the decoration of the Salon d'Hercule at Versailles, and many of his paintings were engraved by Laurent Cars, engraver of Watteau's *fêtes galantes*.

With Gilles-Marie Oppenord (1672–1724) the tendency towards

rococo became more marked. Oppenord was architect to the Regent and influenced Cressent's furniture-designs. He owes something to Francesco Borromini (1590–1667), an early baroque architect whose influence can be seen in some of Oppenord's designs. Oppenord is now probably most widely known for his wrought-ironwork designs, then becoming fashionable for balconies and staircases (plate 87) in addition to the gates which had always been popular for the entrances to *châteaux*. He also turned his attention to *console* tables on supports of wrought and cast iron and other items of iron furniture, including even a *prie-Dieu*, which seem to have been intended for gardens and exterior courts rather than for interiors.

Nicolas Pineau (1684–1754) was a pupil both of Mansart and of the architect, Boffrand. He appears to have been at first a *menuisier* (page 59) principally concerned with the carving of *boiseries*, especially at the Court of St Petersburg where he stayed for ten years. In Russia he functioned also as an architect and a designer of interiors, and on his return to Paris in 1726 he became a leading designer. His work was less emphatically asymmetrical than that of some of his contemporaries, and earned the approbation of the architect, J.-F. Blondel, who was one of the early critics of rococo extravagances.

Jacques Verberckt (1704–71) from Antwerp was a *menuisier* and carver who worked principally on *boiseries*, especially in collaboration with the architect Gabriel, in a rococo style less pronounced than that of Meissonnier.

Despite early examples of asymmetry already mentioned (page 49) the especial characteristics of the developed rococo style did not become obvious before the time of Juste-Aurèle Meissonnier (1695–1750) who was born in Turin. He worked principally as a goldsmith and *ornemaniste*, becoming *orfèvre du Roi* (goldsmith to the King) in 1726. Two years later he was appointed *dessinateur du cabinet du Roi* in succession to Jean II Bérain, but little or nothing of his work in this capacity is extant. Indeed hardly anything can be attributed to Meissonnier apart from his design books, but these were probably the greatest single influence on the development of rococo. A good deal of his work was done for foreign nobility, and included clock-cases, lighting fixtures, *console* tables and other furniture, *boiseries*, and – somewhat naturally – silver of all kinds. Among his silver designs some shell salts were an obvious inspiration for several of the porcelain factories, including Chelsea and Bow in the 1750s. Other silver designs with marine subjects on a base of asymmetrical scrollwork influenced porcelain-making in Saxony and England, although little such work was done at either Vincennes or Sèvres, where the kind of porcelain employed was hardly suited to it and gilt-bronze bases were substituted (plate 92). Meissonnier's table-supports and seat-furniture were almost as elaborately ornate as his silver. Even more advanced were the designs of an engraver and goldsmith, P. E. Babel, whose vignettes and ornamental work were popular.

More or less contemporary with Meissonnier, and working in a style which resembles his, but without his emphasis on asymmetry, were the brothers Slodtz. Three of them worked for the King as designers and sculptors. Antoine Sebastien (1695–1754) was a *dessinateur de la chambre du Roi*, a position in which he was succeeded by his brother Paul Ambroise (1702–58). The design of the *commode* illustrated on plate 2 has been attributed to one of the Slodtz. In 1739 they were associated with the engraver Cochin *le jeune*, later discussed, who assisted them to design settings for Court *fêtes* and state ceremonies. The Slodtz were, according to one present-day critic, good at designing festivals, but they really let themselves go at funerals.

Jean-Jacques Bachelier (1724–1806), painter and *ornemaniste* and a follower of Chardin's, helped to decorate *châteaux* and *hôtels* before he was appointed director of studios at the Vincennes porcelain factory. Encouraged by Mme de Pompadour he became Art Director in 1751 and was largely responsible for the development of the Sèvres style in porcelain decoration, introducing the use of *biscuit* (i.e. unglazed) porcelain for figure-making.

The influence at mid century of François Boucher (1703–70), son of a designer of embroidery, can hardly be over-estimated. One of the most facile painters of his generation, he could turn his hand to scenes of gallantry, mythological subjects, *chinoiseries*, animal paintings, religious subjects, theatre scenery, porcelain-designing, tapestry cartoons, and many other things. Although he is best known today for his nudes, these in fact formed a comparatively small part of his work. In 1743 a *List of the Best Painters* refers to him as a . . .

history painter living in the rue Grenelle Saint-Honoré, opposite the rue des Deux-Écrus, pupil of Lemoyne, excelling also in landscapes, grotesques and ornament in the manner of Watteau, and equally skilled in painting flowers, fruit, animals, architecture, and subjects of gallantry and fashion.

Boucher, who was elected to the Academy in 1734, was an intimate of Meissonnier's, who stood godfather to his son in 1736. In this year a series of engravings by Ravenet and Le Bas from Boucher's *Cris de Paris* was published, and later became a source of inspiration to the Meissen porcelain factory for a series of figures. In 1736, at the suggestion of the director, Oudry, he submitted designs for a new series of tapestries illustrating 'Don Quixote' to Gobelins, which were the forerunners of many more. By 1737 his paintings were selling as quickly as they were taken from the easel, both cabinet pictures and those intended for more permanent positions, such as overdoors. He had been accumulating a collection of Chinese porcelain perhaps from about 1740 when he began a series of *chinoiseries*, 'The Five Senses, representing various Chinese pastimes', followed by the '*Suite de Figures Chinoises*', which inspired porcelain figures and groups at Meissen later copied in England. This phase of Boucher's work seems to have started when he engraved a design for Gersaint's catalogue, the latter specializing in Oriental art of all kinds.

Boucher was on the staff of the Paris Opera, designing costumes and scenery for the ballet, *Indes galantes*, in 1743. Less well known are his designs for the fashionable gilt-bronze mounts and for interiors. His friendship with Mme de Pompadour and his designs for the Sèvres porcelain factory followed, the marquise obtaining for him the position of *premier peintre du Roi*.

Among the mistresses taken by the King from the lower classes was an Irish girl named Murphy – the model for Boucher's *Petite Morphil*, and Boucher was also commissioned to paint erotic pictures for the King's private apartments.

By 1754 Boucher had turned to pastorals, setting a new fashion, and in the following year he became director of Gobelins in succession to Oudry. His connection with Vincennes began just before 1754 when Bachelier asked for his assistance, and he provided sketches for the modellers Fernex and Suzanne.

Boucher's influence diminished after the death of his friend and patron, Mme de Pompadour, in 1764, although his reputation survived his lifetime. He died at his easel in 1770.

The more extravagant aspects of rococo never found universal favour. An early critic was Jacques François Blondel (1705–74) whose *Architecture française* in eight volumes published between 1752 and 1756, and the *Cours d'architecture civile* (1771–7), were both influential. His designs for *boiseries* while not departing from the prevailing spirit of the time are, in conformity with his published views, much less extravagant than a good deal of the work of his contemporaries. Of some plates based on the work of Pineau he says that they are 'varied without being too much in the taste of the time'.* The chimney-pieces of Charles Étienne Briseux (1680–1743), who published a book on the art of building country-houses in 1743, with plates engraved by Babel, and who employed Pineau for some of his commissions, are notable for the large space allowed for mirrors. By this time chimney-piece mirrors were complementing the pier-glasses opposite, adding an air of spaciousness to the room. Babel engraved other interior designs notably for Boffrand, and he was much influenced by Meissonnier, but how much his work of this kind was original is problematical.

A designer of *chinoiseries* who requires mention is Jean Pillement (1728–1808), painter, water-colourist, and engraver, who worked for the Prince of Liechtenstein and Stanislas Leczinski. In England his characteristic *chinoiseries* inspired the decoration of porcelain, enamels, and *objets d'art*.

* As early as 1737 he apologizes for giving a few examples of asymmetrical designs, explaining that they are merely a concession to the taste of the moment, and referring to the absurd mixtures of shells, dragons, reeds, palms, and foliage then coming into vogue.

Less well known is his landscape painting in the manner of Boucher.

The origins of the neo-classical style are less easy to trace. In its earlier manifestations it was first termed *le style grec* and later *le style étrusque*, neither of which is particularly appropriate. It is true that some early Greek *motifs* occur, especially the wave-pattern used as a frieze ornament, and that some Roman *motifs* were derived from Etruscan art of a kind which, in its turn, had been borrowed from Greek sources, but so little was known of the Etruscans that all kinds of things were claimed for them to which they were not strictly entitled. When Josiah Wedgwood, for instance, started his factory in Staffordshire to manufacture neo-classical pottery he called it 'Etruria'. There was a revival of this 'Etrusco-mania' in the nineteenth century, but, in general, neo-classical sources were usually Roman, and provincial and *bourgeois* Roman at that, from Pompeii and not from the capital.

Perhaps the most important single influence was the publication of the compilation of the comte de Caylus which began in 1752. Its influence on the decorative arts can hardly be measured, although it was a culminating point of a series of attacks on the more extravagant aspects of rococo which Caylus had started almost twenty years before. The catalogue of Sir William Hamilton's collection was published in a sumptuously printed and engraved edition in 1766–7. Sir William (1730–1803), was Ambassador to the Court of Naples from 1764 to 1800, and is popularly known as the husband of Nelson's mistress, Emma.

The numerous engraved designs, as well as the writings, of Charles-Nicolas Cochin le jeune (1714–90) contributed to the same end, and the influence of Piranesi, acquainted both with Clérisseau and Robert Adam, was certainly not negligible.

The nature of contemporary attacks on rococo may be illustrated by a quotation from Cochin published in the *Mercure de France* in 1754. He begins by entreating goldsmiths, bronze workers and woodcarvers who decorate apartments to observe certain laws dictated by reason. He writes

When they have a candlestick to make we beg them to make it straight and not twisted as if some rogue had taken pleasure in spoiling it. We will not venture to quarrel with the taste of the interior decoration of our buildings. We will not even ask for reticence in the use of palm-trees which are cultivated in such profusion in apartments, on chimney-pieces, round mirrors, against walls, and everywhere. To suppress these would be to deprive our decorators of their last resource. But we may at least hope that when a thing may be square without offence, they will refrain from distorting it, and that when a pediment may legitimately be semicircular they will not corrupt it with S-shaped scrolls, which they appear to have borrowed from a writing-master.

Nearly ten years later Diderot wrote:

Eccentricity in ornament reached its crowning point in France, [but] for some years past antique forms and ornaments have improved considerably . . . and the new fashion has become so general that everything is now made in the Greek manner. . . . [plate 113] The taste has passed from architecture into our milliners' shops. Our ladies dress their hair *à la Grecque*, and our dandies would think it disgrace to be seen with a snuff-box not in the Greek style.

The early lack of outstanding designers in the new style is to be explained by the fact that those of established reputation were already being employed by the King, whose attachment to rococo was unswerving. Cochin states that an obscure and little-known artist, Louis Le Lorraine, was the first to use such typical Louis Seize *motifs* as swags, urns, and plaited cable ornament, and the part played by the German *ébénistes* (page 64), beginning with Oeben, must not be overlooked. At Sèvres the models for *biscuit* figures of Étienne-Maurice Falconet were by no means uninfluenced by the new movement, although his work for the porcelain factory owes something to the designs of Boucher. Falconet's 'Leda and the Swan' of about 1760, and the maquette for 'Cupid and Psyche', appeared in the Salon of 1761. The bases are plain and no longer the rockwork associated with Vincennes and early Sèvres figures. Of his earlier '*Baigneuse*' and his '*Nymphe qui sort du Bain*', both before 1760, Falconet remarked that they were '*plus noble, d'un goût plus général et moins sujet à révolution de la mode*' (more noble, and in a general taste less subject to the changes of fashion), which implies a concession to the prevailing changes. In the making of the popular vases for chimney-piece decoration or for *pot-pourri* the Louis Seize style was well marked by 1765, and in 1772 a vast table-decoration in *biscuit* reproduced one of the ceiling-paintings of the Galerie d'Apollon in the Louvre, executed in the seventeenth century.

Jacques-Germain Soufflot (1713–80), architect of the Panthéon, who, with Cochin, accompanied Marigny on his Italian journey, had studied at the Academy in Rome in his youth. At first a rococo designer hardly distinguishable from the remainder, he was nevertheless dissatisfied with the style, and as early as 1744 had expatiated on the 'wise and rich simplicity of the Greeks and Romans'. The second journey to Italy was his road to Damascus, and on his return he vigorously promoted the return to classicism.

Looking at the new developments across the Channel inspired by the Adam Brothers, where Robert Adam was appointed architect to George III in 1762, the conclusion is difficult to escape that revived classicism in England was not without influence in France. The rococo style had never found more than a precarious foothold in England, principally because Palladianism was so strongly entrenched. The porcelain factories and the Huguenot silversmiths adopted it, and Horace Walpole made a light-hearted excursion into revived Gothic at Strawberry Hill, but the mainstream merged almost insensibly from Palladian classicism into the Adam version. Both Charles-Louis Clérisseau and Jean-Simon Rousseau de la Rottière – the latter's work, represented here by plate 59, the *boudoir* of Mme de Sérilly, formerly part of an *hôtel* at the rue Vieille-du-Temple in Paris – drew something from Adam designs. Associated with Rottière was the sculptor Claude Michel, called Clodion (1738–1814), who is later discussed (page 102), and another sculptor to influence the new movement, patronized by Caylus, was Edmé Bouchardon (1698–1762), who returned from Italy in 1733, and whose work inspired porcelain models at Meissen and elsewhere.

Despite a gesture towards the early phases of the new style by Mme de Pompadour in her private apartments, the fashion appealed considerably more to some of the up-to-date *fermiers-généraux*, such as Grimod de la Reynière whose *salon* was designed by Clérisseau, perhaps as early as 1769, and whose mansion in what is now the rue Boissy d'Anglas eventually became the American Embassy. Jean Demosthène Dugourc (1749–1825), who was attached to the Garde-Meuble, exerted considerable influence on later neo-classical design, while Jean-Charles de la Fosse (1721–90) who began as a rococo designer turned increasingly to a more classical style. Richard Lalonde published many furniture designs, some obviously influenced by Roentgen and Riesener.

A painter whose work merits attention is Hubert Robert (1733–1808), one of Fragonard's intimates. Later Designer of the King's Gardens and Keeper of the Royal Collection, he fell under the influence of Winckelmann in Italy, whither he journeyed in 1754 with an introduction to Pannini. His choice of subject, usually architectural, earned him the soubriquet of Robert des Ruines, and his success as a decorator of *salons* was probably due to the interest of Diderot, who much admired his work. His friendship with Mme Geoffrin helped the youthful Robert to establish himself.

This brief chapter takes account of some of the more influential designers whose work will be discussed later, but French decorative art during the century and a half with which we are concerned was the work of many, some of whom will be mentioned hereafter. Every craftsman at the tapestry looms, in the porcelain factories, in the workshops of the goldsmiths, the *ébénistes*, and the *menuisiers*, every painter, engraver, and sculptor who added something new which was taken up elsewhere, contributed to the complete picture. The painters here mentioned were also designers of one kind or another, or painters of walls and ceilings in addition to easel-pictures, who noticeably influenced general trends. But we should not overlook those others, who confining themselves rather more to easel-pictures, often influenced the decorative arts by acting as a source of inspiration. The same is to be said of sculptors, some of whom are discussed in Chapter 5. As a general rule sculptors were rather more intimately connected with the decorative arts than painters.

Louis Quatorze, Louis Quinze, and Marie-Antoinette as patrons of the arts played influential roles in the evolution of styles during the seventeenth and eighteenth centuries, Louis Quinze with the help of Mme de Pompadour and to some extent of Mme du Barry, but they were at the apex of the pyramid which broadened out towards its base to take in the nobility, the *fermiers-généraux* and the financiers of Paris, and then the provinces in direct proportion to their distance from the capital and the state of communications with it.

4
Furniture

In a book devoted to the decorative arts, furniture must inevitably play a major part, and this chapter examines briefly the development of furniture in France during the seventeenth and eighteenth centuries.

It is essential to clarify the picture at the outset with definitions that will lead us to a system of classification which although not watertight is nevertheless helpful. Three schemes of classification are possible:

1. According to the prevailing style. Broadly into baroque, rococo, and neo-classical; more closely according to the progression of styles outlined in Chapter 2.
2. Into *menuiserie* and *ébénisterie*, a distinction which is usually fairly clear-cut.
3. According to the degree of permanency in the decorative scheme awarded to the furniture in question.

During the sixteenth century furniture was the province of the *menuisier* who worked in solid wood. The nearest English equivalent to the term is 'carpenter and joiner', but this is not entirely satisfactory. At this time the technique of inlaying, extremely fashionable in Italy, was in France the province of the *menuisier*, but when it was replaced by more sophisticated techniques such as veneering and marquetry in the early years of the seventeenth century, the most skilled *menuisiers* became known as *ébénistes*, a term often translated as 'cabinet-maker' which again is not strictly accurate. The *menuisier* proper continued to be responsible for seat-furniture, table-supports, such furniture as *buffets* (a kind of cupboard) and *armoires* (wardrobes) of solid wood, the decorative carved panelling for walls (*boiseries*), door-cases and overdoor mouldings, and window-cases and shutters. In this he was assisted by wood-carvers, and by painters, varnishers, and gilders.

Ébénistes were so called from the fact that when ebony (*ébène*) was first introduced into France towards the end of the sixteenth century it was an exceedingly rare and expensive wood used principally for veneers and inlays. They became known as *menuisiers en ébène*, later shortened to *ébénistes*, and since veneering was almost invariably done on case-furniture of one kind or another the *ébéniste* was necessarily also a cabinet-maker. The term, however, can be applied correctly to any kind of furniture decorated with veneers or marquetry, and with related techniques.

The elaborate mounting and applied decoration of metal, which became especially fashionable towards the end of the seventeenth century, required yet another category of craftsman – the *ciseleurs-fondeurs* who cast and finished the mounts, and the *doreurs*★ who were responsible for gilding.

French furniture of the period under discussion is commonly referred to either as *menuiserie* or *ébénisterie*, and these terms will henceforward be used without further explanation, since to translate them would be needlessly confusing. They are both in use today, and the workshops of these craftsmen are a not uncommon sight in provincial France, even though the *ébénistes* are rarely as skilful as their forebears.

Classification according to position in the decorative scheme, whether fixed or not, is not an entirely new concept. The French word for the furnishings of the house – *meubles* or movables – is sufficient indication of this, because the notion of movables implies the existence of immovables, apart from the building itself, which is always an *immeuble*. These immovables have usually been taken to be the *boiseries*, the door-cases and chimney-pieces, and similar kinds of architectural woodwork. Pierre Verlet, however, has recently drawn attention to the fact that the distinction allows room for a good deal of extension. *Console* tables supported in front and attached at the back to the *boiserie* (the *console d'applique*), the carving of the support matching the remainder of the panelling, were certainly not mobile. The large cupboards called *armoires*, built-in and forming part of the *boiserie*, must also be regarded as permanent, even though they were later detached and are sometimes to be found today in the storerooms of the *brocanteur* seeking the support of a new *boiserie*. But these are obvious examples. The notion may be taken a good deal further. The independent *armoire* by its very size and weight is semi-permanent, and if it was originally carved to match a particular *boiserie* it was even more static in intent, even though it has today been divorced from its original setting. Such movable furniture as the *canapé* (a kind of sofa), often by etiquette and because the framework was carved to match the *boiserie*, may be regarded as having been fixed in its position, and some *fauteuils* (armchairs), and even a proportion of the chairs, were destined to occupy a fixed point in relation to the rest of the interior scheme. Plans dating from the eighteenth century exist showing the exact position of all these pieces of furniture. Verlet has also shown how contemporary terminology recognized the existence of this classification, for instance in the case of certain small tables without a fixed position which were termed *ambulantes* (strolling).

In these days when the original scheme has been scattered to the winds of heaven – the *boiseries* in New York, the *commodes* in Los Angeles, the pier-glasses in Chicago, and the *fauteuils* perhaps gracing a London flat, it is not always easy to understand how complete was the harmony between all the elements of decoration – fixed, semi-permanent, and movable – in its original form, and this kind of classification is therefore

★ Gilding of bronze mounts, nearly always by the mercuric process described by Pliny and Cellini, is discussed at greater length on page 87.

often difficult and the line of demarcation vague. Nevertheless, the distinction is an important one to a proper understanding of the period.

II

The principal methods of decoration in wood during the period under review, apart from carved work, are marquetry, veneering and parquetry. Veneering on a flat surface is simple enough. Thin sheets of rare wood of good figure are sawn and glued to a carcase of some commoner wood like pine or oak. Little difficulty is presented in veneering the simple curve, but the problem of securing a veneer to a surface which is a section of a sphere or a spheroid – a kind of swelling outline termed *bombé* – was not solved until towards the end of the Regency.

Marquetry is a more or less elaborate pattern formed from inlays of differently coloured woods. These can be exceedingly complex, and floral and pictorial marquetries decorated some of the finest *ébénisterie* (plate 28). The term can also be applied to inlays of different materials, such as the tortoiseshell and brass marquetries associated with the name of André-Charles Boulle (page 62). Boulle cut them from a sheet of brass and one of tortoiseshell clamped together. These, when separated, gave two sheets of alternating brass and tortoiseshell, the first, in which the tortoiseshell forms the background, being termed *première partie*, and the second, with brass predominating, the *contre-partie* or *deuxième partie*. Marquetries of ebony and ivory cut in the same way, from sheets clamped together, are occasionally to be observed.

Parquetry is decoration with sections of veneer of the same wood but with contrasting grain, the simplest form being the parquetry floor of blocks laid in the so-called herring-bone pattern. Much more complex designs are to be found, however, both as floor decoration and as furniture veneering.

Other ways of decorating furniture include painting, gilding, and varnishing with imitations of Oriental lacquer discussed on page 63. Applied bronze mounts, and porcelain as furniture decoration, are both treated under the appropriate headings (pages 97 and 124). Carved and gilt wood, an especially prominent feature of decoration under Louis Quatorze, hardly calls for explanation. Such work is at its best when seen by candlelight, when it seems incomparably rich in appearance.

The opening of trade with the East and the exploration of the western hemisphere in the sixteenth and seventeenth centuries brought many new woods to Europe, and French furniture in general is noted for the decorative use made of these rare and exotic varieties. Among many we notice amboyna (*bois d'amboine*) from the East Indies, violetwood (*bois violet*★)

★ Violetwood is often termed kingwood, but the latter term was not introduced before the nineteenth century, and then probably in England. *Bois de rose* (literally, wood of the rose) is sometimes mistranslated as rosewood. The term, in fact, refers to tulipwood.

from South America, rosewood (*palissandre*) from Brazil, thuyawood from North Africa, satinwood (*bois satiné*) from the West Indies, *acajou* (mahogany) from the same region, and tulipwood (*bois de rose*) from Brazil. Many unusual native woods were employed for particular purposes, such as wild cherry, and limewood. Limewood, because of its softness, even texture, and peculiar suitability for the rendering of detail, was a preferred wood for carving in France as well as in southern Germany.

III

Before proceeding to a more detailed consideration of the furniture of the period, it is desirable to glance briefly at a few of the craftsmen who contributed to its evolution and pre-eminence.

André-Charles Boulle (1642–1732), *ébéniste du Roi*, was a man of many skills. The typical brass and tortoiseshell marquetry associated with his name (plate 15) was developed by him from techniques introduced early in the seventeenth century from Italy and the Low Countries. He can hardly be said to have originated it. So closely has he been identified with this kind of work, however, that it is nearly always called *boulle*.* His earliest furniture was decorated with marquetries of wood, and Verlet comments that Boulle shared with Louis Quatorze a taste for magnificence, a somewhat overcharged richness, sumptuous materials, and an almost tyrannical symmetry. The King installed him in the Louvre, which made him independent of the craft guilds, and he soon acquired the reputation of being the most highly skilled craftsman in the Paris of his day. But his fame does not rest only on his skill as an *ébéniste*. He was a bronzeworker, an engraver, an architect, and also a talented painter in the best tradition of the Renaissance. Most of his work was done for the royal palaces or for members of the Court.

Many of the designs for brass and tortoiseshell marquetry seem to have been based on those of Jean I Bérain, although no record exists of contact between the two men. He may, of course, have used Bérain's published designs, but it is difficult to conceive that they worked entirely independently when their respective positions at Court are remembered. The fashion in furniture design for which Boulle was largely responsible at the end of the seventeenth century continued until well into the nineteenth. He had several sons who followed their father's craft – the *ébéniste du Roi* Charles-Joseph Boulle, for example, who was the master of J. F. Oeben – and many imitators.

Almost equally outstanding was Charles Cressent (1685–1768) who was *ébéniste* to the Regent. His influence was neither so strong nor so persistent, but he worked for many important people – for the marquis de Marigny, the *fermier-général* Blondel de Gagny, and the banker Pierre

* Quite inaccurately it is sometimes referred to as '*buhl*'.

Crozat, for instance.* Like Boulle, Cressent was skilled in several crafts, with training as a sculptor and bronzeworker in which spheres he excelled. He sometimes made his own bronze mounts, and he played an influential part in developing the characteristic disposition of the mounts of the rococo period. One in particular representing a small female head with a plumed head-dress and a lace collar, termed an *espagnolette* and to be found at the angles of *commode* stiles and sometimes those of mirror-frames, was often employed by him. During his lifetime three sales were held of his furniture which he seems to have catalogued himself, and it is worth observing the emphasis which he laid on the richness and quality of the bronze mounts, such as 'a *commode* of the most elegant form adorned with bronzes of extraordinary richness'.

Working mainly in the rococo style Antoine Gaudreau was one of the principal *ébénistes* to the King from 1726 until his death in 1751, supplying a good deal of furniture to Mme de Pompadour. Some of his work was based on the designs of one or other of the Slodtz family. A *commode* in the Wallace Collection with mounts by Jacques Caffiéri (page 102) is closely based on a drawing presumed to be by the Slodtz which is in the Bibliothèque Nationale. This *commode* was once in the new apartments of Versailles begun by Louis Quinze in 1727 (plate 2).

An *ébéniste* known formerly only by his initials stamped on furniture, BVRB, has recently been identified as Bernard Van Ryssen Burgh (or Risenburgh). He supplied Mme de Pompadour by way of Duvaux, and from what little is known of him he seems to have become a *maître* of the guild in 1736, and to have died or ceased working about 1765. His work, of extremely fine quality, is much sought today, and was usually decorated with floral marquetry or with lacquer.

Lacquer was so often employed for furniture-making during the currency of the rococo style that it is appropriate to discuss it here. Oriental lacquer comes from a tree, the *rhus vernicifera*, the sap of which hardens on contact with the air, and it was among the earliest imports from the Far East. At first mainly from China, the superior quality of Japanese lacquer panels was soon recognized, and these came to be the more highly valued of the two. The panels came to Europe either singly, or made up into caskets which were broken down for remounting as case-furniture or screens. Demand was so great that the various East India Companies found it impossible to maintain a sufficient supply, and many attempts were made to produce a satisfactory substitute utilizing varnishes of one kind or another. In England John Stalker and George Parker published their *Treatise of Japanning and Varnishing* in 1688, inquiring, 'What can be more surprising than to have our chambers overlaid with varnish more glossy and reflecting than polisht marble?', and the use of the term 'japanning' is sufficient indication of the kind of lacquer most in demand.

63

---

* Known as 'poor Crozat' because his brother Antoine was even wealthier.

The Dutch had produced imitation lacquers before this, and the first record of such manufactures in France goes back almost to the middle of the seventeenth century, when work of this kind was being done by Louis Le Hongre. In 1692 there is record of three factories in Paris producing imitations of Oriental lacquer and Chinese furniture, but it was not until the early years of the eighteenth century that these began to develop into the *chinoiseries* so characteristic of the rococo period.

In 1730 two of the brothers Martin, Guillaume and Étienne-Simon, devised a varnish, a considerable improvement on anything known hitherto, which became extremely fashionable under the name of *vernis Martin* – Martin's varnish. It was widely employed in furniture manufacture, for musical instruments, for the decoration of carriages and sedan chairs, and even for such small objects as *étuis* and snuff-boxes. The prepared surface, sometimes ornamented in relief, was often painted by artists of repute, or in their styles by journeymen-painters. The technique proved equally applicable to interior decoration. The Petits Cabinets of Louis Quinze at Versailles where the King retired from the formality of the Court – 'At supper in the Cabinets', wrote de Luynes, 'he becomes an ordinary person' – were decorated in this way. The varnish known as *Chipolin* had a glossy surface almost like a porcelain glaze, or Stalker and Parker's 'polisht marble', and it provided a new and colourful way of decorating *boiseries* especially when painted in the manner of some of the more fashionable artists of the day.

Although Mme de Pompadour was fond of lacquer furniture, and paid the Martins 58,000 *livres* in 1752 for work done at Bellevue, it was a taste which the King did not share with her. Now in the Wallace Collection is a *commode* once in the bed-chamber of Queen Marie Leczinska at Fontainebleau. It was made by Marchand and Joubert, and is described in the *Journal du Garde-Meuble* as 'of Chinese lacquer with a black ground and Oriental figures and flowers, the top of brecciated violet marble'. The Queen also patronized the Martins, who supplied her with an *encoignure* (or corner-cupboard) decorated with imitation lacquer in 1738.

About mid century we see the arrival of the South German craftsmen who were to exert so remarkable an influence during the second half of the eighteenth century. The first of the great German *ébénistes* was J. F. Oeben (1720–63), who arrived in Paris in the late 1740s and became a pupil of C.-J. Boulle in 1751. He worked for Mme de Pompadour and was appointed an *ébéniste du Roi* in 1754. Oeben developed the *bureau à cylindre*, a writing-desk with a semicircular closure at the top, either a slatted roll-top (*bureau à lamelles*) or a solid section of a cylinder. This was the beginning of a fashion for complicated mechanical furniture fitted with a variety of ingenious devices by which it was made to serve several purposes, such as the combined writing and toilet tables with rising mirrors, and tables with rising backs and falling fronts and concealed drawers (plate 44). The shutter of Oeben's finest work, the *bureau du Roi Louis Quinze*, completed in 1769 by the great Jean-Henri Riesener, was so delicately counterpoised that it slid open when the key was turned in the lock. A copy of this desk is in the Wallace Collection together with the *bureau du Roi Stanislas* somewhat similar in design which was made for Stanislas Leczinski. This, too, may have been started by Oeben, although it bears the stamp of Riesener. Since Stanislas died in 1766 the *bureau* cannot have been delivered, and it appeared in the Beckford sale of the contents of Fonthill Abbey in 1823, when the catalogue described it as having come from the Garde-Meuble in Paris (plate 31).

Riesener took over Oeben's workshop after his death in 1763, becoming *maître ébéniste* in 1768 and *ébéniste du Roi* in 1774. During the decade which followed he received numerous commissions from the Court by which he became extremely wealthy, but the favour with which he was regarded proved ephemeral, largely because of the high prices he charged. He continued to enjoy the patronage of Marie-Antoinette however, even during the early years of the Revolution.

Riesener took the place of Joubert as an *ébéniste du Roi* in the same year as the King died. Joubert's preference for the now outmoded rococo style was a product of his age (he was eighty-four when he retired) and of the King's love for the style he had done so much to foster. The King's death in 1774, however, removed an influence which might have persuaded even Riesener to remain in some degree faithful to his master's preferences, and for almost the next twenty years he supplied furniture to the royal family of unmatched quality, superbly decorated with marquetry and veneering, and magnificently mounted in gilt-bronze, sometimes perhaps by Gouthière, which was more to the taste of Marie-Antoinette than was the relative severity of the *neo-grec* of the 1760s. Riesener commonly used legs in the form of *gaines* which he protected with laurel leaves of gilt-bronze, and his *secrétaires* were given chamfered corners decorated at the top with a console (using the word in its architectural sense) which was also of gilt-bronze.

David Roentgen also specialized in mechanical devices of the kind already mentioned, and his furniture was decorated with elaborate pictorial marquetries of dyed woods. His bronzes do not equal those of Riesener for quality. Roentgen's furniture was made in Germany, at Neuwied in the Rhineland, and he enjoyed the patronage of Catherine the Great (Appendix IV). Although overshadowed by Riesener in France, he was widely considered elsewhere to be the finest European *ébéniste*.

Adam Weisweiler (*fl.* 1774–1809), whose small and elegant tables sell for such fantastically high prices today, became *maître ébéniste* in 1778 after serving an apprenticeship with Roentgen at Neuwied. Much of his furniture was commissioned by the well-known dealer, Daguerre, and lacquer was one of his favourite materials. Despite the statement that he seldom used Sèvres porcelain plaques, several small pieces reasonably attributed to him are thus decorated. Jean-Guillaume Benemann, another German *ébéniste*, was making furniture for the Court by 1784 and became *maître* of the guild in the following year. At first he worked under the supervision of the sculptor Hauré, who was employed as an overseer at the Garde-Meuble. Benemann took some of Riesener's trade, but his furniture is pompous, pedestrian in design, and much inferior to that of Riesener in its decoration.

From the Low Countries came Roger Vandercruse (called La Croix) who employed the initials R V L C as a stamp. He specialized in fine marquetry, especially of Oriental subjects, and like several other *ébénistes*, he seems to have worked with Joubert, the latter perhaps manufacturing the frames or providing the designs.

There is space here only to refer to some of the more notable native-born *ébénistes* of the eighteenth century. Prominent among them was Gilles Joubert (1689–1775), already *maître ébéniste* during the Regency, who began to work for the King about 1748, succeeding Oeben as *ébéniste du Roi* in 1763. In consequence of the large number of commissions with which he was entrusted he often worked in collaboration with others. Jean-Francois Leleu (1729–1807) was apprenticed to Oeben, but left the workshop after his master's death as the result of a violent quarrel with Riesener. *Maître* in 1764, Leleu worked for both Mme du Barry and Marie-Antoinette, as well as for the Prince de Condé at Chantilly. He used Sèvres porcelain plaques to ornament his furniture and worked occasionally in the manner of Boulle. He has been credited with the introduction of inlaid brass stringing. Martin Carlin (*c.* 1785) made especial use of Sèvres plaques in the ornamentation of furniture, probably working to the orders of either Poirier or Daguerre, both dealers who supplied the Court. He also specialized in lacquer furniture, some perhaps made from dismembered Oriental cabinets, caskets, and screens, which were broken down and refurbished in a more up-to-date style. He is especially noted for the quality of his bronze mounts.

One of the most influential of the *menuisiers* engaged in the production of seat-furniture was Georges I Jacob (1739–1814), who flourished between 1765 and 1796. Jacob was a pupil of Louis Delanois, and a skilful *ébéniste* as well. Some of his designs for *ébénisterie* influenced the later Directoire style (page 161), and his Paris workshop was continued after his death by his sons, one of whom became a noted *ébéniste* of the Empire period under the name of Jacob-Desmalter. Jacob began by designing the new and lighter chairs which mark the early years of the Louis Seize style. He was among the first to adopt mahogany for chair-making, and it is probably to him that we owe the introduction of the old Roman sabre leg. Jacob supplied the French Court, and his work is also represented at Windsor. Jean-Baptiste Sené made chairs for the Queen in association with Hauré of the Garde-Meuble, as did J.-B. Boulard (1725–89) who also worked on the bed of Louis Seize at Versailles. J.-B. Lelarge (1743–1802) became *maître-menuisier* in 1775 and worked for the royal family. Michel Gourdin, *maître ébéniste* in 1752, also made chairs for the royal *châteaux*. One made by him in the 1770s, probably for the Prince de Conti (a cadet branch of the family of Bourbon-Condé) who was Grand Prior of the Temple, is in the Wallace Collection. It is still in the Louis Quinze style despite its date. These are a few of the more prominent names. These who wish to pursue the subject in detail are referred to the Bibliography.

Ébénistes were inclined to specialize in particular techniques. Such well known names as Bernard Van Risenburgh (BVRB), Carlin, Levasseur, Riesener, Topino, and Weisweiler were among the foremost craftsmen to utilize lacquer panels, while Carlin and Riesener both employed porcelain plaques. Roentgen was probably the greatest of the *ébénistes* to employ such *motifs* as vases of flowers, urns, and musical instruments executed in marquetry, although these were fashionable and done by others. Topino, *maître* of the Guild in 1773, specialized in small furniture, and he employed these *motifs* to great effect, as well as executing elaborate pictorial marquetries. The Germans, Oeben and Riesener especially, specialized in pieces with secret drawers and ingenious mechanisms which enable an apparently simple piece to serve several purposes.

The number of masters of the Guild of *Menuisiers-Ébénistes* working in Paris from the time when figures first become known in 1723 to the Revolution fell only a little below a thousand, although not all of them made furniture, some being engaged on *boiseries* and other forms of architectural woodwork. From 1751 every master of the Guild possessed a stamp with which he was compelled to mark the furniture sold by him, even the pieces he repaired which is sometimes a cause of confusion. Craftsmen who, because they worked for the King or for some other reason, did not belong to the Guild were neither allowed nor required to use a stamp, which is one reason for unstamped Paris furniture of the eighteenth century. Another reason, of course, is that it may not be an eighteenth-century production.

IV

Marks on French furniture are of several kinds–those of the *ébénistes* and *menuisiers*, marks denoting that the piece was at one time in one of the numerous royal *châteaux*, and sometimes the monogram of the Guild, the letters *ME* joined thus. The subject is a vast one, and there is insufficient space to pursue it in any kind of detail here. In the first category only the name of the craftsman is usually given, generally in full, but sometimes only initials. Most such names are stamped in a straight line; a few are in circular form. Very few provincial workshops added the name of their town or city, although exceptions include the well-known Hache family of Grenoble, Joseph Oeben (or Open) of Tours, Parmentier of Lyon, and Roentgen of Neuwied. A few stamps are usually informative, such as *Ferdinand Schwerdfeger ME Ébéniste, à Paris, 1788* (page 176). It is not unusual for the letter N to be reversed, thus Я, even in a name where it is elsewhere correctly used, which suggests that the Я stamp was sometimes employed upside down in a name stamped letter by letter.

The marks on pieces made for the royal *châteaux*, which can occasionally be linked with surviving inventories, were sometimes branded, sometimes painted or stencilled, but rarely struck. The royal mark is usually the fleur-de-lys in conjunction with a crown. Under Louis Quinze this sometimes became the double *L* monogram under a crown. Bellevue is represented by *BV* under a crown; Chanteloup is *CP*, but the name, Chanteloup, is also that of an *ébéniste* of the Louis Seize period. The mark of Chantilly was a hunting horn, which also appears on porcelain made at the Prince de Condé's factory. Interlaced *C*'s beneath a crown is the mark of Compiègne, and Fontainebleau is represented by an *F* or *FON*, sometimes in conjunction with a crown or the fleur-de-lys. *GR* and *F* beneath a crown refer to the Garde-Meuble de Fontainebleau, and the Garde-Meuble de la Reine is that of Marie-Antoinette. *MLM* is the stamp of Malmaison, *SC* refers to Saint-Cloud, *CT* or *T* to the Palais de Trianon, *GT* to the Grand Trianon, and *T* beneath a crown, or *TH*, to the Tuileries, so called because tile-kilns were once situated in the grounds. *GM* signifies Garde-Meuble, *V* means Versailles, and *MRCV* within a shield and under a crown is the mark of the Mobilier Royal of the *Château* de Versailles.

Old French furniture has been extensively forged and reproduced, often very cleverly, and a close study of genuine examples is essential to sound judgement. False stamps are sometimes added, and these cannot be accepted as proof of genuineness except in conjunction with a favourable verdict on all other aspects – style, relationship to other known and accepted works, patina, bronzework, and so forth. When everything agrees a stamp is very desirable, and one of those listed above as indicating its origin in one or other of the royal *châteaux* an extremely important addition.

V

Nothing can be created out of nothing. The furnishing of Versailles was stylistically a continuation of what had gone before. It evolved from the many foreign influences which competed for attention. Not the least of the achievements of Louis Quatorze and his talented administration, the designers and artists they employed, was the resolution of these often conflicting currents into one style which could be called truly French.

The revived classicism of Italy came to France at the beginning of the sixteenth century, but, like the English, French designers were at first inclined to regard ornament as the essence of the new style. Thus we find old Gothic forms tricked out with the new classical *motifs*. To a considerable extent the dissemination of the new styles was a product of the art of printing from engraved copper plates, newly discovered at the beginning of the sixteenth century. Particularly were these employed to delineate the popular *grotesques* which we can trace in varying forms through the ensuing three centuries, those of Jean I Bérain being discussed on page 48. *Grotesques*, an ancient Roman form of ornament discovered in the excavated ruins of Nero's Golden House, inspired Raphael's decorations for the *loggie* of the Vatican, and they became exceedingly popular in all forms of decorative art, first in Italy, and then in the northern countries in conjunction with an angular strap-work (plate 6) derived from the Low Countries.

François Premier brought many Italian artists to France, including Primaticcio, Cellini, and Leonardo da Vinci, to help with the decoration of Fontainebleau. Both Catherine de' Medici (1519–89) and Marie de' Medici (1573–1642), as Queens of France, helped to strengthen Italian influence, and both came from a family with a long tradition of art-patronage. During the reigns of Henri Quatre and Louis Treize Flemish influence was also strong, and that of Spain, and even of Portugal, may be traced. Henri Quatre sent French craftsmen to Holland to study the art of working in ebony, installing them in the Louvre as the first *menuisiers en ébène*, and Louis Treize brought craftsmen from Germany, Flanders, and Switzerland. There is evidence to suggest that one of the latter, a Swiss named Pierre Boulle, was an ancestor of André-Charles Boulle.

It was, however, the craftsmen of Italy who brought many of the techniques later developed in France. The Italians were adept at the art of inlaying in a great variety of materials – stone, ivory, tortoiseshell, and mother-of-pearl – as well as being makers of extremely elaborate marquetries in coloured woods. They employed gold and silver mounts for the cabinets of the day, and they anticipated the brass and tortoiseshell marquetries of Boulle, and his gilt-bronze mounts.

The fashion for luxurious cabinets in France was the product of their popularity in Italy, and those imported from Holland are almost indistinguishable from their Italian prototypes, so well did the northern craftsmen assimilate the southern style. Cabinets imported from southern Germany were less Italian in style, but often of superb quality, with locks and similar furniture by the metalworkers of Augsburg.

Neither Richelieu nor Mazarin attempted to stem the tide of Italian influence, and among the many Italian craftsmen taken into French royal service at the time were the metalworker, Domenico Cucci, and the carver, Philippe Caffiéri, whose work will be later discussed.

The origin of the *Manufacture Royale des Meubles de la Couronne* is to be found in an attempt by Henri Quatre to collect the foremost French craftsmen under one roof in the Louvre, but it needed the genius of Colbert to organize them on a scale large enough decisively to direct the course of art in France.

The principal item of furniture in the seventeenth century was undoubtedly the cabinet of *ébénisterie*, often on an elaborate stand made by the *menuisier* and the carver. It was usually fitted with drawers in an interior closed by two doors. The cabinet itself was more or less richly decorated, often with chiselled silver. For a glance at the cabinets of mid century we may profitably turn to the Inventory of Mazarin's possessions, made in 1653. He possessed no fewer than twenty cabinets, described as having columns of lapis lazuli, jasper, and amethyst outlined with gold, inlays of ivory and tortoiseshell, and mounts of gilt-bronze. Those of the King were even more sumptuous. Cucci was paid 30,000 *livres* for two for the Louvre. Of another made for Versailles the description mentions the

covering of jasper, lapis lazuli, and agate, enriched in the front with four figures of heros in gilt-bronze on a lapis ground, in the middle with a portico supported by two columns of lapis with bases and capitals of gilt-bronze, and the Arms of France crowned on the front supported by two gilt-bronze angels also on a lapis ground. In the recess beneath the portico a figure in gilt-bronze of [Louis Quatorze] seated and carrying in his left hand a shield chiselled with His Majesty's device.

The carved and gilded stand was no less rich, the four legs being in the form of pilasters with an azure ground, and four figures representing the principal rivers of the world.

The cabinet is basically a chest on stand. Related to it are the marriage-chests on stands and the *commode*. The latter first appears a little before 1690. It means 'convenient' or 'commodious', and it was not only an extremely decorative object, to be placed under a pier-glass between windows, but it was useful for storing the multitude of valuable trifles which the eighteenth century accumulated.★

The term does not seem to have become current immediately. In 1718 we find the duchesse d'Orléans using it in a letter and describing the object for the benefit of her correspondent as 'a large table with two large drawers'. The number of drawers is, in fact, variable, and until a little after mid century the customary arrangement was either two long drawers, or two small ones at the top and two long drawers below. The stiles also form the legs, the feet sometimes being of *pied de biche* form, i.e. deer's hoof. The stiles are slightly curved (plate 20) in a fashion termed *profile en arbalète*, from a resemblance to the *arbalète* or crossbow. There was usually little ground clearance in the case of *commodes* made before the Regency, the lower apron approaching the floor quite closely, and specimens have survived mounted on a stand (*gradin*) a few inches in height. A serpentine front is an early feature, but swelling curves to the

70   ★ How, and why, the word became a euphemism for what the French call so much more accurately the *chaise percée* I cannot say, but I suspect it became current during the nineteenth century.

panels – usually termed *bombé* – are a Regency innovation at a time when *ébénistes* first solved the problem of applying veneers to this kind of surface. Some of the *commodes* designed and made by Boulle were based in form on the antique sarcophagus and are termed *en tombeau* (page 75).

Boulle's greatest skill as a craftsman and designer was probably lavished on the *armoire*, of which a specimen is illustrated on plate 32. The *armoire* is a large cupboard perhaps once for the storage of arms as the name suggests, but later adapted to the storage of many other things – clothes, silver, porcelain, and so forth. The *armoire* resisted change rather more than other kinds of furniture. It was made far more often by the *menuisier* than most case-furniture, and the plainer *armoires* of the reign of Louis Quinze often echo the style of his predecessor on the throne, even when made in Paris, while the mid-century style still survived sixty years later.

The *buffet à deux corps*, which dates back to the sixteenth century, is also a tall cupboard like the *armoire*, but in two separate parts, one on the other, and the earliest examples are very richly carved, although the decoration became simpler as these massive objects were made for more purely utilitarian purposes. Divorced from its top and surmounted by a marble slab it became the *armoire basse*, the low *armoire* (plate 36), often a *meuble à hauteur d'appui*, a piece low enough to lean on.

Both the *armoire* and the *buffet à deux corps* must, because of their size, be reckoned among the least mobile pieces of furniture, and the *armoire* was often built into the *boiserie*, being little more than a pair of doors, solid, glazed, or with a trellisage of brass backed with silk to exclude dust. Provided with shelves for the storage of books, the *armoire* became a bookcase (*armoire-bibliothèque*).

There is a danger, since this discussion is largely confined to the finest specimens, that we shall think of the *armoire* as an elaborately decorated cupboard, but the term is equally applicable to the plain specimens of *menuiserie* in oak or pine which furnished the homes of the *bourgeoisie* or the less important rooms of palaces.

A development of these two pieces of furniture was the *encoignure* or corner-cupboard, which first appears in the reign of Louis Quinze in two parts, the top being either open shelves or closed with doors. These have now, all too often, been parted from one another, as have the two parts of the English corner-cupboard, although one sees the lower part fitted out with a marble top as a complete piece of furniture. They were later made in this form. Like the *armoire*, the *encoignure* was often built in.

The basic 'table' takes many forms. Verlet has adduced ample evidence in favour of his contention that the word without qualification was employed only to refer to what we should call the table-top. The distinction between the *console* table attached to the *boiserie* (*console d'applique*) and the *table de milieu* placed in the centre of the room is an important one.

The most precious part of the *console* table was undoubtedly its marble top. The carved gilt-wood support, however fine, was considered to be expendable, to be changed in accordance with the dictates of current fashion. Verlet refers to the various sale catalogues of the eighteenth century which describe 'tables of rare marble on their supports', and tops (or 'tables') were not only of marble, but of jasper, porphyry, onyx, alabaster, polished granite, and mosaic. The same distinction is to be observed in the appropriate entries in Duvaux's account book, and it was current in England at the end of the seventeenth century.

The marbles themselves were of the most exotic kinds – turquoise blue, Egyptian green, red and brown Italian *griotte, antin* streaked with red, grey, and violet, *portor*, black with a veining of grey splashed with golden yellow, and *brèche d'Alep* which was a brecciated marble of grey, black, and yellow pebbles. For the less affluent *bourgeoisie* there were imitations of marbles, either painted in *trompe l'œil* or made from marble chippings embedded in *stucco* (the Italian *scagliola*), such as that of Grisel who advertised in the *Mercure* that he had discovered a composition which imitated all marbles, even to the most precious, so perfectly as to deceive connoisseurs. It would not, of course, be difficult for a skilled workman to recut an old marble top to a more fashionable shape, and this we must assume was done occasionally.

During the reign of Louis Seize *console* tables were rarely attached to the wall, being placed instead on four or more legs, when, strictly, they become side-tables. The term, however, is to be used with care. English side-tables are more often than not serving-tables, whereas the Louis Seize variety were frequently intended to be ornamental, for carrying a clock or a garniture of Sèvres porcelain vases.

The dining-table in France until quite late in the eighteenth century was nearly always of common *menuiserie* – boards placed on folding trestles such as had been used in the Middle Ages. The expandable table of *ébénisterie*, into which leaves could be inserted in the English manner, did not come into use until quite late in the eighteenth century. There were several reasons for this. The trestle-table could be adapted to the seating of a very large number of guests; it could easily be taken down and stored when not in use; and it was large enough, and strong enough, to provide room for the elaborate table-decorations customary during the seventeenth and eighteenth centuries.

The art of table-decoration was carefully studied. At first of silver or silver-gilt (*vermeil*) and later of porcelain, the complete ensemble often took hours to set out. English readers can get an impression of the appearance of an eighteenth-century banqueting table at Apsley House, where the Duke of Wellington's Portuguese silver table-decoration is set out on a table extending for most of the length of a large *salon*, but this is a relatively late survival of what was customary in the more exalted eighteenth-century circles.

In the eighteenth century the porcelain of Meissen was popular as table-decoration, and many of the small figures modelled by Kändler and Eberlein in the 1740s were originally in large sets intended for this purpose, even though they are now treasured singly in cabinets. Meissen porcelain marked *KHC* (*Königliche Hof Conditorei*) testifies to its presence in the cupboards of the Court kitchens and confectioneries, and ultimately on the royal table. These figures were inspired by those made from sugar which decorated Roman banqueting tables in the seventeenth century, and whether of silver or porcelain they were usually provided with a large centre-piece having a definite theme, with figures contributing to the same theme dotted about among the plates, dishes, and tureens, which they matched in form and ornament. It was also far from unknown for two sets to be used, one for dessert which was laid at a separate table.

The trestle-table was essential to seat the large number of guests customarily invited to dine with the King on formal occasions. The movement towards greater informality, of which the rococo style is one aspect, perhaps began with the Regent who, like Louis Quinze, was impatient of ceremony, but it was certainly well in evidence after the construction by the King of the Petits Cabinets at Versailles, referred to by those who were not invited to share the intimate suppers there as 'the rat's nest'. Guests were usually drawn from the King's hunting companions of the day, and many were the intrigues to gain an invitation when the list of guests for the particular evening was marked off.

Informality marked the eighteenth century increasingly as the years passed. Rooms became smaller, more intimate, and more varied in their purposes. State occasions were fewer. Louis Quinze observed the retirement ceremony in the State bedchamber, but he slipped out through a side door to his real bed when the courtiers had left, to return the next morning in time for the *lever*. This may also be seen in the progress towards smaller tables, which multiplied in their variety as the century unfolded. The *ambulantes* were the equivalent of the occasional tables of eighteenth-century England, where a similar evolution may be observed in the introduction of the Pembroke table, the tip-up tea-table, and small tables with a tray-top and tripod feet for placing near the chair. In France these small tables evolved in great numbers, usually inspired by the more important of the dealers, such as Poirier and Daguerre. The seventeenth-century *guéridon* had been a candlestand with a tray-top, a stem, and a tripod foot.★ The eighteenth-century piece of furniture termed a *guéridon* was very different. It was a table, usually circular, quite small, and with a shelf or shelves between the legs. Frequently it was provided with a top of *porcelaine de Sèvres* for tea and coffee cups, such as Carlin made a speciality. A pierced gallery was added to protect the precious Sèvres coffee service from being knocked off by a passer-by.

★ The first *guéridons* thus to be named were in the form of a blackamoor holding aloft the tray on which the candelabrum was placed. The figure represented a Moor named Guéridon.

Work-tables were almost infinite in their diversity, and rarely are two alike. They were made to hold the implements for sewing and embroidery. '*Chiffonnière*' is a term among many, some of which are obscure, and probably the invention of the dealers of the period. Night-tables or bedside-tables (the *table de nuit*, the *table de chevet* for the head of the bed, or the *vide-poche* into which the pockets were emptied, are some eighteenth-century terms for them) housed the chamber-pot in the cupboard below which was provided with a marble shelf, while the tray-top carried the candlestick and the requirements for the night. These tables commonly had pierced hand-holes on either side for ease of carrying, since they were stored in the *garde-robe* during the day. Tip-up tables in the English style enjoyed a limited vogue with the fashion for English things generally, to which the letter from Wedgwood to Choiseul quoted (page 115) testifies.

Also in great diversity were the tables which pandered to the eighteenth-century passion for gaming, which continued unabated until the Revolution.* One of the panels of Huet's *Petite Singerie* at Chantilly depicts monkeys in the costume of the day playing at cards, but card-tables apart, special tables for all kinds of games – chess, backgammon, roulette, and billiards – were placed wherever company gathered.

Belonging to a group of furniture classifiable as a kind of table is the *bureau-plat* – a large flat writing-table (*table à écrire*) with drawers in the frieze. It was first introduced about the beginning of the seventeenth century, and the name comes from the stuff used to cover it – *drap de bure*, a sort of drugget. Although it resembles a table, however, the *bureau* also seems to have been a variety of *cabinet*, a seventeenth-century record referring to a *cabinet ou grand bureau*. The term '*bureau*' seems to have been reserved for the more imposing examples with large drawers, while '*table à écrire*' referred only to small tables for this purpose. Thus we find in an inventory of 1677 'a small table in the form of a *bureau* with five drawers'.

The familiar English desk flanked by pedestals of drawers supporting the top on either side of a knee-hole is comparatively rare in French furniture, although it occurs occasionally. The more usual arrangement in the eighteenth century was the addition of a *cartonnier* or *serre-papiers*, (untranslatable terms for what are essential ornamental racks of pigeon-holes and drawers), often to the flat top on one side or the other. These, like the *bureau* itself, were frequently superb specimens of *ébénisterie*, whether separate from or integral with the table. The great *bureau du Roi Louis Quinze* is strictly a *bureau-plat* on which has been placed an unusually elaborate *cartonnier* extending over the whole of the upper surface and closed with a cylinder-front. The type is illustrated on plate 31, but this

*. . . it is no dishonour to keep a public gaming-house; there are at least a hundred and fifty people of the first quality in Paris who live by it. You may go into their houses at all hours of the night and find hazard, pharaoh, &c. Horace Walpole, *Letters*. 1739.

and the *bureau du Roi* are among the masterpieces of their kind, and smaller and much less elaborate versions are the rule.

The true *bureau-plat* with its *cartonnier* was immense in size, fit for formal occasions and great houses. It was made for the offices of Ministers and *fermiers-généraux*. Hardly to be regarded as belonging in the same category is the *bureau* or *secrétaire à dos d'âne* (the ass's back), with a sloping front, which is also called a *bureau à pente*, in the eighteenth century a *bureau à dessus brisé* (with a broken top), and sometimes a *secrétaire en tombeau*. Verlet points out that it is a mistake to call the single desk an ass-back, a term which could only be applied to a back-to-back partner's desk on this plan, with a slope on both sides, but in any case '*à dos d'âne*' is a relatively recent dealer's term for such desks. *Bureaux* of this kind have fall-fronts which rest on two pull-out slides on either side, or are supported on the upper side by two brass pieces shaped like a compass. The place of the *cartonnier* of the *bureau-plat* is taken by an arrangement of small drawers and pigeon-holes above the level of the opened writing surface, as in the case of some similar English desks.

At the other end of the scale, testifying to the amount of letter-writing customary before the invention of the telephone, are numerous *bureaux* made for a variety of purposes, such as the *bureau de dame* (the lady's desk) for the *boudoir*, which is sometimes a small *dos d'âne* on slender legs, or the *bonheur du jour* (plate 49),★ a small flat writing-table with an additional receptacle at the back for papers and oddments, usually drawers or shelves enclosed with doors. Under this frivolous designation the *bonheur du jour* became increasingly popular during the second half of the century, but seemingly it did not receive its name until about 1770, and it was probably given to it by one of the dealers although there are entries in Duvaux's account book apparently referring to pieces of this kind.

Many pieces of furniture, apparently small tables intended for other purposes, were fitted for writing with pull-out slides which were leather-covered, and a small drawer at the side for ink and pens. Others had a reading-slope incorporated rising from the top and supported at the back with an adjustable stand, with a ledge at the bottom on which the book was placed. In some pieces the whole of the top lifted upwards.

Toilet-tables of *ébénisterie* often had a writing-slide incorporated, or even a reading-stand, in addition to various compartments for toiletries and the mirror. The top frequently opened in the middle to reveal the mirror which lifted upwards and was held by a stand, and the top folded back on either side to provide access to small compartments fitted with hinged or sliding covers. The interiors of these compartments were lined with satin or padded, and they contained cosmetic pots and jars of silver and Sèvres porcelain. This, however, was an almost standard

★ Meaning literally, 'the happy hour of the day', the name given to this piece of furniture is probably derived from the passionate eighteenth-century pursuit of happiness, which by mid century assumed almost the proportions of an obsession.

version, of which many variations in shape and size are to be seen. These tables were *ambulantes*, often on casters, to enable them to be moved from the bedroom to the *boudoir*, and to the *garde-robe* when not required. A less elaborate kind of toilet-table, often of *menuiserie*, was draped with one or other of the decorative materials of the period, with toilet accessories of silver, porcelain, or *faïence* on the top, and an independent mirror which could be removed at will.

Another variety of writing-desk, which developed from the *armoire* rather than from the table, is the *secrétaire en abbatant*, sometimes called *en armoire*. In general plan it closely resembles certain walnut *bureaux* made in England at the beginning of the eighteenth century, but in France it is an innovation of the reign of Louis Quinze. In its usual form it has a large fall-front which, when let down, uncovers a series of drawers, and provides the writing-surface. The lower part was usually given double doors enclosing shelves (on one of which was placed a strong-box) instead of drawers in the English manner. Often it was provided with a companion piece – the *chiffonnier*, not to be confounded with the *chiffonnière* which is a work-table. Both these objects, because of the large surface presented by the doors and the fall-front, offered exceptional opportunities for elaborate decoration in marquetry.

A provincial variation is essentially a *commode*, the top of which was adapted for writing by the addition of pigeon-holes and drawers at the back enclosed by a sloping front, like the *dos d'âne*, and surmounted by a bookcase with glazed doors, the whole being very similar in appearance to the English bureau-bookcase.

Perhaps the only entirely new development of the Louis Seize period was the *vitrine*, a glazed cabinet for the display of such trifles as porcelain figures, small bronzes, Oriental curios, and *bibelots* of one kind or another which had formerly found a place on the mantelshelf or on a corner *étagère*, a tier of shelves which sometimes surmounted a lower *encoignure* or was attached to the wall. *Vitrines*, usually simple in design, often have a pierced gallery at the top, another introduction of the period, but more elaborate specimens, Louis Quinze in style, especially those decorated with paintings after Watteau and Lancret in the sort of varnish associated with the Martins, are of nineteenth-century date.

Screens were the province either of the *menuisier*, when they are carved and gilded, or of the *ébéniste*, when they are veneered or of solid polished wood of exceptional quality. In the seventeenth century draught-screens (*paravents*) of very large size were sometimes made of incised and coloured Chinese lacquer which gained its name from the port of trans-shipment on the Coromandel coast of India. From years of exposure to light and dust these have now lost their original brilliance, but the rare enclosed cabinets of this kind of lacquer, when finely preserved, are evidence of the colourful appearance of these screens when they were new.

Eighteenth-century draught-screens were of many materials, quite often in a frame of *ébénisterie*, the panels perhaps of silk, embroidered fabrics, Chinese painted paper, or painted lacquer and varnish. In front of the chimney-piece was the firescreen (*écran*), which was generally rectangular on a double support at either side. They were often quite elaborate, with sliding panels, and sometimes a shelf in addition for small articles, and even a drawer. The adjustable pole-screen of the English type made its appearance at mid century, and hand-screens were usually of Chinese paper with a turned handle. Chinese paper, termed *papier des Indes*, was especially popular during the reign of Louis Quinze.

The tendency throughout the century was for screens to follow room design and to become smaller. The great seven-foot twelve-leaved Coromandels of the seventeenth century were no longer necessary, nor was it possible to house them. Large *paravents* began to disappear, to be replaced by the *écran*, which became more elaborate as its usefulness as an additional piece of furniture became apparent. The firescreen *en secrétaire*, for example, was provided not only with a drawer but with a small shelf and an inkstand.

Throughout the eighteenth century Paris furniture of good quality was usually veneered, whilst much provincial furniture was of solid wood. Provincial pieces are, for this reason, in native woods of one kind or another – oak, walnut, beech, wild cherry, olive, ash, and so forth, while elm was usually reserved for *boiseries*. Care was taken to select wood with a good figure, and knots and burrs were valued for their decorative effect. Pear wood, which takes dye well, was often stained black, and such wood is termed 'ebonized'. It is met quite frequently in eighteenth-century records as '*bois noircy*'. Until the beginning of that century few imported woods were employed, apart from the much-valued ebony, but the interest in the West Indies, awakened during the Regency, led to the import of mahogany (*acajou*), which came particularly into the ports of Le Havre and Bordeaux. Provincial furniture from the latter area was often carried out in mahogany and early *armoires* of solid mahogany are not unknown. By mid century it was relatively common, and Lazare Duvaux delivered several pieces of mahogany furniture to Mme de Pompadour. Soon it had almost replaced walnut for the finest work.

Other woods were imported freely. Satinwood, violetwood, rosewood, tulipwood, and amaranth (which is a variety of mahogany), were among them. The demand for exotic woods suitable for coloured marquetries and veneers rose steadily. For the most part they were needed for marquetries – a field in which the possible range of colours had hitherto been very limited. Violet, green, yellow, red, black, grey, and white became possible, some in a variety of shades, while the decorative possibilities of grain and figuring were also explored. These techniques replaced the combinations of wood with other materials common in the seventeenth century, and the *motifs* employed became extremely complex, ranging from the simplest chevron pattern, called *point de Hongrie*, to panels of elaborate geometric marquetry bordered and outlined with inlaid fillets of contrasting colour, and to coloured pictures in inlaid woods. The latter were the culminating point – floral bouquets, trophies, and even figure and architectural subjects, some of which necessitated the use of dyed woods which have now lost their original colour. Roentgen was the greatest exponent of this kind of marquetry, and he developed a fashion which first appeared soon after mid century. By using smaller pieces of wood he produced pictures in far greater detail than the earlier *ébénistes*, and by heating the surface and by engraving it he attained a much more varied effect.

Equally colourful, and always expensive, were lacquer panels, both genuine and simulated, and a certain amount of furniture, especially seat-furniture, was always painted and gilded, a fashion more marked towards the end of the century.

During the reign of Louis Seize there are few technical innovations of consequence in the realm of furniture-making. Mahogany was common enough to be used in solid form, especially for chair-frames, and Marie-Antoinette even had the parquetry of her *boudoir* floor made from it. Brass stringing began to take the place of stringing of inlaid wood, and was probably less expensive.

VI

If we leave *boiseries* and architectural woodwork to one side for later consideration, the *menuisier* principally devoted himself to seat-furniture, table-supports, and beds.

Almost until the end of the reign of Louis Quatorze the bed-chamber remained the most important room in the house; the *salon* – the large reception room where the company gathered – did not begin to assume a predominant position until the closing years of the seventeenth century. The focal point of the bed-chamber was the bed itself, on which even people of modest means often lavished all, or more than all, that they could afford. Financiers, aristocrats, and especially the King, had beds the richness of which has never been surpassed. This was the product of the establishment of the Court in a fixed position. Until well into the sixteenth century the Court moved about from place to place, from one royal palace to another, at relatively frequent intervals, for the purpose of allowing the King to oversee every part of his dominion, sometimes staying in encampments of large tents and portable buildings. In medieval times one Court official was known as the 'driver of the tapestry sumpter' and was nominally responsible for the movement of tapestries, which were taken down in one place and rehung in another. Portable beds were still common in the eighteenth century, both for campaigning and travelling, although few have survived. Of a kind unknown today, so far as my own researches take me, but which may have existed in France in the seventeenth century, is a Spanish settee in the Getty collection which is completely collapsible, the back folding forward on to the seat of scarlet velvet, the legs, held by wrought-iron supports, collapsing to fold under the seat.

At Versailles the finest beds, fixed in their position and awarded a place of honour, were monumental in size and decorated with the greatest elaboration. They were usually provided with four posts (*quenouilles*), one at each corner, which upheld the canopy. The seventeenth-century bed was mainly the province of the *tapissier* instead of the woodcarver as it had been in the sixteenth century, and the *menuisier* usually provided little more than a plain framework on which the *tapissier* could demonstrate his skill. Canopies became increasingly luxurious, and the top of each post was decorated with costly plumes and ornamental *pommes* or 'apples'. Mazarin's inventories refer to 'four velvet apples to put on top of the posts', while those of Madame's bed towards the end of the century bore 'apples' of gold and silver brocade, with plumes of green, white, and yellow feathers. The plumes were called *panaches*, from the plume of feathers decorating medieval helmets.

The bed was totally enclosed by ample and sumptuous curtains, and when drawn they left a space between them and the bed itself. Additional to the curtains were the *lambrequins*, draperies looped upward at intervals or scalloped and fringed, which hung from the frame of the canopy, the curtains being suspended inside the *lambrequins* on rings sliding on rods. At the back a hanging was permanently suspended, and the bedhead itself was lavishly upholstered. Canopies occur in a variety of forms, attached to all four posts at the top in the case of the bed called *à la française*, at the back only if it was *à la duchesse*, in the form of a crown if it was an *impériale*, *d'ange* when it was suspended from the ceiling, and *à pavillon* if it was in the form of a pitched roof. These are but a few of the many terms used to describe canopies, some of which are now obscure.

The bed itself, its mattress and its coverings, provided a suitable subject for the display of luxurious materials of all kinds, both imported and made in France, which included silks, satins, damasks, *brocatelle*, and delicate *passementeries* (page 131) and fringes, like the bed owned by Richelieu of velvet heavily fringed with gold *passementerie*. Mazarin's bed had curtains of pearl-grey satin embroidered with flowers in scarlet, green, and cream, with a counterpane of the same material, and flowers in scarlet, gold, and silver thread. His State bed was of crimson velvet ornamented with silver flowers alternating with flowers of gold, the curtains of crimson taffeta, and the rest, including the counterpane, fringed with gold and silver, the four posts surmounted by massive silver ornament. The King possessed no fewer than four hundred beds, all more or less sumptuously decorated, and of every conceivable variety, enhanced with scallops and fringes of silk, gold, and silver. Nor was he parsimonious in giving beds to his mistresses. Louise de la Vallière's bed was covered with gold and silver in squares on a crimson ground, with a monogram worked in gold. Less sumptuous beds marked the descent in social scale, but even a simple country gentleman had a bed of violet satin embroidered with small pieces of cloth of gold and bound with silver threads.

From about the middle of the seventeenth century some of the women of the Court received their guests reclining on a *lit de repos*, a day-bed, and both Fouquet and Mazarin possessed splendid examples of this kind. They became popular at Versailles, the cushions covered in luxurious materials and the frames of gilded wood. These are perhaps better classified as seat-furniture rather than beds, and are later discussed.

By the middle of the eighteenth century beds had become far less elaborate. They now fell largely into three different categories – *à la française*, *à la duchesse*, and *à la polonaise*. The *duchesse* bed had a canopy attached only at the back, the front part being suspended from the ceiling; the Polish bed usually had three backs, at either end and on one of the long sides, the canopy, where provided, being upheld by iron rods. These beds were primarily intended for an alcove which was increasingly being provided for the purpose, the three walls taking the place of the earlier bed-curtains which were now to be found only in the front. The bed *à la française* had a head-board only. Canopies of great luxury and varied form were still customary, and the head-boards for French and *duchesse* beds were handsomely decorated. Occurring less frequently were the beds *à la turque* and *à la romaine*, but these terms are imprecise and obscure, and it is now difficult to be certain exactly what they meant.

Most of the more exotic names given to beds of the Louis Seize period principally mark differences in the type of canopy and the arrangement of the hangings – such as *l'Impériale* (with a crown-shaped canopy), *à la Panurge*, or *à la Militaire*. There was also a revival of the four-poster of the Louis Quatorze period, but with fewer drapes, the woodwork as often of *ébénisterie* as of *menuiserie*. Legs, now no longer concealed beneath voluminous draperies, were characteristic of the furniture supports of the time. The emphasis on woodwork rather than on textiles is the reason why more beds have survived from this period.

If the bed proper largely remained the province of the *tapissier*, the day-bed (the *lit de repos*) was the work of the *menuisier* and the carver, the *tapissier* providing the coverings and the cushions in the same way as he did for seat-furniture generally.

The *canapé* (which is a basic term for the settee) first appeared in the middle of the seventeenth century, but seemingly the word first occurs in an inventory of the possessions of André Le Nôtre in 1700. The *canapé* probably developed from the *banquette* (a bench without a back) or the *lit de repos*, but in effect it is an enlarged armchair made from two or more chairs put together side by side with an arm at either end. At first of considerable length, and more or less fixed in its general design, it became smaller during the reign of Louis Quinze and its varieties multiplied. Some variations were of a relatively minor character to which exotic names were given by the dealers of the day, and these are now often difficult to separate one from the other.

The *canapé* proper nearly always occupied a designated position and was often carved with its frame matching the *boiserie*, but some of its variations were less fixed, it frequently being placed in a lady's bedchamber at the foot of the bed. Here she reclined to receive her visitors, and sometimes even the tradesmen.

Terms of Turkish derivation are fairly common. The principal one was the *sopha*, an overstuffed *canapé* which was often of great length. The *ottomane* (not to be confused with the English 'ottoman') was a *sopha* the ends of which were usually rounded to form a semicircle (*en gondole*). *Sultane* and *turquoise* are also terms of similar derivation denoting relatively minor differences. The term *paphose* is seemingly of Greek origin, but even André Roubo, a *menuisier* whose *L'Art de Menuisier* published between 1769–74 is a primary source of information on the *menuiserie* of the period, confessed an inability to do more than define it as a kind of *sopha* unusually ornate. The *duchesse* was a kind of *chaise-longue* or *bergère* (see below) with a back at one end only, to which was added a stool (*tabouret*) with two sidepieces and a footstool with a low footboard called a *bout de pied* or foot-end, when it became a *duchesse brisée*. Alternatively it took the form of two *bergères* at either end with an intervening leg-rest. The *veilleuse* was a day-bed large enough for night-time use.

The *canapé* small enough to seat only two people was called *à confident*, and sometimes *à marquise*, the latter a term dating from the last quarter of the eighteenth century and probably the invention of one of the dealers.

The evolution of the chair requires discussion. The strict etiquette governing the positioning of chairs in the eighteenth century was partly a product of the fact that the woodwork was carved to match the *boiserie* of a particular room, and the coverings were similar to the fabrics of curtains and *portières*, and often the wall-hangings. Occasionally tapestries from Gobelins or Beauvais were accompanied by matching sets of covers woven for the chairs and *canapés*, although this was a luxury reserved only for the finest houses.

In the seventeenth century, however, chairs were not so numerous as in the eighteenth, and they were, at formal gatherings and even at informal ones, allocated strictly according to social rank. Nor must we omit reference to the kind of chair to which one was entitled. For the greater number of minor Court officials no seating at all was provided. For the lowest rank of those entitled to sit a high stuffed cushion had to serve. Next in order were those whose rank was high enough to be awarded a *pliant* – a folding stool. Slightly higher in the scale was the *tabouret* or stool proper, and the *banquette* or bench on which several people could sit side by side. Next came the chair with a back, and finally the *fauteuil* with a back and arms, the latter being a very rare honour, the finest specimen always being reserved for the King. Status was also equated with the richness of the chair offered. Invited to sit in the chamber of a nobleman of high rank, a minor country gentleman, a *bourgeois*, or a poet might be offered a chair with turned rails and a rush seat.

In the Middle Ages the chair without arms did not exist, and even the chair with arms – the *chaise à bras* – was a great rarity, stools or benches being the rule. The Old French from which '*fauteuil*', meaning an arm-chair, is derived is *fauldsteuil* – the equivalent of the Old English *faldstool*, derived from the Old High German, *falden*, to fold. It once meant a folding-stool or chair similar to the Roman curule chair, of which a seventh-century example is preserved in the Louvre – the chair of Dagobert which has a back and arms added in the twelfth century.

The chair without arms was a by-product of the fashion for the *vertugadin* or farthingale, a kind of hooped petticoat, in vogue during the last quarter of the sixteenth century, and the term *fauteuil* for an arm-chair did not become current until the second half of the seventeenth century, when the voluminous wigs of the period necessitated a chair with a modified back, in contrast with the high backs of the old Gothic chairs which were usually of solid wood elaborately carved, the hardness of the seats alleviated by cushions. The *chaise à bras* had always been a prerogative of the most powerful and influential personages in any assembly, and at Versailles it was reserved for the King and his immediate family. The custom was preserved throughout the reign of Louis Quatorze, a stickler for etiquette and protocol. The *fauteuil* of this period had a relatively high back, rectangular in form, which was overstuffed like the seat. The frame was of carved wood, usually gilt, and the legs were linked and strengthened by a stretcher (*entretoise*), either in the form of an H, or, on the finest examples, an X-stretcher, curved and handsomely carved. Covering was of the richest materials, including brocade, satin, damask, velvet, tapestry, the piled fabric of the Savonnerie carpet factory, silk, embroidery, and, on the least important examples, *moquette* or serge. Leather coverings, usually on chairs influenced by Spanish work, were embossed in imitation of wall-hangings, hammered over an *intaglio* plate so that the design was imprinted on the surface and ornamented with metal. Rush-seated chairs (*à la capucin*), popular in the reign of Louis Treize for the less important rooms, were replaced by seats of woven cane during the second half of the century, but they continued in use for rustic interiors.

A departure soon after 1680 was the *fauteuil en commodité* or *en confessional*, analogous to the English wing armchair, which was primarily designed for comfort, and exempt from the strict rules governing the use and disposition of the more formal seats. These anticipated the attention to comfort which was to be a feature of eighteenth-century design.

The eighteenth century saw the introduction of many new kinds of seat-furniture, much of which had comfort as its principal objective. The *bergère*, for instance, introduced during the Regency, was an arm-

82

chair with a deep seat and comfortable upholstery, and cushions on which one could half-recline in luxury, which, with the addition of a stool or stools on which to rest the legs, became something very close to a *duchesse brisée*. It was sometimes designed on the same principle as the wing-chair, when it became a *bergère en confessionnal*.

The *fauteuil* proper, as well as the chair without arms, is divided into two classes – *en cabriolet*, with a curved back, and *à la reine*, with a flat back. Of these two, the former was an occasional chair, to be moved at will, and the latter more or less fixed in its position, not merely by custom and etiquette but often by its relationship with the *boiserie* and the remainder of the furnishings.

Under Louis Quinze the cabriole leg was invariable, and the frame was handsomely carved in the taste of the period, being painted or gilded in addition. The *menuisier* prepared the frame for the carver, who passed it on to the painter or gilder. Then it went to the upholsterer (*tapissier*), who delivered it to the customer. The *accotoirs* (the upright part of the arms) were recessed and curved backwards during the Regency to accommodate the enormous skirts of the period, and the arms themselves were usually padded with *manchettes*, except in the case of some *cabriolets*. Desk-chairs were sometimes given a low semicircular back termed *en gondole*, and the same term is sometimes employed for *canapés* the ends of which are shaped in a similar fashion, or for *bergères* with this kind of back.

Throughout the eighteenth century the etiquette governing the position of chairs was progressively relaxed – beginning with the Regency and the emphasis on comfort. A contributory factor was the popularity of smaller and more numerous rooms. The large *salon* lent itself to formal seating arrangements, the chairs *à la reine* occupying their position against the wall, and those *en cabriolet*, movable at will, grouped in the centre according to the needs of the company, but this was hardly essential in more intimate apartments.

With the decline of rococo, cabriole legs began to disappear, to be replaced by those which were straight and tapering, often fluted, and sometimes with spiral ornament. The legs terminated at the top in a cube carved with a rosette. Backs were often square or trapezoid in form, frequently of an oval medallion shape, and generally *en cabriolet*. The *accotoirs* of early Louis Seize chairs are usually curved backwards, but towards the end of the period they often become straight. A fairly common back, termed *à chapeau*, has a slightly curved top rail terminating at either end in short, sharp counter-curves just before it joins the two stiles on either side. Other terms include the *lyre*, with a back in the form of a lyre; the *corbeille de vannerie* (wicker-basket), also an open splat; and the *montgolfière* or balloon shape, testifying to contemporary interest in the ascents of that intrepid aeronaut. *Bergères* continued to be popular; the *fauteuil en bergère* was a comfortable *fauteuil* somewhat in this form and not so large as the *bergère* proper.

83

The emphasis on comfort so noticeable as a feature of the rococo period is no less obvious during the second half of the century, and coverings were of such rare stuffs as silk and velvet of one kind or another, but printed cotton (page 137) also makes its appearance as an upholstery material. Leather-covered dining-chair seats were stuffed with horsehair, and provincial chairs for the same purpose with rush seats on turned legs are light and well proportioned. The backs are usually à chapeau, and the seat was often given a square cushion tied to the stiles and the front legs with tape. Oak and walnut were commonly used for chairs, and for the first time we meet mahogany (*acajou*) which became popular under English influence in the case of chairs which are not unlike those designed by Hepplewhite and Sheraton. With some of the more ornate chairs of the period the influence of Louis Quatorze is also apparent.

Carved work drew freely on classical ornament; at first such *motifs* as the Greek wave-pattern were used as a frieze, and a little later patterns such as the *entrelac* (interlacing circles), all of them derived from ancient sources.

VII

The greater number of mirrors were made by the *menuisiers*, who prepared them in rough form for the carver and gilder. But frames were not always of wood. Those surrounding the mirrors of the Galerie des Glaces, for instance, are of bronze. From the beginning of the seventeenth century onwards great ingenuity and the most luxurious materials were lavished on mirror-frames. Mazarin's inventory refers to one of ebony decorated with Augsburg silver pierced in the form of foliage, and there are several contemporary references to German silver mirror-frames from Augsburg being imported into France. Tortoiseshell, ivory, gold, silver, silver-gilt, and all kinds of exotic stones, such as lapis lazuli, ornamented the finest specimens.

Mirror-frames attracted the attention of the *ornemanistes*. Jean Le Pautre, Jean I Bérain, and Daniel Marot, to name only three, left many such designs. Boulle made mirror-frames in his characteristic marquetry, of which an example is illustrated on plate 10; this should be compared with the toilet-mirror displayed in the view of Gersaint's shop on plate 9. Louis Quatorze had nearly five hundred mirrors of all kinds, some of which had frames of gilt-bronze additionally embellished with coloured glass.

The mirrors of the reign of Louis Quatorze are usually rectangular, in a heavy frame finely carved with the *motifs* of the period. Most have an elaborate cresting, usually foliate, sometimes with figures, and sometimes with trophies. The mouldings of the frame are often multiple, the intervening spaces filled with narrow strips of mirror-glass. Most are gilt, although colour combinations such as crimson and gilt are not unknown. Among the most handsome of these are mirrors in scarlet lacquer frames bordered by carved gilt wood and decorated with *chinoiseries* in gold. A frame of cartouche shape sometimes occurs in gilt wood.

The fashion for narrow strips of mirror glass inset into the frame itself had not entirely disappeared with the Regency. Regency frames are among the first objects of the period to foreshadow the development of the rococo scrollwork of Louis Quinze, and scallop-shell ornament is fairly common, especially in the form of an *agrafe*. While still rectangular, some Regency mirrors are both longer and narrower, proportions familiar in the case of English mirrors of the Queen Anne period, and these sometimes have arms terminating in candleholders (*bras de lumière*) on either side at the bottom.

The exotic materials of the early years of Louis Quatorze gave place to carved wood before the end of the century, and the lowering of the mantelshelf of the chimney-piece, a fashion perhaps initiated by Robert de Cotte, provided more room for overmantel mirrors. Almost all the eighteenth-century *ornemanistes*, from Pineau to Lalonde and Salembier, made designs for mirrors in great variety. The carved wood of the frame was especially adaptable to the *motifs* and swirling curves of rococo, and some of the finest mirrors belong to this period. Contemporary records refer to mirrors in bronze frames, and one 15 feet by 8 feet was the work of Caffiéri. In silver, toilet-sets made for the draped dressing-table were provided with a mirror in a handsomely chiselled silver frame which was often extremely elaborate, but most went to the Mint and few have survived.

Louis Quinze mirrors have asymmetrically carved frames, the cresting forming an *agrafe* which is usually of characteristic pierced scrollwork, and sometimes formed from a scallop-shell. Often the frame had multiple curves, sometimes restrained but, at the culmination of the rococo style, extremely elaborate, with proliferating C- and S-scrolls and luxuriant acanthus foliage.

At this time mirror-frames of porcelain were being made at Meissen, and they were well known in France where the products of the royal Saxon factory were wildly fashionable. *Faïence* mirror-frames also exist, but neither variety approaches in size those of more conventional materials. No such frames of Sèvres porcelain are known to me, but the kind of porcelain employed by the French royal factory probably precluded their manufacture. Although no record of one seems to exist, I would not be unduly surprised to hear of a mirror-frame of Chantilly porcelain, especially after the discovery of the cartel clock sold at Christie's in 1966.

The asymmetry of the mirror-frame was occasionally carried to unusual lengths, the top of the scrolled cresting being distinctly to one side of the centre line. An unusual site for a cartel clock was in the centre of a tall overmantel mirror, about one-third of the way from the top. I do not know of a surviving example, but an eighteenth-century engraving shows a clock in this position.

Louis Seize mirrors, while returning to symmetry and to the earlier classical *motifs*, are often in elaborately carved frames, usually crested with an urn or sometimes a trophy, and sometimes with the quiver. The sumptuous independent toilet-mirrors of the Louis Quinze draped *menuiserie* dressing-table, however, gave way to the new enclosed tables of *ébénisterie* with a plainly framed mirror concealed beneath the rising flaps of the top.

Although the finest mirror-frames were of carved wood, increasing demand towards the end of the eighteenth century led to the production of frames ornamented with *stucco* mouldings, sometimes with free-floating and semi-floating parts supported on stiff iron rods. Convex mirrors were limited in number, and largely regarded as curiosities. They had existed for centuries. Van Eyck's *Jan Arnolfini*, for instance, has a mirror of this kind on the wall. An interesting by-path is to be found in the development of burning-mirrors in the seventeenth century, principally for scientific purposes. These focused the sun's rays, and they generated sufficient heat to melt metals of all kinds. One such mirror was employed in the preliminary experiments which led to the development of Meissen porcelain.

5

Metalwork and Small Sculpture

I

French silver of the seventeenth and eighteenth centuries is now exceedingly rare, very much rarer in fact than English silver of the same period, and most surviving examples are comparatively humble in origin or purpose. Indeed, for French silver of the finer kinds it is now necessary to look outside France.

The reason for this scarcity is that not only were Louis Quatorze and Louis Quinze compelled by circumstances to send vast quantities of silver to the Mint to be turned into coin to pay for military adventures, but the Revolution (which, however arguable its effect may have been otherwise, was an unmitigated disaster to French decorative art, particularly that associated with the royal house and the aristocracy) destroyed much of what had survived. I have earlier mentioned the Revolutionary sales of royal furniture, which denuded France of the finest examples and enriched English collections, but this furniture has at least been preserved with care down to our own day. Silver and gold, however, have an intrinsic value as metal, apart from workmanship, and at a time when economic conditions saw to it that there were no buyers of manufactured silver, old or contemporary, looters, official and free-lance, melted it down and disposed of it for what it would fetch as bullion. Not only were royal palaces looted in this way, but *châteaux* outside the ambit of Paris were systematically pillaged, and a few ecclesiastical treasuries escaped only because their custodians had the common sense to bury the most valuable objects before the Revolutionaries could get at them.

The scarcity is not in France alone; other Continental countries were similarly denuded. This was a consequence of the Napoleonic Wars, when the ragged, ill-fed soldiery of Napoleon, living off the country, eagerly looted collections of silver, hammering it flat so that it could easily be packed in the knapsack or the baggage-train. Nor was this confined to other ranks; even high-ranking officers took their share, although Old Master paintings were more to their taste.

Nevertheless, in times of the greatest stress a desire to possess gold and silver still remained, even though it was necessary to make do with a simulation. Gilded bronze was in great demand for mounts of all kinds, as well as silvered copper (*cuivre argenté*), although table-services were replaced first by those of *faïence* and then by porcelain.

Plating with silver and gilding was done by the mercuric process. This is very ancient. It is not only mentioned by Pliny, but instructions for gilding in this way are to be found in medieval texts, and it is described at length by Cellini in his treatise on the art of the goldsmith. Finely divided particles of gold or silver were added to mercury to form a pasty amalgam which was applied to the surface of either copper or bronze. Mercury vaporizes at a relatively low temperature, far lower than the melting-point of any of the metals with which it was alloyed or to which it was applied, and by moderately heating the object the mercury could be driven off as vapour, leaving the precious metals adherent to the base metal. For those readers inclined to experiment with this relatively easy and efficient method of covering base metal with the noble metals, it is essential to add that the fumes evolved are exceedingly poisonous. Pliny says that gilding of this kind was carried out by Roman craftsmen only when the wind was blowing strongly away from the oven so that the fumes were safely dispersed. There is a fourteenth-century record of payment to a Flemish gilder of a bronze tomb of thirty guilders as compensation for the loss of his teeth. The life of the eighteenth-century gilder was relatively short, but payment was very high in relation to that for most other operations, and the cost of gilding formed a disproportionate part of the total cost of making bronze mounts.

So far as the precious metals are concerned, a system of hall-marking was introduced into France early in the fourteenth century, when the shops of the goldsmiths clustered on the old Pont au Change in Paris, so called because it was here that the money-changers had their booths. The houses on the bridge were not demolished until 1786, and its present appearance dates from 1858. From an inventory of Edward I of England, c. 1300, we have the following entry: 'Item, eight silver spoons marked on the neck or stem with the Paris mark, that is to say, a certain *fleur-de-lis*.' At this time gold heavily alloyed with copper was being passed off as fine gold, and regulations were drawn up by Étienne Boileau, provost of Paris, about 1255 which established a Guild of jewellers and goldsmiths. This, to quote the original charter, laid down that 'no Paris goldsmith may mark gold in Paris which is not of Paris standard, which standard surpasses all the gold which is worked in any other country'. Certainly Paris goldsmiths achieved an enviable reputation for skill, and the account of his journey to Karakorum, to the Court of Mangu Khan, left by the Franciscan William of Rubruck, describes the work of one such goldsmith, Guillaume Boucher, who was attached to this Court. In 1313 Philip the Fair ordered that gold should be tested for purity and stamped accordingly, the duty of making the tests being imposed on provincial city governments soon afterwards. At the beginning of the Revolution 186 cities had been empowered to test and stamp gold and silver as a guarantee of purity.

Unlike English hall-marking, however, the systems adopted were sometimes complex, and despite the use of date-lettering it is not always easy to assign a year of manufacture to French plate with any degree of certainty. Style is usually the best guide.

At first, two marks were added – the maker's mark, an emblem surmounted by the fleur-de-lys, and an assay mark impressed by the Guild which was a letter of the alphabet changing yearly with each new guild master (the *garde de métier*). This date-letter, however, is a little unreliable, especially during the seventeenth and eighteenth centuries. From 1789 to 1797 no stamp was added at all, the reason being the complete disorganization of the Guilds by the events of the time followed by their abolition by the Revolutionaries, and for some years virtually no works in either gold or silver were produced.

Some of the salient events occurring during the period under review include, in March 1672 (the year of the invasion of Holland), the levying of a duty on gold and silver, which was doubled in 1674 when the allied armies threatened Lorraine. In 1687, the year before Louis sent his silver to the Mint, works in gold and in massive silver were forbidden altogether. Another decree of 1700, renewed in 1720, limited the weight of gold objects to one ounce and of silver to twelve marks, and prohibited the making of massive plate, although, as before, no limit was placed on ecclesiastical silver. In 1721 the regulations were relaxed to allow the making of gold snuff-boxes, *étuis*, and similar small objects up to a weight of seven ounces, at the same time reducing the standard demanded for watch-cases.

Regulations had been promulgated in 1689 relating to the refining of gold and silver, and in 1724 death was the penalty decreed for anyone who forged hall-marks, or who transferred a hall-mark from one object to another.* A regulation of 1746 governed the making of galloons and lace of gold thread or its imitation, and a decree of 1760 directed the *fermier* of the tax not to affix his discharge stamp unless the object had previously been stamped by the Guild (*Maison Commune*). This needs explanation. The *fermier* bought the right to levy the duty on plate, and when the goldsmith brought his work to the *Maison Commune* to be assayed he paid the duty to the *fermier*, who added his stamp in discharge of the obligation. Subsequently the system was altered, and when the work had reached a certain stage of manufacture the *fermier* stamped it with a *charge* mark, entering it in his records, adding the *discharge* mark when the work was completed and the duty paid. Before the discharge mark could be added, however, the work had first to be submitted to the *Maison Commune* for assay, and if found to be below standard it was broken up, returned to the maker, and struck from the *fermier's* records.

In 1765 all articles of silver plated with gold were required to be stamped *Argent* (silver), and the discharge mark stamped over the letter A. The year 1769 saw a decree concerning duty on foreign works of silver and gold, and 1779 regulations referring to duties chargeable on

---

* The latter has always been one of the commoner kinds of fraud practised in connexion with the sale of antique objects of gold and silver, and offences of this kind have always been heavily punished. In England, for instance, the penalty for possessing false punches is still fourteen years imprisonment.

plate sold at the Mont de Piété – the Paris pawnshop. The first decree of consequence after the Revolution was in 1795 when the metric system was introduced, and in 1797 the old standards, disused since 1789, were re-established and new punches decreed.

During the early decades of the seventeenth century France had imported a good deal of goldsmiths' work from Italy and Germany. The opening up of the New World, and the flow of precious metals into Spain and other European countries from this source, made gold and silver more plentiful than at any time since the first century A.D. Until 1672, when the demand for coin began to limit the quantity available for works of art, massive objects, rivalling for size and weight those described by Pliny, had been made in France. In the declaration of intent which accompanied the levying of the duty at this time the King stated that his principal aim was to reduce the weight of silver vessels so that sufficient metal should be available to the Mint for conversion into coin. He reserved the right to give permission to individuals to exceed the permitted weight and since massive plate continued to be made, despite the decree, royal permission was apparently dispensed with a certain freedom. Colbert especially fostered the goldsmiths' art (a term which includes silver), no doubt with the object of providing reserves of precious metal against contingencies, and the principal goldsmiths were lodged in the Louvre, an honour later more frequently reserved for painters and sculptors.

Goldsmiths' work in France is termed *orfèvrerie*. Strictly, an *orfèvre* is a man who makes, and usually sells, relatively large works in gold and silver, although in general use the term is extended to include gold and silver of all kinds, as well as jewellery (*bijouterie*). The eighteenth-century *marchand-bijoutier* was primarily a dealer in jewellery and small works in the precious metals, such as snuff-boxes, but the term was often employed loosely. Lazare Duvaux, for instance, was a *marchand-bijoutier*, although he sold almost every kind of decorative art, including furniture (see Appendix II).

When, in 1644, John Evelyn visited the Louvre he noticed the apartments of the artists and craftsmen there.

Under the long gallery . . . dwell goldsmiths, painters, statuaries, and architects, who being famous for their art in Christendom have stipends allowed them by the King. Into that of Monsieur Saracin [James Sarazin, 1590–1660 – a celebrated goldsmith and sculptor who later worked at the *Manufacture royale*] we entered, who was then moulding for an image of a Madonna to be cast in gold of great size, to be sent by the Queen Regent as an offering for the birth of the Dauphin, now the young King.

It will be noticed that Evelyn selects goldsmiths for first mention in keeping with their status at the time. With the establishment of the *Manufacture royale* work was superintended by Le Brun, and among the massive objects of silver made for the King were *chenets* (andirons), tables, stools, mirror-frames, *jardinières*, and *torchères*, as well as *cassolettes* (perfume-urns), ewers and basins, and toilet services. Among them was the work of the goldsmith, Claude I. Ballin, who is referred to in this extract from a contemporary record:

[The King] melted down tables, *torchères*, and large seats of silver, decorated with figures, bas reliefs, and chasing by Balin which had cost ten million *livres* [about £5 million today] and brought three.

Since the tables no longer exist it is impossible to be certain how they were made, but solid silver was probably unusual. There is a serving-table at Windsor of this kind, and several pieces of silver furniture, including a table and two *torchères*, at Knole in Kent. The Knole specimens, which I have examined, are of chased silver over wooden formers, approximating in technique to similarly ornamented Roman furniture described by Pliny and others. This, of course, reduces the weight of metal considerably (plate 52). *Jardinières* on the other hand were probably always solid, with a lead liner.

A *fête* at Versailles in 1668 was especially notable for its display of vast quantities of magnificent silverwork, with a gold *nef* (a centre-piece in the form of a ship), and many silver-gilt vessels for the use of the King. Four of the *torchères* were six feet in height and surmounted by silver *girandoles* (candelabra). Twenty-four large silver *jardinières* were filled with flowers. This fantastic display of a weight exceeding 800,000 ounces, chased and chiselled with superb skill, was all melted, with much else besides, in 1688.

The Edict of 1687 (page 8) was more effective than the one of 1672, probably because, in the serious financial situation then prevailing, the King in the following year set the example and sent his own silver to the Mint, and his courtiers were compelled to follow suit. The Mint paid only the intrinsic value of the metal, and these things are now known only from drawings made at the time. Almost the only thing to be saved from the royal plate was the gold *nef* which weighed 1,200 ounces. Ecclesiastical plate and humbler specimens of domestic plate, chiefly in the provinces, also escaped. French taste in silver precariously survived, chiefly in England and especially at Whitehall Palace, where in the time of Charles II even the dressing-tables of the maids of honour were furnished with silver toilet-services. But these were melted by Dutch William for the same reason as that which had activated the French King.

This enforced economy in France led to the manufacture of more luxurious and elaborate kinds of *faïence* discussed in Chapter 6, and to the import of vast quantities of porcelain from China, and later from Saxony. Ships of the Compagnie des Indes put into French ports with vast quantities of porcelain of all kinds from the Far East on board, and Louis Quatorze set an example by ordering a *faïence* service from Rouen to replace his silver-gilt services which had been melted.

The first relaxation of austerity came in 1721 during the Regency,

91

when an evanescent prosperity followed the inflationary schemes hatched in the fertile brain of John Law. French taste persisted in England, and grew stronger again in the early decades of the eighteenth century. The rococo style was adopted by Paul de Lamerie, of Huguenot descent, whose work is now avidly sought, and it is to be observed in a more developed form in the silver of Nicolas Sprimont, the founder of the Chelsea porcelain factory, of which notable examples are preserved in Buckingham Palace. A page from a contemporary design book – that of Meissonnier – appears on plate 67, from which may be seen the influence he exerted on porcelain design at Chelsea during its first period, although in the French porcelain factories of Vincennes and Sèvres this kind of ornament was reserved for the bronze mounts accompanying porcelain figures and vases. The association of the two arts of porcelain and silver may also be seen in Saxony, where Johann Melchior Dinglinger, who had studied at Augsburg and in Paris, worked in the late baroque style which was the immediate precursor of rococo – the style adopted by the Meissen porcelain factory who were exporting large quantities to Paris.

For a few years the revival of the silversmith's art in France was on a relatively lavish scale, although hardly matching that of the previous reign. Silver furniture also appears to have returned to favour but on a much diminished scale, since there is record of a silver toilet-table being melted during the Seven Years' War (1756–63), when coin once more became scarce – a time when a good deal of German silver met a similar fate at the hands of Frederick the Great.

Louis Quinze did not compel anybody to send silver to the Mint, but he extended a pressing invitation to do so – one hardly to be ignored. His own plate went in cartloads, sent with deliberate ostentation, and Mme de Pompadour, the duc d'Orléans, the duc de Choiseul, and other prominent people followed suit. 'Everybody', said a contemporary writer, 'feels uneasily that he cannot resist.' Even the more patriotic citizens, however, felt the need to decorate their homes with at least a simulation of silver and gold, turning to *cuivre argenté* and bronze gilded *d'or moulu*, and the *ciseleur-fondeur* prospered at the expense of the goldsmith. The desire to save small treasures from the Mint may have been the reason for covering with white paint two silver figures of the period which I was able to recognize some years ago.

There is space only to refer briefly to a few of the more notable of the silversmiths of the period, beginning with Claude I Ballin already mentioned. He was received Master of the Guild in 1627 and died in 1678. For the reasons discussed his work is known almost entirely from contemporary records, including the royal inventories. It was on a grand scale, recalling the silver of Imperial Rome. He was the principal maker of silver furniture, among which was a superb table described in the inventory of Louis Quatorze, that had Apollo driving the quadriga of the sun as its subject, with figures representing the Four Quarters of the globe and the Arms of the King. In the centre was a sunburst and a relief portrait of Louis in medallion form upheld by four cupids astride dolphins. This was 4 feet 7 inches long, 3 feet in depth, and almost 3 feet high, with a weight of 1,515 marks of Paris, or more than 350 kilogrammes in modern terms.*

Among the silver orange-tubs with their pedestals we find those described as being made by Ballin, chiselled with Bacchanalian figures and vine branches and bunches of grapes, while massive basins chiselled with three trophies of Arms and six symbolic figures between them, 3 feet in diameter, were matched with vases 2 feet 4 inches in height, with the arms and cypher of the King, as well as other ornament.

Claude II Ballin (1667–1754), nephew of the first Claude, was a silver-smith, a maker of medals, and an engraver of seals. He was especially talented, and worked both in the baroque and rococo styles. As *orfèvre du Roi* he was lodged in the Louvre in 1702, having become master of the Guild in 1701. A eulogy published after his death in the *Mercure* enumer-ated some of his more notable works. In a style which was a precursor of the rococo he executed a basin and a casket for Maximilian Emmanuel, Elector of Bavaria, which were delivered in 1713 and are now in the Munich Residenz. Ballin delivered two *surtouts de table* to the Russian Court in 1728, and these are preserved in the Hermitage; in 1745 he made a table-service for Elisabeth Farnese, Queen of Spain, at a cost of 38,000 *livres*.

At a sale held soon after his death it could be seen that he was a man of considerable taste, a collector of paintings, bronzes, porcelain, and Boulle *armoires*, but his goldsmith's work had, for the most part, vanished, and only the examples preserved in the Hermitage and at Munich remain to testify to his skill. It would, perhaps, be true to say that his work helped to bridge the transition from baroque to rococo, although he never adopted the *motifs* which characterize the full-tide of the latter style – the crayfish, plant-forms, tureens in the form of vegetables, and so on, which inspired so many European porcelain factories – preferring instead to draw inspiration from the old seventeenth-century themes of the chase and of classical mythology.

Nicolas Besnier (d. 1754) was among the important silversmiths of the first part of the eighteenth century. He became *orfèvre du Roi* in 1714, with lodgings in the Louvre. In 1724 he was appointed administrator at the Beauvais tapestry factory, obtaining the position of *orfèvre du Roi* for his son-in-law, Jacques Roettiers, a move which was distinctly unpopular with the Guild. A bowl by Besnier for the duchesse d'Orléans is in the Louvre, and he made a toilet-set for the Infanta of Spain in 1724, at the time of her projected marriage to Louis Quinze. He executed numerous orders for the King both in silver and silver-gilt.

93

* The old French *pied* is here translated as *foot* to which it approximated. The *pouce* was roughly an inch.

Members of the Germain family were Pierre (1647–84) who made *guéridons* and chandeliers for Louis Quatorze, and his son, Thomas (1673–1748), who was the greatest of the eighteenth-century silversmiths. His life was written by the comte de Caylus, and he was said to have united the skill of the craftsman with the genius of the designer and the sculptor. Thomas was sent to Rome by Louvois in 1688, where he studied at the Académie de France. He entered the profession in Rome, and supplied designs to the Vatican, working also for Cosmo III of Tuscany for whom he made a basin ornamented with scenes from the history of the Medici family. He returned to Paris in 1706, and was received Master of the Guild in 1720 with lodgings in the Louvre. Thomas Germain was principally noted for the perfection of his rendering of detail in the tradition of his craft, but he was also a talented sculptor, bronzeworker, and *ciseleur*. He did a great deal of work for the French Court, but his work was also sought abroad – in Portugal, Spain, and the Two Sicilies, for instance. Examples are now to be found as far apart as New York, in the Metropolitan Museum, and in the Hermitage at Leningrad.

His son, François-Thomas Germain (1726–91), became *orfèvre et sculpteur du Roi* in place of his father. He worked principally in the rococo style. Like his father he had frequent commissions from foreign Courts, but, as with so many others, he found difficulty in collecting payment, and he became bankrupt in 1765. Some of his work for the Portuguese Court is preserved in the museum at Lisbon, and a pair of candlesticks he made for Mme de Pompadour is in the Musée Nissim de Camondo in Paris. Of his work in bronze, a pair of rococo *chenets* made for the Bernstoff Palace in Copenhagen was signed by him.

Pierre Germain belonged to a family of goldsmiths established at Avignon, and at Marseille where he was born in 1716. He seems to have been related to Thomas Germain, and was apprenticed to Nicolas Besnier, being received Master of the Guild in 1744. This Pierre Germain was the author of two design books depicting ornament in the rococo style which were published in 1748 and 1751 respectively. With Thomas Chancellier he made a toilet-service in the manner of Philippe Caffiéri for the Princess of the Asturias in 1765.

Jacques Roettiers, born at Saint-Germain-en-Laye in 1707, was the son of Norbert Roettiers, *graveur-général* to the Mint during the reign of Louis Quatorze. Jacques became master in 1737, without a formal apprenticeship, in recognition of his father's services. He married the daughter of Nicolas Besnier, was awarded lodgings in the Louvre, and became Member of the Academy of Painting and Sculpture in 1773. After 1765 he was associated as *orfèvre ordinaire du Roi* with his son, Jacques-Nicolas, and retired in 1772. He contributed seven of the plates to Pierre Germain's design-book published in 1751, but he was among the earliest to explore the neo-classical style for which he became noted. Both father and son are remarkable for quality of design and workmanship.

Among his many works of importance may be numbered the Berkeley Castle dinner-service (plate 62) which was sold at Sotheby's in 1960. This service of 168 pieces, the finest now existing, realized £207,000.

His son, called Roettiers de la Tour, retired only five years or so after his father, with a large fortune. His style was neo-classical, and a good deal of his work was done for the Russian Court. A few of these pieces have since found their way to the West as the result of the Soviet sales of former royal property in 1928–9.

Although little now remains of the work of these, or any other of the silversmiths who have been left unmentioned, contemporary records and design books testify to the large amount of silver which formerly existed, and to the quality of the workmanship. The reader who wishes to pursue the subject is referred to the Bibliography.

The course of design and ornament in silver during the eighteenth century broadly followed the progression of styles described in Chapter 2.

In its details rococo was largely the product of the silversmith, who was, at first, in advance of his time, especially in the adoption of asymmetry and the rockwork and scrolling *motifs* so characteristic of the style. During the period which followed, however, the silversmith tended to be slower to adopt new ideas or to abandon old ones. A coffee-pot in the Victoria and Albert Museum for example, made by Roquillet-Desnoyers in 1780, is remarkable for swirled flutings which are rococo in spirit rather than neo-classical. The work of Paul de Lamerie and Nicolas Sprimont already mentioned may be regarded as characteristic of much of the work which was done between 1740 and 1750 and melted soon afterwards. Nevertheless, the new style was apparent before the end of the reign of Louis Quinze, when the swags and medallions, to be seen on Sèvres porcelain vases mounted in gilt-bronze, became popular decorative themes, and perhaps an inspiration as well. Animal legs as supports copied from old Roman tripods, and rams' heads, were also characteristic *motifs* of the new fashion.

The gaps existing in our knowledge of later French silver can be filled without too much conjecture by reference to English silver designed in the style of the Brothers Adam, who were, in their turn, influenced by contemporary movements in France. It is probable that today our knowledge of the art of the silversmith in France during the second half of the eighteenth century is a little out of balance. Comparatively, so much gilt-bronze and so little silver has survived that we are apt to assume that only small quantities were made and to discount the holocaust of the Revolution. To some extent, also, the acquisition of silver may have become almost an antiquarian taste, limited to people with a stronger sense of tradition than those who moved in fashionable Court circles, where the insatiable demand for novelty reached almost present-day proportions. Bronze, at least in small quantities, had no intrinsic value however, and only church bells and large statues attracted the attention of the cannon-maker; small objects may have been dispersed, they were not usually destroyed.

Even though important examples of plate are rare, we can gain some slight notion of its design from the superb gilt-bronze of the period, however different the techniques. There can be no doubt that cast gilt-bronze, usually in conjunction with some other material such as porcelain, which also largely replaced the silver dinner-service, was substituted in many instances for silver raised by traditional methods. Such objects as urns which would formerly have been made of silver came to be made from porcelain, or from such decorative stones as jasper, alabaster, and porphyry, with embellishments of gilded bronze. Truly massive decorations disappeared, of course, when Louis Quatorze sent his silver to the Mint and, with a few very rare exceptions, nothing like them has been seen since, especially in France. Of course *bibelots* of silver and gold were unaffected by the changes in fashion, and rich snuff-boxes, *étuis*, and handsomely decorated gold boxes continued to be made, but these hardly call for notice here.

II

Throughout the period discussed in this book bronze played a major part in the formation of the Court style, from the statuary and fountains cast by the Brothers Keller at the Paris Arsenal for the gardens of Versailles to furniture mounts, hearth-furniture (especially *chenets* or andirons), clock-cases, vase mounts, all kinds of lighting appliances, and many small decorative sculptures and *objets d'art*.

Almost always these mounts were mercurically gilded, and gilders were usually highly paid, the cost of gilding forming a substantial part of the total cost of manufacturing mounts at all periods. A record survives, for instance, of a *bureau* made for Versailles in which the gilding alone accounts for one-fifth of the total cost, and the same proportion was expended on the chiselling of the bronze-work. These two operations cost together the sum of 2,400 *livres* (about £1,200) out of a total of £2,900, leaving £1,700 for the *ébénisterie* and the original casting of the mounts, as well as for all the other expenses involved in a work of this kind.

The process known in France as *dorure d'or moulu* (literally, 'gilding with gold paste'), which means using an amalgam of gold and mercury, was the origin of the term 'ormolu' sometimes applied to work of this kind, an anglicization which took place soon after the middle of the eighteenth century. The word, however, has been much abused and employed inaccurately to describe light brass alloys which are not gilded, of nineteenth-century or modern work, and later bronzes electrically coated with gold. It is perhaps less confusing to refer to eighteenth-century mounts as mercurically gilded, but it is hardly necessary here to be so pedantic. The term 'gilding' applied to the application of gold to base metal always means mercurically gilt unless otherwise stated. Leaf-gilding of metal was always rare.

Most bronzes were cast by the 'lost wax' or *cire perdue* technique by which a model was first prepared in wax, usually over a fireproof core unless the cast was required to be solid, and over the wax a mould of fireproof material (made from plaster and brickdust or refractory clay) reproduced the surface of the model. Before the molten metal was poured in the wax was melted and run off, leaving the outer mould and the inner core, the latter supported by metal pins. The work of making the moulds and pouring the metal was the province of the *fondeur* or founder, and, after casting, the object was handed to the *ciseleur* or chiseller, who proceeded with chisels and burins to remove cast-marks and blemishes, to sharpen the detail, and to punch the background lightly in preparation for gilding where this was required. The finished cast then went to the gilder.

After the gilder had added the layer of gold the cast was in fit condition to be sent to whoever had ordered it – the *ébéniste*, the porcelain-maker, or even the dealer. Dealers such as Duvaux ordered mounts to be cast for all kinds of *objets d'art* belonging both to themselves and to their clients.

The *ciseleurs-fondeurs* kept stocks of mounts suitable for various kinds of mounting, and these stock designs led to a certain amount of repetition in the finishing of furniture of the period. One or two of the *ébénistes* were also *ciseleurs-fondeurs* who made their own mounts (Cressent was one of them), but this led to frequent disputes with the guild, who claimed the right to be the sole makers. It is therefore only on the finest furniture that one is likely to find mounts of especially distinguished quality which were purposely cast for the piece in question.

Bronze mounts were not only intended to be decorative. They had other and more practical uses. Particularly in conjunction with delicate marquetries, such as those of Boulle, they gave protection from accidental damage. Mouldings to the edges of tables preserved them from being bruised, and corner-pieces served to strengthen the frame. In the case of large *bureaux* a *filet* of bronze protected the place where the two sheets of leather essential to cover the top joined each other. The escutcheon plates which covered keyholes, finally chiselled and gilt, were nonetheless essential, and handles, while not strictly protective, were as utilitarian as they were decorative. The *sabots* or *chaussons* – the bronze toes – often to be found ornamenting the bottom of the legs of case-furniture especially, were necessary to resist damage from accidental contact with feet and brooms. In fact very few mounts are purely decorative, and most have some kind of primary practical purpose to fulfil.

Gilt-bronze as a furniture-mount came into its own during the latter part of the reign of Louis Quatorze, and it has rarely been absent from the

97

best French furniture ever since that time. There was nothing new in this way of decorating furniture. The Romans applied bronze mounts, which were no doubt gilded, to their furniture in the first century A.D. and medieval chests were heavily reinforced with metal strapping used decoratively, as well as handsomely engraved escutcheon plates to the keyholes. That the mounts of seventeenth-century French furniture, and metalwork of the period generally, owe something to the particular genius of the craftsmen of Augsburg and Nürnberg can hardly be doubted, especially when we remember German influence on furniture-design during the early years of the century. German metal-workers were capable of producing work of a very high standard throughout the sixteenth century and later. But it was the Italian, Domenico Cucci, who first made such mounting fashionable by casting figures of gold and silver to ornament cabinets which were largely in the Italian style. Cucci became a naturalized citizen of France in 1664, and probably came in the first place at the behest of Mazarin for whom he worked until the latter's death. Cucci is described in contemporary records as an *ébéniste et fondeur*, and between 1674 and 1679 he made the gilt-bronze balustrade for the great staircase of Versailles for which he was paid 31,200 *livres*. He is also credited with the framing of the Venetian mirrors in the Galerie des Glaces. Another Italian called to France by Mazarin was Philippe Caffiéri, who became *sculpteur du Roi*, and was primarily a wood-carver who also worked in bronze. He was assisted by the gilders La Baronnière and Gougeon.

The use of metal, gilt-bronze especially, was continued by Boulle, who was both an *ébéniste* and a bronze-worker. His designs undoubtedly led to the characteristic employment of the metal mount which distinguishes French furniture throughout the eighteenth century, although it has been truly said that all the Paris *ébénistes* who mounted their furniture during the rococo period were but pupils of Cressent.

During the seventeenth century gilt-bronze largely took the place of gold, silver, and silver-gilt. Mercuric gilding was the rule, but a few instances of leaf-gilding are known. Even more rarely some bronzes were silvered, and throughout the reign of Louis Quatorze, and the two following reigns, we meet occasional examples of silvering on both wood and metal. These may have been even more numerous at the time, but silver has the drawback of oxydizing easily, with the formation of a black tarnish, and it is likely to have been replaced by gilding when this occurred. Throughout the eighteenth century it was the custom to regild mounts which were no longer in pristine condition, to which Duvaux's account book testifies.

The *fondeurs* were organized into a guild which was finally amalgamated with the guild of *doreurs* (or gilders) in 1776. They functioned on similar lines to the guild of *menuisiers-ébénistes*, with whom they were closely connected in the manufacture of furniture. For the clock-maker the *fondeurs* made elaborate cases (which are considered later), and for the porcelain-maker they provided not only the scrolled mounts ornamented with delicate and detailed *motifs* appropriate to the period, but they made the stalks and leaves necessary to carry the porcelain flowers which were a speciality of the Vincennes factory, and often the *jardinière* as well. No doubt some of these were to the factory's order, but others must have been made for dealers of the period, since the porcelain sometimes came from China or from Meissen and was often a mixture of the two, such as a vase of white Chinese porcelain from Fukien flanked by two Meissen figures of swans and mounted on a gilt-bronze scrolled base with added ornament of rushes and leaves, once in the collection of Louis Quinze's finance minister, Machault, and sold in the Chavagnac Collection in 1911. Porcelain plaques used to ornament furniture were surrounded by delicately moulded gilt-bronze framing, both as an ornament and as protection.

I have already commented on the profound and far-reaching effect of metalwork design on the course of furniture styles and the decorative arts during the eighteenth century, but bronzeworkers are, in general, neither so well known as the principal *ébénistes* and designers, nor is it usually possible to attribute their work with certainty in the absence of a signature or some other material evidence of authorship. During the eighteenth century about three hundred *fondeurs* and a like number of gilders were working in Paris as members and *maîtres* of the Guild.

A few of the more important *fondeurs* and *ciseleurs* are mentioned below. Boulle and Cressent were both bronzeworkers who are discussed elsewhere. The sculptor, goldsmith, and bronzeworker Jean-Claude Duplessis (d. 1774) was one of the original appointments to the Vincennes porcelain factory in 1745. He designed both porcelain and its bronze mounts, as well as the mounts for the *bureau du Roi Louis Quinze*. Much of his work was influenced by Meissonnier, and his porcelain-designing was also usually based on contemporary metalwork. To him may be attributed the *vaisseau à mât* illustrated on plate 99, as well as the well-known 'elephant' vases the trunks of which form candle-sockets. One of his finest works as a maker of mounts for porcelain is that for the rare coloured figure of Sèvres porcelain called 'La Source' which is now in the Louvre.

Duplessis was succeeded at Sèvres by Pierre-Philippe Thomire (1751-1843), who had worked as a *fondeur* for the sculptors Pajou and Houdon, and who made furniture-mounts for Benemann. Later he organized the manufacture of mounts of all kinds almost on a factory basis as Thomire-Dutherme et Cie. A similar organization in England was that of Boulton and Fothergill at Birmingham, who exported mounts to France during the last decades of the eighteenth century. A clock in a combination of porcelain, marble, and bronze was made by Thomire for Marie-Antoinette.

Jacques Caffiéri (1678–1751) was the son of Philippe Caffiéri already mentioned. He worked for the King at several of the royal palaces, and was one of the principal exponents of the rococo style, perhaps working to the designs of the brothers Slodtz. A number of signed examples by him are known, and provide a foundation for the attribution of others on grounds of style. These include furniture-mounts, lighting fixtures, clock-cases, and porcelain mounts. Jacques Caffiéri worked with Jacques Verberckt on the Salle du Conseil at Versailles, the former carving the *boiseries* and the latter providing the bronzes for the chimney-piece.

One of Caffiéri's sons, Jean-Jacques, who was a pupil of Lemoyne's, became chief modeller at Sèvres in succession to Falconet, while another son, Philippe (1715–74), assisted his father and succeeded him as *fondeur-ciseleur des Bâtiments du Roi*. Thomas Germain – goldsmith to Louis Quinze – was also a bronzeworker who was vigorously attacked by Cochin for the extravagance of his rococo ornament.

Pierre Gouthière (1732–1813) was by far the most noted bronzeworker of the reign of Louis Seize. He worked for the duc d'Aumont and Mme du Barry at Louveciennes, to whom he also acted as artistic adviser – a connexion which, as I have noted earlier, proved disastrous for him. For the duc d'Aumont he enriched some marble columns bought in Rome with bases and capitals of gilded bronze. Signed works by his hand have survived in one or two instances. One is illustrated on plate 83. His output seems to have been prolific, and traditionally he is said to have provided Riesener with mounts, although satisfactory evidence of a connexion between the two is lacking. Gouthière also introduced a technique of matt gilding which was an effective contrast with the more usual burnished surfaces.

III

We are not concerned here with large sculpture, but only with small examples of the art employed to decorate *salons* and galleries, placed in a niche or on a *console* table or a *commode*. These small pieces were sometimes of marble, sometimes of terracotta, but most often of bronze. The latter are usually classified as *bronzes d'ameublement* – furnishing bronzes, and they were quite often simply a reduction of large-scale statuary, which was also fashionable in the porcelain of Sèvres. The eighteenth century was the period during which the portrait bust was particularly fashionable, and these were made in ever increasing quantities by the notable sculptors of the day, to be repeated by those who modelled for porcelain and furnishing bronzes.

During the early part of the seventeenth century native French sculpture was extremely dependent on Italy for inspiration, especially on Giovanni da Bologna who was much admired. The influence of Bernini began to be perceptible after mid century and it persisted into the eighteenth century, especially in the dramatic form sometimes taken by French sculpture of the period.

Two names are outstanding in any consideration of the decoration of Versailles – François Girardon (1630–1715) and his rival, Antoine

Coysevox (1646–1720). Girardon worked in a pronounced classical style, as can be seen in some of his sculpture for the gardens of Versailles, and his bronze equestrian statue of Louis Quatorze, which stood until the Revolution in what is now the Place Vendôme, was a masterpiece of casting. 'There was', wrote Lister, '100,000 lb. weight of mettal melted, but it took not above 80,000 lb. It was all cast at once, Horse and Man.' Girardon told Lister that it had occupied him almost daily for eight years. All that remains of this vast statue, apart from reductions, is a solitary foot twenty-six inches long in the Louvre.

Coysevox worked in a baroque style. A version of the crouching Venus, taken from the well-known antique model, is at Versailles, cast by the brothers Keller who were gun-founders at the Paris Arsenal and who also cast the bronze statues for the Parterre d'Eau. From the windows of his Salon the King could see perhaps the most important assemblage of statuary bronzes in Europe. Lister writes of 'incomparable brazen Vasa, and large Brass figures couchant of the best Masters in sculpture', which refers to the bronzes decorating these twin lakes devised by the King and based on a design by Le Nôtre. Lister also visited the 'Atelier' of Coysevox (to whom he refers as Quoisevox), seeing there many rare pieces. Coysevox is noted for his portrait busts, and he completed Mazarin's tomb in 1692.

Pierre Puget (1620–94) was perhaps the only strictly baroque sculptor working during the seventeenth century, and he was much influenced by Bernini. Puget was commissioned to make the statuary for the gardens of Vaux-le-Vicomte, but the fall of Fouquet prevented their execution. His masterpiece, the *Milo of Croton*, is now in the Louvre, and this was also the subject of Falconet's *morceau de réception*.

The influence of Bernini was still potent in the early decades of the eighteenth century. The nephews of Coysevox – Nicholas and Guillaume Coustou – were also his pupils, much influenced by the older man. The latter carved the famous Marly horses in marble which were brought to the Champs-Elysées in 1796. They were originally executed in 1740 for the entrance to the Marly riding-school, and they are best known, perhaps, from numerous reductions in bronze, most of which belong to the nineteenth century (plates 72 and 73).

In the work of Étienne-Maurice Falconet we see the early stages of the neo-classical style. He was a favourite of Mme de Pompadour's, and his designs were strongly influenced by Boucher, at any rate so far as his work as chief modeller for the Sèvres factory was concerned. He disliked the increasing exuberance of rococo, but he was opposed to the indiscriminate adoption of neo-classical severity. The transition between the two styles can be seen in his 'Baigneuse', exhibited at the Paris Salon of 1757 and originally made for M. Thiroux d'Epersenne. Falconet later went to Russia where he executed an enormous equestrian statue of Peter the Great for Catherine. Jacques Saly, whose work was much esteemed, worked in a not dissimilar style, and was adjudged by some to be even better. A statue by him of Louis Quinze, which was at Valenciennes, did not survive the Revolution, and his 'Faune', extremely popular, was probably copied from an antique original by way of an Italian bronze by Massimiliano Soldani.

Jean-Jacques Caffiéri (1678–1756) was the son of the *fondeur-ciseleur*, Jacques Caffiéri, and grandson of the *sculpteur du Roi* to Louis Quatorze, Philippe Caffiéri. He became chief modeller to Sèvres in succession to Falconet, and executed many portrait busts in marble. To him was due the fashion for reductions of statuary in *biscuit* porcelain of the 1760s. His father made furniture mounts in gilt-bronze for Versailles, Fontainebleau, and Marly, as well as portrait busts in bronze and other small works.

Augustin Pajou (1730–1809), a neo-classicist, was a pupil of J.-B. Lemoyne and a favourite of Mme du Barry. Among his other works may be noted a bust of the comtesse which was done for the Sèvres factory. But Mme du Barry proved a troublesome sitter who, urged on by her hairdresser, Legros, continually quarrelled with Pajou's hair styles. A partly nude portrait of Mme de Pompadour by Falconet may later have suggested to Pajou a model of Marie-Antoinette in similar fashion. This, in terracotta, is illustrated on plate 78, and it was also reproduced in porcelain at Sèvres, although such positive indications of the sitter as fleur-de-lys on the scanty drapery were removed by royal command. An allegorical centrepiece of porcelain with Marie-Antoinette similarly modelled also exists.

Jean-Baptiste Pigalle (1714–85) was Falconet's rival for the patronage of Mme de Pompadour, and a one-time pupil of Lemoyne. Much of his work is typically rococo, although it later became less extravagant. A statue of Louis Quinze at Rheims, destroyed during the Revolution, was adapted as the centrepiece of a vast porcelain table-decoration made to celebrate the marriage of the Dauphin to Marie-Antoinette. Lemoyne himself, who had an uncle of the same name, was a sculptor who influenced a number of the younger mid-century sculptors, and his work, also, was occasionally reproduced in porcelain, particularly the 'Hercules and Omphale'. The designs of Edmé Bouchardon (1698–1762) were employed by the porcelain factories, who were always important employers of sculptors. A large equestrian statue of Louis Quinze by Bouchardon was later destroyed, but small bronze versions still exist.

In the second half of the century the most notable sculptor was Claude Michel (1738–1814) called Clodion, who was Pajou's son-in-law. He worked largely in terracotta and modelled for the Sèvres factory. The greater part of his work consisted in naturally modelled nudes – nymphs and fauns – most of which are erotic. These he produced on a very large scale with the aid of assistants and employees, often adapting his figures to the decoration of clock-cases, candelabra, and so forth. Small bronzes based on his terracottas are not uncommon. Jean-Antoine Houdon (1741–1828) was largely independent of any particular style or school, but he conformed in general to the prevailing neo-classical style. He was especially noted for realistic portraits, some of which were subsequently cast in a bronze version.

IV

Among the decorative works in gilt bronze with a utilitarian purpose, to the decoration of which sculpture often contributed, we must number the *chenets* or andirons, of silver in the great houses in the middle years of the seventeenth century, and of gilt-bronze thereafter. Occasionally silvering, or a combination of silvering and gilding, is to be found, and under Louis Seize burnished gilding was contrasted with matt gilding in the manner introduced by Gouthière.

Chenets occur in a very wide variety of forms, and they became especially elaborate in the middle of the eighteenth century, when those decorating the finest rooms were veritable masterpieces of small sculpture. They followed the prevailing fashion in exhibiting marked asymmetrical characteristics during the currency of the rococo style, and they regained symmetry during the classical revival, when they sometimes assumed the form of urns. The finest had figures as their subject, and today one sometimes finds isolated figures of uncertain purpose which probably once formed part of a *chenet*, or perhaps a clock-case.★ Fire-irons matched the *chenets* in their ornament, and the steel was often blued as a decorative addition.

Chenets, clock-cases, and lighting fixtures were perhaps the three principal objects to be made in gilt-bronze during the eighteenth century, but there were many others, ranging from *cassolettes* to small statuary, and all harmonized with the mounts so lavishly provided for the finest furniture.

French clocks are not merely to be regarded as scientific instruments; they were also among the most decorative of interior accessories on which some of the finest workmanship was lavished. The cases were handsomely ornamented with metal, usually gilt-bronze and more rarely silver, and many – the cartel clock especially – were entirely of bronze.

Augsburg was the principal centre of clockmaking in the sixteenth century, and many notable developments in the design of movements were made in this city. François Premier granted a charter to the Paris Guild of Clockmakers, and French clocks of the period were indebted to those of both Augsburg and Nürnberg in form and decoration.

By the middle of the seventeenth century the development of Galileo's discovery of the pendulum had made the clock a much more accurate time-measuring instrument, but long before this the clock-case itself

★ Mercier (*Tableaux de Paris*) writes: 'Observing one of these clocks I found that its capricious owner had more than once changed the gilded figure on its top.'

had assumed an elaborately decorative form. The early French clock partook, for the most part, of two elements – the clock movement proper, and automata of a kind which had been popular from Roman times onwards. Automata – figures made to move mechanically in a variety of ways – were popular in Byzantium and later at the medieval Court of Burgundy. The French goldsmith earlier mentioned, Guillaume Boucher, made a fountain for Mangu Khan with the figure of an angel holding a trumpet. When more drinks were needed, according to William of Rubruck, the steward shouted to the angel to blow his trumpet, which it then placed to its mouth and blew 'right loudly' as a signal to the servants outside to pour drinks into the conduits from which flowed a variety of liquids. This work touched off a fashion for similar works in the Far East. A hydraulic clock in Pekin, for instance, had a peafowl on top which moved every half hour, two peacocks who screamed loudly below, and one at the bottom which spread its tail.

By the end of the sixteenth century clocks with automatic figures were commonly being made at Augsburg, although few have survived intact. In the seventeenth century the figures became stationary, without a mechanism to operate them, although a late example is to be found in a clock made for Louis Quatorze with figures representing the German Electors and the Italian Princes which moved on the hour, and the Kings of Europe who actually struck the hours while a figure of Louis himself bowed acknowledgement.

It is not part of my purpose to discuss details of clock mechanism, which would be out of place in a book of this kind, but to describe cases and their ornament. Clocks during the seventeenth and eighteenth centuries may be classified into three principal categories – the *régulateur*, or long-case clock; bracket, and chimney-piece or mantel clocks, the former placed on mural *consoles* attached to the *boiserie*; and cartel clocks attached directly to the wall without the intervention of a bracket. A few clocks fall a little outside these categories, such as those mounted in *cartonniers* and *armoires* or as part of a *bureau* (plate 32), and those resembling bracket-clocks in form but standing on a *gaine* (a tapering pedestal) instead of a mural *console*, and therefore similar in appearance and effect to a long-case clock. These are termed 'pedestal' clocks.

Clockmakers were very highly regarded and the best of them lodged in the Louvre. Towards the end of the reign of Louis Quatorze Boulle made some important contributions to the design of clock-cases, of which an example appears in *L'enseigne de Gersaint* by Watteau.

The decline in popularity of the porcelain garniture, and its replacement on the mantel-shelf by a central clock with flanking candelabra, began in the early years of Louis Quinze.* It led to fresh developments,

104   * Mercier writes: 'Every chimney-piece has its clock . . . . Clocks are everywhere . . . clocks like little temples, or with domes of gilded bronze, or perhaps globes of white marble with figures running round like an equator.'

and the design of the clock-case was modified to suit its new position, tending to become an object of special interest, executed and finished with skill more appropriate to goldsmith's work. An example is the well-known elephant bearing a clock strapped to its back in the Victoria and Albert Museum, the movement by Jérôme Martinot (*fl.* 1695–1732) and the case by Caffiéri. The name of Martinot first appears as that of a royal clockmaker in 1572, during the reign of Henry III.

The cartel clock is represented here by plate 81, a very well-known clock with a case by Charles Cressent, and adequate testimony to his skill as a bronzeworker. This case has for its subject 'Love triumphing over Time', and it is an excellent example of the general form of clocks of this kind.

Combinations of different materials became more usual after 1750. The use of silver and bronze together, the dial surrounded by brilliants, is to be found about 1750, at the same time as the clock supported by figures, sometimes of Chinese, amid a *bocage* of bronze-mounted porcelain flowers from Vincennes with added metal leaves. Finely painted vases of Sèvres porcelain adapted with the aid of bronze mounts to the functions of a clock-case are a new and less happy departure. Of these, the most conventional is the least attractive, with the usual dial and hands to indicate the hour, but another variety in the form of a classical urn (where the figures are carried on revolving bands situated immediately below the junction of the cover with the body, the hour being indicated by a stationary pointer), is a much more satisfactory design. This novel way of recording the time is also to be found in clocks entirely of gilt-bronze, the bands sometimes revolving round the equatorial region of a terrestrial globe which has a flanking symbolic figure.

The lyre-shaped clock of the Marie-Antoinette period is another innovation, the dial and movement being placed at the bottom of the lyre, the open ring pendulum, through which the dial was seen, being suspended from the neck of the lyre above so that it performed its short swing in front of the actual dial. This ring pendulum was studded with brilliants.

Designs of this kind, even when carried out with the instinctive good taste of the eighteenth century for combinations of materials and colours, and with the superb craftsmanship which we associate with the period, only just avoid vulgarity. The nineteenth-century repetitions of this design are far less fortunate.

Plate 83, the Avignon clock, designed by Boizot (chief modeller to the Sèvres factory) and executed by Pierre Gouthière, will serve equally well as an illustration of one of the finest mantel clocks of the period and as a specimen of Gouthière's craftsmanship. The figures symbolize the city of Avignon, and the two rivers, the Rhône and the Durance. The inscription reads '*Boizot fils sculpsit et exécuté par Gouthière cizeleur et doreur du Roy à Paris quay Pelletier à la Boucle d'or, 1771*', that is to say, 'Modelled by

Boizot the younger and executed by Gouthière, chiseller and gilder to the King, at the Golden Knocker on the Quay Pelletier in 1771'. This clock is one of Gouthière's few signed works, but it supports the high reputation which he enjoyed at the time. One would be hardly surprised to find the subject also in the *biscuit* porcelain of Sèvres, but there seems to be no record of it having been made.

An unusual variety is the musical clock, very popular at the time, which played a melody or a series of melodies on the hour, employing a carillon of bells for the purpose, the hammers being actuated by pins set in a revolving cylinder. French clocks of this kind are now rare, although English specimens are relatively frequent. Equally popular were astronomical clocks which recorded the phases of the moon and the movements of the heavenly bodies on a series of dials. Because of the elaborate trains of wheels required for movements of this kind such clocks are of the long-case variety, sometimes much wider than usual. Unlike the smaller spring-driven clocks, the long-case clock was actuated by weights, which were heavy in proportion to the number of trains of wheels to be driven. Astronomical clocks often took many years to make and were sought as status symbols by the wealthy.

Régulateurs or long-case clocks were often elaborate pieces of mechanism, the heavy pendulums being fitted with temperature compensatory suspensions consisting of alternating steel and brass rods. Many such clocks included a barometer set high up in the trunk, the dial protected by a glass window. Windows were also provided to enable the swing of the pendulum to be seen, and pendulum bobs were extremely handsome, often a gilded bronze mask surrounded by a sunburst. When such clocks are of Paris manufacture they are especially notable for their bronze decoration.

Like other objects of metalwork, clocks exhibit all the changes of style and ornament of their period. It is noteworthy that until the reign of Louis Quinze the width of the case is almost invariably less than the height, and a case not surmounted by a figure of one kind or another is a distinct rarity. These were usually symbolic, the symbolism connected in some way or another with Time. Cronos with hour-glass and scythe is perhaps the most frequent, and such elaborate representations as that of Apollo driving the chariot of the sun extremely rare. Diana frequently surmounts early clock-cases.

Cartel clocks are especially remarkable for fine bronzework, and they are among the most notable examples of the rococo style, the characteristic scrollwork being especially pronounced and floral *motifs* present abundantly. The clock by Cressent (plate 81) aptly illustrates the happy marriage between rococo and the cartel form and, no doubt the product of the necessity for designing the case round a circular dial, the cartel clock continued to retain a rococo air almost to the end of the century.

By 1770 styles in clock-cases changed. The Avignon clock still preserves a few rococo affinities, perhaps the stronger because of the occurrence of water as its principal theme. Nearly all Louis Seize mantel clocks are mounted on a low marble pedestal, often with applied gilt-bronze friezes. In general the mantel clock of the period is wider than it is high, a ratio first to be seen at the end of the reign of Louis Quinze, although this is far from invariable, and there are a good many later instances of the old more or less triangular composition, even if the apex is no longer a single dominant figure. Long-case clocks of the Louis Seize period, and a good many mantel clocks, are topped with a classical urn. A minor recurrence of the fashion for automata occurred towards the end of the century, when clocks were made in the form of a bird-cage with a bird which moved and sang on the hour, but these are now extremely rare.

Lighting appliances of all kinds have always played an important part in the best French interior decoration. By the time Louis Quatorze ascended the throne candles had become smaller and of a standard size, which made the provision of candleholders and drip-pans practical. Apart from the royal *châteaux* gilded wood was more common than metal, although in the King's apartments chandeliers suspended from the ceiling by a silken cord were of chiselled gilt-bronze or of silver. *Girandoles* were additionally ornamented with rock-crystal drops prismatically cut to reflect the light, and their soft and glittering illumination added to the splendour of the scene beneath them. Appliances of this kind later came to be termed *lustres*, although not until towards the end of the eighteenth century. Candelabra embellished with crystal drops were called *candélabres à girandoles*, and they reinforced the effect of the suspended lighting.

Sconces (*bras d'applique*) of bronze with several arms, were sometimes provided with polished metal reflectors. *Guéridons* – tall *torchères* usually on a single stem with a tripod foot, and not to be confused with the eighteenth-century small tables called by the same name – were often of wood, although reference has already been made to those of silver belonging to the King. Lanterns for suspension were primarily a handsomely ornamented top and bottom joined by glazing bars into which were set small panes of bevelled glass. These, of copper or bronze, were often of great size, and were commonly provided with a means of lowering them from the ceiling for cleaning and lighting.

The lighting appliances of the reign of Louis Quinze were especially notable for the manner in which the bronzeworkers gave free rein to their fancy, and for the sinuosity of their curves. Wall-lights especially were often small works of art of great beauty. Wood and silver were by now rarely employed for this purpose and gilded bronze was almost universal, sometimes in conjunction with porcelain flowers and leaves of white iron. Perhaps most of them took the form of scrolling acanthus foliage, with nozzles and drip-pans similarly based, and there are one or two rare examples of sconces of this kind in the porcelain of Sèvres. Chandeliers of iron adapted for the burning of oil first appeared shortly before 1750, and lanterns were still imposing pieces of metalwork, although smaller than in the preceding reign. *Girandoles* replete with crystal drops, often with a crystal bowl beneath, glittered in the candle-light, an effect reinforced by the multi-branched sconces at the sides of the pier-glasses which were reflected and multiplied by the mirror. A few hand-candlesticks mounted with Meissen figures have survived from this reign (plate 68), and small candlesticks designed by Meissonnier and Germain especially are often considerable works of art.

At this time lighting was greatly increased everywhere in the house, especially in the corridors, and many parts were constantly illuminated after dark, even when they were not in use. Street-lighting also made its appearance, and journeys on foot at night became a less hazardous adventure.

Under Louis Seize the curves of the previous reign were abandoned, and the lines of lighting appliances became more severe and the ornament more purely classical. In many ways the style of this period is reminiscent of the earlier reign of Louis Quatorze, particularly in its ornamental *motifs*. Wall-lights with from two to five branches sometimes had a stem in the form of a quiver, a device associated with Marie-Antoinette, or a tapering pedestal surmounted by the body of a woman, reminiscent of much earlier Renaissance ornament. An innovation of this reign was the *cassolette* with a reversible cover, one side of which formed a candleholder.

It is often regarded today as bad taste to convert the sconces of the eighteenth century to electricity with simulated candles, but this is precisely what was done during the last quarter of the eighteenth century, except that oil and not electricity replaced the candle as an illuminant.

For the greater part of the eighteenth century the more elaborate chandeliers were hired for special occasions from dealers in works of art, and all were accompanied by dust-covers which were only removed on special occasions.

It is, perhaps, relevant to turn to the manufacture of metalwork of this kind in England, where the products of the *fondeurs-ciseleurs* were extensively imitated by Matthew Boulton in Birmingham. As Boulton & Fothergill this firm made elaborate mounts of excellent quality, and instances of the native 'Blue John' or Derbyshire spar mounted in this way are far from unknown. At his Soho factory Boulton made objects of 'or-molu', rivalling those of France, which he exported to places as far away as Russia, and what is more significant, even to France itself. Wedgwood wrote to his partner Bentley in 1776, after visiting Boulton's factory,

I had no conception of the quantity of D'Or Moulu [notice Wedgwood's correct use of the term] they have sold, chiefly abroad, you remember a poor Venus weeping over the tomb of Adonis – a Time piece. How many would you imagine they have sold of this single group? 200 at 25 guineas each [now equivalent to about £250], including the Watch. They now sell as much of this manufacture in Tripods, Vases, Groups &c. as they can get up.

Boulton was, at this time, exporting heavily to the Russian Court.

He told me that they now had very great interest at the Russian Court, Mr Boulton having paid the Empress many compliments, both in Sculpture and Painting . . . and they hoped to supplant the French in the Gilt business.

Catalogues of early English metal-founders are preserved in the Victoria and Albert Museum, and they list candelabra, lamps, inkstands, flower-vases, and paperweights in bronze or 'Or-molu', the latter probably a kind of brass rather than gilt-bronze. Vases are listed as 'Lac' (or laquered), or 'rich gold colr. also bronz.', as well as 'chamber candlesticks in Bronz'. 'Bronz.' was probably a commercial euphemism for 'bronzed', much in the same way as 'art. silk' is a deliberately misleading form of 'artificial silk'. The term 'bronzed snuffers' occurs later in the same catalogue. Some catalogues list furniture-mounts, such as handles and escutcheon plates, and it is apparent that these were intended for circulation among French and American buyers. One of 1785 refers to 'French handles' which were in the Louis Seize style, and 'Escutcheons to match French Handles'. Quite probably they were exported to France in the rough and chiselled there.

V

Tôle peinte was a form of metalwork extensively employed for a variety of decorative purposes during the second half of the eighteenth century – for *jardinières* and plant-pots to contain the fashionable flowers and bulbs that people of all stations loved to cultivate, for inkstands, for *verriers* or monteiths for cooling glasses, for ice-pails (*rafraîchissoirs*), for *cassolettes* or urns used as perfume-burners, for *pots-pourris* or containers for sweet-smelling mixtures of herbs and flowers for scenting rooms,* for wall-fountains, for lanterns, candlesticks, and lighting fixtures generally, and for food-warmers, to name some of the more common uses.

The forms were as diverse as the uses to which these vessels were put. Some are based on porcelain and others on contemporary silver. Painted decoration of the more elaborate examples often owes much to porcelain from Sèvres, with scenes more or less finely painted and surrounded by a less elaborate version of the gilded borders of the porcelain factory.

* No doubt essential because of the primitive methods of sanitation which Young describes as an abomination. '*Sous les arbres, monsieur,*' is still quite often the reply to an inquiry for such facilities in provincial France. On the other hand, Young saw and commended the *bidet*, which had not then, and has hardly now, reached England.

Tôle is sheet-iron, the term referring to metal in a sheet form from which the objects were manufactured. (*Tôle de cuivre* is sheet-copper). *Peinte* refers both to the ground and to the decoration. The ground was the product of quite an elaborate process. According to a contemporary source the surface was first scoured with a mild abrasive to remove all smoothness, and the first coat of paint applied and subjected to moderate heat. A second coat was applied in the same way, the surface being blackened where required with smoke from a resinous torch. On the smooth surface thus attained several successive coats of coloured varnish were laid, the last being smoothly polished.

The origin of *tôle peinte* in its familiar form can be traced to the development of a heat-resisting varnish in the 1740s, although manufacture was not undertaken on a considerable scale until the 1760s, the first recorded factory being started by one Clément in 1768. *Tôle peinte* soon became exceedingly popular. Not only were objects made in this way extremely decorative, but they had the merit of being cheaper than porcelain and the elaborately mounted vessels of gilt-bronze. By far the greater quantity, however, was produced in the nineteenth century, although eighteenth-century production was by no means inconsiderable.

Decoration of the earlier examples is often of high quality. A few specimens were even sent to China to be painted in the Canton enamelling shops, and others were decorated in imitation of Oriental lacquer. The palette of those painted in France was diverse, shades being obtained by mixing coloured varnishes, gold being simulated by yellow ochre.

This chapter would be incomplete without mention of the popularity of wrought-ironwork, especially during the reign of Louis Quinze. The balustrade illustrated on plate 87 came from the *château* of Mme de Pompadour at Bellevue, and it is characteristic of much work of its kind. An interesting survival of this fashion where there may still be found a few eighteenth-century specimens are the wrought-iron balconies of New Orleans, in the former French Colony of Louisiana. Garden furniture of the same metal in the prevailing style of the period was also fairly common. Tables and seats are the most frequent survivals.

Handsomely decorated locks were, of course, common throughout the period, the exterior furniture often being of gilt-bronze. One has only to recall the skill of Louis Seize as a locksmith to appreciate the importance attached to locks.

Architectural metalwork in bronze includes balustrades and balcony railings which were usually partly gilded. These are rare, but are comparable in design with wrought-ironwork, although the quality of workmanship is usually better.

This aspect of French metalwork may be studied in the museum at Rouen where examples of all periods have been assembled.

6
Ceramics

I

Porcelain and *faïence* were so widely employed both for serving meals and for decoration that they require consideration in a certain amount of detail.

Faïence is a kind of pottery or earthenware covered with a glaze opacified by the addition of tin oxide. It is then white, and provides an excellent surface for painted decoration. Sometimes blue pigment was mixed with the glaze material to produce a coloured ground on which painted decoration was then executed, usually in white or yellow.

The secret of this kind of glaze came to France from Italy (where it is known as *maiolica*) during the early years of the sixteenth century, although it had been known and employed to a very limited extent at an even earlier date. It was fashionable not only for table-ware, but for all kinds of decorative purposes, including stoves and wall-fountains, and even for such relatively massive and architectural items as chimney-pieces. Louis Quatorze astonished France by building the so-called Trianon de Porcelaine, finished in 1674, in the grounds of Versailles. This consisted of *faïence* tiles and ornaments employed in a manner inspired by the porcelain pagodas of China. Inside 'everything was adorned in the manner of the works of art which come from China'. According to Saint-Simon it was 'a porcelain house where one could go to eat and drink'. This Trianon had been built, as everyone knew, for Mme de Montespan, and in 1687, probably to please Mme de Maintenon, it was demolished.

Porcelain is a much more sophisticated material which might well be termed an artificial hardstone. It somewhat resembles glass inasmuch as it is translucent, although not transparent. It is also extremely hard, and its glaze provides an excellent surface for painting.

Porcelain was of two kinds. The variety made in China, and in Saxony at Meissen, was a mixture of white clay and a powdered feldspathic rock fused under intense heat. Much of the porcelain made in France was of clay mixed with powdered glass fused at a slightly lower temperature, and with a lead glaze instead of the glaze made from powdered feldspathic rock which covers Oriental porcelain.

The decoration of porcelain is either painted under the glaze (in Europe always in blue), or with enamel colours which are added after the preliminary firing of body and glaze and fixed with a much lighter firing. The great advantage of enamels is that they provide a varied palette, to be seen at its best in the decoration of Sèvres porcelain.

During the seventeenth century porcelain was extensively imported from China, often by way of Holland, and manufacture in France began during the last decade of the seventeenth century, although several attempts had been made throughout the second half of the century. *Faïence* was manufactured throughout the seventeenth and eighteenth centuries in increasing quantities, the best work after the middle of the eighteenth century being much influenced by contemporary porcelain decoration.

Outside France porcelain similar in most respects to that of the Chinese was first made at Meissen about 1710, and this became immensely popular in France under the name of 'Saxe'.★ Some notion of the popularity of Meissen porcelain at the French Court at mid century, before the development of manufacture at Vincennes and Sèvres on a scale sufficient to supply the market, may be derived from the remarks of a lady of the period:

Saxe is certainly rather expensive, but I have eight complete dinner-services, quite apart from what I have spent on having my mirrors, candelabra, clocks, toilet-sets, and wardrobes mounted in Saxe. I have a passion for it which is almost adoration – I am Saxe from top to toe.

Before discussing wares made in France, however, it is essential to glance at the fashion for Chinese porcelain, to the popularity of which Cardinal Mazarin made so great a contribution.

Small quantities of Chinese porcelain as a highly valued curiosity had existed in France since the fifteenth century, either brought back by returning Crusaders from the Near East or imported by way of Venice or Portugal, but it was not until the Dutch began to sell porcelain captured on the high seas from Portuguese or Spanish carracks that it became available in significant quantities. The Dutch sold table-services of this kind to both Louis Treize and James I of England, and porcelain thus acquired came to be called in Holland '*kraak*' or 'carrack' porcelain, because the ships in which it was carried were called carracks. Evelyn's observations in the shop called Noah's Ark have already been quoted, and Beurdeley recalls a contemporary satirical verse to the effect that Cardinal Mazarin entertained the King and two Queens on dishes of porcelain and silver. By the time when Mazarin began to collect Chinese porcelain the Dutch East India Company's ships, spurred on by the watchword 'Jesus is good, but trade is better', were sailing to China whither the Jesuits had preceded them, bringing back enormous quantities of porcelain, lacquer, silk, and spices which they distributed throughout northern Europe, and the activities of *faïenciers* and *entrepreneurs* were continually directed towards the making of an acceptable substitute for the fashionable Chinese porcelain. This was by no means easy, since no way existed of analysing porcelain to find precisely what it contained, and what little information the Jesuits were able to send back to Europe was not merely imprecise but completely inaccurate. To the potters of

★ In England it was once erroneously termed 'Dresden'.

the seventeenth century the difference between *faïence* and porcelain was that the latter had the property of translucency, which it shared with a kind of Venetian glass opacified with tin oxide, and for this reason it was thought to be some kind of glass modified in a way which allowed it to be formed by normal pottery methods. This led to experiments with clay to provide plasticity and glass to give the translucent quality, and few manufacturers at the beginning of the eighteenth century, apart from one or two German experimentalists, recognized the fact that this was not, in fact, the porcelain of the Chinese.

As early as 1644 Claude Révérend, a *faïence* importer and probably a manufacturer as well, sought a privilege from Louis Quatorze for a material which he described as 'undoubtedly as good, if not better, than Chinese porcelain', but this material was almost certainly a kind of *faïence*, and French potters did not succeed in elaborating their formula for a porcelain substitute which was translucent until the last decade of the seventeenth century.

The first seventeenth-century imports of Chinese porcelain into France were decorated in blue under the glaze and made at the Imperial centre of Ching-tê-chên, but the French market later grew tired of blue alone and demanded polychrome decoration using enamel colours. This fell under two heads – polychrome painting, largely in the native taste, now usually grouped into such categories as the *famille verte, famille rose, famille noire*, and *famille jaune* in reference to the predominant colour, and polychrome decorations done to order from patterns provided by European merchants. The former were often executed at the factory itself, the latter always in enamelling shops established on the waterfront of the treaty port of Canton.

Of these colours, the *rose* – introduced about 1700 – was an import from Europe, sometimes called the 'purple of Cassius', which had been invented by Andreas Cassius of Leiden about 1670. This pigment, derived from gold chloride, was also widely used in Europe as a colouring agent for glass, and as a basis for enamels for all purposes. A later ground colour, sometimes employed at Sèvres until the death of Mme de Pompadour in 1764, was a variant of this *rose* which was termed *rose Pompadour*, sometimes known in England (quite inaccurately) as *rose du Barry*.

Particularly popular were vases and services decorated with the Arms of the French owner, but many subjects were taken from engravings which were copied with varying degrees of fidelity and competence. The fashion for Chinese porcelain, which played a great part in establishing the vogue for the *chinoiserie*, began to disappear with the onset of the rococo style, and the demand for sets of vases for the mantelshelf (*garnitures de cheminée*) lessened with the increasing popularity of gilt-bronze clocks and candelabra used for the same purpose. Chinese porcelain also had to meet growing competition from Meissen and from the French factories – from Sèvres especially.

The trade with Japan began in the middle of the seventeenth century, when the Dutch secured a monopoly, not only as traders between Japan and Europe, but as carriers between the various countries of the Far East based on Batavia as an *entrepôt*. The first imports were of wares decorated in underglaze blue, today often mistaken for Chinese porcelain. These, like similarly decorated Chinese wares, were much favoured by the Dutch, and copied meticulously by the *faïence* potters of Delft on to a tin-enamel glaze. Towards the end of the century polychrome wares painted in the manner of Sakaida Kakiemon first made their appearance, and they were soon being widely sought in France as the *première qualité du japon* mentioned earlier. The extent of their popularity, not always apparent today, may be judged from the fact that these were among the earliest Far Eastern polychrome wares to be imitated at the Meissen factory soon after it was established, and a palace bought by the Elector of Saxony, Augustus the Strong, to house his own collection was renamed the Japanische Palais. When a porcelain factory was established at Chantilly under the aegis of the Prince de Condé it soon achieved fame for its close copies of Japanese porcelain (plate 92), and the asymmetrical nature of the decoration no doubt helped to inspire the same feature in rococo scrollwork.

A little later than the Kakiemon wares was a kind of decoration often based on native brocades which came from the same factory of Arita (Hizen Province). This was called 'Imari' from the port of shipment not far from Arita. In France it was regarded as second quality.

Although the Japanese copied European forms to order, decoration with European subjects is relatively uncommon and mostly confined to representations of Dutch ships and merchants. Porcelain imported into Holland in white was enamelled by Dutch *faïenciers*, but these wares form a special group not worth discussing here. Testimony to the popularity of Japanese porcelain, however, may be found in the imitations of Imari designs by the Chinese about 1700.

Perhaps the finest example of Chinese painting-to-order surviving from the early years of the eighteenth century is an enormous trumpet-shaped vase in the Louvre bearing the Arms of the Regent, and it is noteworthy that an inventory of the Palais-Royal, made after his death, lists many Oriental *objets d'art* of all kinds, including furniture and lacquer as well as porcelain. In this taste, however, he was only following Louis Quatorze and the deceased Dauphin, and Mazarin before them.

Chinese export porcelain included not only forms in native taste, such as the vase mentioned above which was based on a bronze of the first millennium B.C., but tureens which were sometimes of pronounced rococo form, centre-pieces, monteiths (or glass-coolers), pepper-pots, sugar sifters, butter-dishes, and a vast number of other European shapes based either on *faïence* or metalwork. Production ranged from ewers and basins for the toilet table, chamber-pots, *bourdaloues*,★ and *bidets*, to snuff-boxes and cane-heads, and lighting appliances of all kinds – candlesticks, chandeliers, and sconces. The Chinese, however, never did succeed in overcoming the technical difficulties of producing plaques for furniture, and these always came from Sèvres.

Much Chinese porcelain was elaborately mounted in gilt-bronze. A pair of vases treated in this way by Gouthière is reputed to have cost no less than 10,700 *livres* in 1782, and Lazare Duvaux's account books list numerous examples of the mounting of Chinese porcelain of one kind or another in this way (page 165 ff.).

Porcelain, including that of China, became less fashionable with the onset of the neo-classical style. As a material it was much more suited to rococo, and both design and decoration in the classical style presented problems which no European porcelain factory successfully surmounted. Chinese copies of neo-classical forms are rare, although urns of the period exist, probably based on drawings of those produced by Sèvres. *Faïence* was even more unsuited to the new forms, and likewise began to decline. The place of both this and porcelain was increasingly taken by creamware, a kind of fine transparent glazed earthenware developed by Josiah Wedgwood, who vigorously promoted it on the French market and sold a large service to Catherine the Great. The *faïence* factories of France were forced, as self-protection, to imitate Wedgwood's productions, calling their creamware *faïence-fine*. This is also an appropriate place to mention Wedgwood's jasper ware, a fine stoneware which is usually decorated with white reliefs on a blue background, less often on backgrounds of other colours. These were employed to decorate French furniture in place of Sèvres painted plaques, beginning a few years before the Revolution. The Sèvres factory itself imitated Wedgwood's jasper plaques in similarly coloured *biscuit* porcelain, as did the Meissen factory, where it was called '*Wedgwood-arbeit*'. The situation in France in 1770 is amusingly underlined by a letter which Wedgwood addressed to the duc de Choiseul in that year:

'My Lord:

Knowing the taste they have in France for every thing that comes from England I thought your Excellency would freely pardon the liberty I have taken to send you a box that contains a complete assortment of [creamware] Urns and Vases in the antique taste, and after the Greek, Roman, and Etruscan models, and used for ornamenting appartments. . . . The assortment I take the liberty of addressing to your Excellency is the same as the one that hath been made here by order of the Empress of Russia [Catherine the

★ The *bourdaloue* is a chamber-pot somewhat like a sauce-boat in shape, intended for feminine use. Tradition has it that the name derives from Louis Bourdaloue, a seventeenth-century Jesuit whose sermons at Versailles were of such great length that the ladies of the Court found these vessels indispensable.

Great], afterwards by that of the King of Prussia [Frederick the Great], and hath since been sent to the Kings of Denmark and Poland. . . . I know my Lord, that this composition is not comparable to those Manufactures of France that are carried on at Sceaux [a small factory under the patronage of the duc de Penthièvre] and Vincennes [i.e. Sèvres], and give it no other name than earthenware.

I know my Lord, that all this is counterband in France, but the liberty I have taken in sending this Marchandise to your Excellency is not with a desire to open a trade betwixt this country and France, it is only to show my zeal and attention to your Excellency. I am not ignorant that with regard to curioseties the Nobility of France have the priviledge of procuring for themselves what the rigour of the Law would not permit to be sold publicly, and indeed it would be pity too liberal and pharasaical an observation of the Law should deprive people of taste of what all the rest of Europe enjoy. It is only with this view my Lord that I have taken the liberty to send you this parcel. . . .'

Numerous catalogues in French, of which the earliest is dated 1773, appeared subsequently. Those who are acquainted with Wedgwood's normally easy style as it appears in his numerous letters to his friends will be able to guess the hours of careful cogitation which went into the phrasing of this letter, which delicately suggests that, in return for the gift of creamware, Choiseul – powerful Minister of State – should close his eyes to infractions of the King's edicts in favour of his own factory at Sèvres. But it could hardly have been better done. Whether Choiseul did find the gift acceptable we do not know, but the letter testifies to the fashion for English manufactures and designs then beginning to cross the Channel and perhaps more evident in certain kinds of furniture. After 1770 the situation began to ease, culminating in a commercial treaty with France in 1786 by which English creamware was no longer 'counterband', Wedgwood acting as expert adviser to Lord Auckland (then William Eden) who was one of the negotiators.

II

There is space only to notice briefly some of the more important centres manufacturing *faïence*. Large numbers of small factories grew up, principally clustering around the larger ones, attracted by suitable raw materials and sources of fuel, and sometimes by the existence of more or less exalted patronage. There are seven centres influential enough to demand discussion here, however brief, and these are Nevers, Rouen, Moustiers, Strasbourg, Niderviller, Lunéville, and Marseille. For the remainder the reader is referred to the Bibliography. Of these factories Strasbourg also produced porcelain.

The Nevers factory dates back to the sixteenth century, when Italian potters were brought to France by the duc de Nivernais. Its early wares were largely based on the popular Italian *maiolica*, especially the *istoriato* decorations – a term meaning history-painting. In the seventeenth century the wares with which we are, perhaps, more familiar were produced at a factory belonging to the Custode family, one of whom was later a potter at Rouen, although Jean Valjean of Nevers was described in 1751 as '*noble faïencier du Roi*'. Of the notable wares of the seventeenth century from Nevers it is essential to notice those decorated with a blue ground termed the *bleu persan*, which had, in fact, little or no connexion with Persia. Designs were painted in opaque white and yellow pigment over this blue ground, some of them inspired by Chinese prototypes, and Chinese forms were also copied more or less faithfully. Towards the end of the century designs imitating Chinese wares painted in underglaze blue, usually figure subjects, were perhaps inspired by Dutch copies emanating from Delft. Forms based on contemporary European metalwork are also to be found, a particular example being a ewer (*aiguière*) with a trefoil lip and the characteristic domed base of silver ewers of the period, which probably once had a basin and formed part of a toilet-set (plate 93).

Nevers produced very little of especial note during the eighteenth century, being content rather to copy the popular wares of Rouen. Figures of excellent quality were made but were always rare, and after mid century, tureens in the form of fruit and vegetables naturally painted are a typical rococo product.

Although Rouen was producing wares in imitation of Italy in the sixteenth century, it does not assume any great importance in the history of the industry until the middle of the seventeenth century with the advent of Edmé Poterat. His son, Louis, was for many years the principal potter in this town. About 1690 a decoration of *lambrequins*, loosely based on such *motifs* as bed-drapes, the engraved designs of Jean I Bérain, and contemporary book-binding ornament, were introduced and became extremely fashionable, appearing also on early specimens of the porcelain of Saint-Cloud (page 120). *Lambrequins* were followed about 1700 by the *style rayonnant*, a form of ornament similarly inspired, but radiating from a common centre, which persisted until shortly after the death of the Regent. This, too, was widely imitated. Both kinds of ornament decorated the *faïence* which replaced table-silver at the Court when Louis Quatorze sent silver to the Mint in 1709. Polychrome wares in a limited range of high-temperature colours date from about 1700, and had become well established by 1720, continuing in favour until after mid century.

The factory of Nicolas Fouquay, Louis Poterat's successor, made some large busts of extremely fine quality, one of which – set on a typical *gaine* of the period – is among the prized exhibits of the Victoria and Albert Museum.

The ability to make and fire large pieces successfully is to be observed also in two globes in the Musée de Rouen, one terrestrial and the other

117

celestial, mounted on pedestals which are Louis Quatorze in style and 150 cm. in height. The celestial globe is inscribed '*A Rouen 1725 peint par Pierre Chapelle*'. The *faïence* of Rouen is best studied at this Museum which has a particularly fine collection.

The rococo period at Rouen is notable for excellent enamelled wares made between about 1750 and 1770 which were decorated with a variety of *motifs* characteristic of the style, often with pronounced asymmetrical scrollwork. The years after 1770 are marked by a slow decline in which little of importance was done.

The small town of Moustiers in the Basses-Alpes was almost equal in importance to the two just mentioned as a centre for the making of *faïence*, although it principally supplied the southern French market. Pierre Clérissy was established here in 1679, and the factory became especially influential under his grandson, Pierre II Clérissy. Another factory which made wares of fine quality was started by Joseph Olerys in 1738, and there were several other lesser enterprises in the same town during the eighteenth century.

Perhaps most notable are a series of wares based on the designs of Jean I Bérain, the finest painted in blue, which were produced between 1710 and 1740. The name 'Moustiers' is especially associated with this kind of decoration. Under Olerys polychrome decorations, often in the prevailing rococo style, form the subject of a central panel bordered by some excellent floral painting, the 'potato flower' border being especially associated with this factory. Moustiers became noted for large table-fountains and wall-cisterns, as well as a great deal of well-painted tableware. A later factory owned by Jean-Baptiste Ferrat specialized in enamelled *faïence* in the manner of Strasbourg, which is sometimes confused with the work of Marseille.

The Strasbourg factory was started by Charles-François Hannong about 1709, with a branch at Haguenau not far away, but the factory did not extend its activities on a considerable scale until it came under the direction of Paul Hannong in 1732. Strasbourg production bridges in style the work of the German and French factories, and a number of German workmen of considerable skill were employed, notable among them Adam Friedrich von Löwenfinck from Meissen who was the director of the Haguenau undertaking. The two factories were brought under the sole direction of Joseph-Adam Hannong in 1762, and he added the production of *faïence* stoves to the factory's output.

The earliest *faïence* from Strasbourg was painted very much in the Rouen style, and it was not until the 1740s that Paul Hannong began to make copies of Chinese and Japanese porcelain in a polychrome palette largely based on Meissen and Chantilly prototypes rather than those of China. The polychrome palette was greatly extended about 1745 by the introduction of enamel colours, and the adoption of European flowers (derived from a popular series at Meissen and there termed *deutsche*

Blumen) may have been suggested by von Löwenfinck. Those of Strasbourg were so popular that they were soon being copied by almost every *faïence* factory in France, although few of them could equal the Strasbourg painters for skill, nor could they reproduce successfully the characteristic carmine enamel. Rococo forms were adopted successfully, especially for relatively large pieces such as clock-cases based on those of gilt-bronze. Joseph-Adam Hannong largely followed and developed the work of his predecessors.

Another Alsatian factory, that of Niderviller in Moselle, was founded with the assistance of the Baron Jean-Louis Beyerlé in 1754, and sold in 1770 to Adam Philibert, the comte de Custine. Apart from imitations of Strasbourg, a good deal of original work was done. Some excellent figure-modelling came from Paul-Louis Cyfflé of Lunéville, who sold his moulds to the factory, and from Charles-Gabriel Sauvage, known as Lemire, many in a kind of *biscuit* porcelain. At Lunéville not far away figures were made by Cyfflé in an unglazed semi-porcelain known as *terre de Lorraine*, and another speciality of this factory was large figures of lions in *faïence* which decorated the entrances of houses and *châteaux* in the eighteenth century, and which were among the earliest productions.

The earliest *faïence* from Marseille largely copied the styles of Nevers, Moustiers, and Rouen, but after the middle of the eighteenth century the factories here struck out in a direction of their own and became known for colourfully painted wares. The best known, and perhaps the largest, of these Marseille factories was that of the Veuve Perrin, who succeeded her deceased husband, a one-time potter at Nevers, in 1748. Much of the painting, excellent in quality, has flowers, fish, birds, fruit, and vegetables as its themes during the rococo period and for some years afterwards. A few *chinoiseries* after Pillement have also been noted. The wares of Honoré Savy's factory are noted for a brilliant green enamel which also appears on some of the later wares from the Veuve Perrin with whom he was associated. Landscape painting, somewhat in the manner of Joseph Vernet, was done at the workshop of Joseph-Gaspard Robert, much of whose *faïence* was influenced by the prevailing style of Louis Seize, a characteristic which marks even more strongly the *faïence* of Antoine Bonnefoy. Robert also made a small quantity of porcelain, but specimens are rare.

French *faïence* is not especially well known outside the country of its origin, but a number of French museums preserve specimens of local work, notably Rouen, where the collection is extremely large. The museum at Montpellier is the best place to study the wares of the numerous southern factories.

III

The origin of porcelain in France is extremely obscure, and contemporary records are conflicting. In a general work such as this a discussion of the evidence in favour of one factory or person and another would be out of place, and we can accept the traditional attribution of the earliest porcelain to a factory at Saint-Cloud, near Paris, without going too far astray.

Dr Martin Lister visited Saint-Cloud in 1698, writing:

I saw the potterie of St Clou with which I was marvellously well pleased, for I confess I could not distinguish betwixt the pots made there and the finest China ware I ever saw. It will, I know, be easily granted me that the painting may be better designed and finished (as indeed it was) because our men are far better masters of that art than the Chinese; but the glazing came not in the least behind theirs, not for whiteness, nor the smoothness of running without bubbles. Again, the inward substance and matter of the pots was, to me, the very same, hard and firm as marble, and the self same grain on this side vitrification. Farther, the transparency of the pots the very same.

I have quoted this at length because it is testimony to the interest then being taken by the layman in this comparatively new and precious substance. As physician to Queen Anne, Lister was no doubt acquainted with the collection of Oriental porcelain brought to England by Queen Mary when Dutch William ascended the throne, and which was carefully preserved at Hampton Court.

Lister was astonished at the prices asked at Saint-Cloud. He writes:

They sold these Pots at excessive rates; and for their ordinary Chocolate Cups askt Crowns a-piece. They had arrived at Burning on Gold in neat Chequer Works. He [the proprietor] had some Furniture of Tea Tables at 400 Livres a Sett.

The porcelain made at Saint-Cloud did not, in fact, so nearly resemble typical Chinese porcelain as Lister seemed to think. It was an artificial type, made from clay and ground glass, and was closer in appearance to southern Chinese manufacture from Tê Hua (Fukien Province) which the French prized and called *blanc-de-Chine*. Indeed, the French factory adopted some of the patterns of Tê Hua, especially the well-known prunus blossom in relief. Other wares were painted in colour with Oriental *motifs* which are a mixture of standard Chinese designs and those of Kakiemon. The influence of contemporary metalwork appears in some of the forms, particularly in the employment of bird's-head teapot spouts, and handles in the form of animals. Specimens mounted in silver are not unusual. *Lambrequins* based on those of Rouen *faïence* and painted in blue underglaze appear on some of the early work. The manufacture of small 'toys', to give them the name current in the eighteenth century, in the form of snuff-boxes, cane-handles, and so forth, was probably on a considerable scale, although survivals are comparatively rare.

The earliest mark adopted by the factory was that of a sun-face which obviously refers to *le roi soleil*, but the factory was, from the beginning, under the protection of the duc d'Orléans.

120

A factory started at Chantilly in 1725 was under the patronage of Louis-Henri de Bourbon, Prince de Condé, who had a large collection of Chinese and Japanese porcelain, much of the latter decorated in the Kakiemon style. The earliest work of this factory was largely based on Kakiemon porcelain decoration, sometimes mounted in gilt-bronze (plate 92). The wares made after 1751 are rarely of interest because production was limited to inferior ware by the King's edicts in favour of the Vincennes factory. Chantilly adopted, for its early wares, the most unusual technique of covering its porcelain body with a *faïence* glaze, which makes them easy to recognize.

A factory at Mennecy at first made *faïence*, porcelain being added about 1735. It was patronized by Louis-François de Neufville, duc de Villeroy, and later (in 1779 when it was removed to Bourg-la-Reine) by the comte d'Eu. Its early wares resemble the later productions of Saint-Cloud, especially in the use of prunus blossom. Hardly later are copies of the less ambitious decorations of Meissen, especially the *deutsche Blumen*, which were of excellent quality, very well painted. With the rise of the royal factory of Vincennes (later Sèvres) attempts were made to copy its work, but specimens are very rare. One with the royal monogram of intertwined Ls adopted by the Vincennes factory, and the mark DV (de Villeroy) of Mennecy, leaves no doubt of the intention. Excellent figures were made here, both white and painted, as well as a small number of unglazed or *biscuit* figures in imitation of Vincennes. Small boxes, especially those in the form of animals, are much sought today.

The work of these three factories, and of numerous minor off-shoots whose products can be identified only with difficulty, led ultimately to the interest of the King in the manufacture of porcelain. Almost all the European porcelain factories of the day, apart from English ones, were patronized by one or other of the ruling princes, or by members of their Courts, and it was not therefore, surprising that Louis Quinze should eventually want a factory of his own.

With the assistance of Orry de Fulvy, brother of the Minister of Finance, and aided by two workmen from Chantilly, a factory was started in 1738 which was housed in some outbuildings in the disused fortress of Vincennes. De Fulvy's brother, Orry de Vignory, used his influence to gain a privilege from the King for the new undertaking, and this was granted in July 1745 in the name of Charles Adam, the sculptor, for a term of twenty years. It referred to the manufacture of porcelain in the manner of Meissen. The porcelain body employed was a sophisticated development of that of Saint-Cloud and Mennecy, and in 1745 Adam referred, in a communication to the King, to 'a new factory just established in England for the manufacture of porcelain more beautiful than that of Saxony owing to the nature of its composition'. This factory could only have been Chelsea, established probably in 1744, which was using a formula undoubtedly derived from French sources.

Orry de Vignory was replaced as Finance Minister by Jean-Baptiste de Machault, who was not at first entirely favourable to the new project, but by 1747 he had been so far converted that he issued orders forbidding the manufacture of porcelain in France otherwise than at Vincennes. The help of Mme de Pompadour was secured at the same time, and she persuaded the King to grant an annual subvention of two hundred thousand *livres*. The directors of the factory were the *fermier-général* Boileau de Picardie, Jean Hellot, director of the Académie de Sciences, and Claude-Thomas Duplessis, goldsmith and bronzeworker, who was the principal designer. Jean-Jacques Bachelier was placed in charge of painting and modelling, and Jean-Adam Mathieu, enameller to the King, gave assistance in the perfection of overglaze colours. With the help and interest of Mme de Pompadour, Bachelier became Director of the factory in 1751 and retained this position until 1793.

The factory became entitled to the status of *Manufacture royale* in 1750 when a new company was formed with the King holding a quarter of the shares to the value of two hundred thousand *livres*, and at the same time the use of the royal monogram was granted as a factory mark. At this time it was strictly forbidden for other factories to make porcelain in France, or even to paint *faïence* in any colour other than blue. Imports of porcelain from abroad were forbidden, and all workmen were prohibited from leaving the factory to engage in porcelain-making elsewhere. That the other factories already mentioned were able to continue clandestinely testifies to the strength of their patronage, but for some years they were able to do very little, and they must have sold their output outside the capital.

Hitherto the most fashionable porcelain had been that of Meissen, imports of which were forbidden under the new edicts, and the earliest products of Vincennes copied Meissen wares more or less faithfully, as well as producing large quantities of porcelain flowers to which leaves and stalks of bronze were added. Lazare Duvaux bought heavily from the new factory, especially flowers which he sent to the bronzeworkers for mounting. As early as 1748 the Queen had acquired a vase of white porcelain from Vincennes mounted in bronze, which held almost five hundred flowers and stood three feet high. Mme de Pompadour created a winter garden of porcelain flowers at her new *château* of Bellevue, and the marquis d'Argenson wrote:

The King has ordered more than 800,000 *livres* worth of porcelain flowers from the Vincennes factory, naturally painted, and especially for the *château* of Bellevue belonging to the Marquise de Pompadour. Paris talks of nothing else, and this unheard of luxury causes great scandal.

The expansion of production in other directions, and the beginning of the characteristic Sèvres style, can be dated to about 1752, and was apparently due to the influence of Duplessis. Although the factory made service-ware of extremely high quality, it concentrated principally on the production of ornamental ware, especially vases in great variety with richly coloured grounds, tooled gilding, and magnificent painting in panels. Duvaux's purchases rose from 36,000 *livres* in 1753 to 102,000 *livres* in 1756, many being made on behalf of the King and Mme de Pompadour.

Boucher began his connexion with the royal factory as adviser and designer soon after 1750, and his influence is nearly always apparent in the products of its best period, which closed with the death of Mme de Pompadour.

By 1756 the factory had achieved such success that it had outgrown its original buildings at Vincennes, and with the King's assistance Mme de Pompadour selected a new site for it at Sèvres, not far from her house at Bellevue. The new factory, badly designed, cost more than a million *livres*, and many difficulties were experienced in organizing production. The porcelain body used, while being the finest in appearance ever to be made, was also one of the most difficult to produce successfully, and the quantity of 'wasters' was exceedingly high. Consequently it was extremely expensive, and the cost was certainly no less when the King became the chief salesman, adding his powerful persuasion to that of Mme de Pompadour. 'He sells the pieces himself,' wrote a contemporary, 'and they are not cheap'. Louis unpacked the new production with his own hands in the library at Versailles, 'breaking', as one factory comment ruefully has it, 'not a few'.

Inspired by the figure-work of Meissen the factory at Sèvres especially turned its attention to figure-modelling, which had first been introduced by Bachelier at Vincennes. Vincennes-Sèvres made a speciality of the unglazed or *biscuit* figure which, because it needed to be perfect and without blemish, was always more expensive. The English Derby factory, where *biscuit* figures were also made, glazed and painted slightly imperfect examples and sold them more cheaply. Although Boucher provided the designs for many of the porcelain figures, the modelling was in the hands of the sculptor, Étienne-Maurice Falconet, until he left for Russia in 1766 to work for Catherine the Great, when he was replaced by Jean-Jacques Caffiéri.

Vincennes-Sèvres porcelain is especially noted for its ground colours, many of which – the work of the chemist, Hellot – were new to porcelain manufacture. Among them the best known is the *rose Pompadour*, which may have been the invention of the painter Xhrouet, and which was discontinued in 1764. The *gros bleu* is an underglaze blue ground, the *bleu céleste* a fine turquoise, the *jaune jonquil* a rare pale yellow, and there were many others.

Much of the painted decoration was inspired by Boucher, usually little *putti*, at first in monochrome and later in polychrome. Subjects taken from the painter, Teniers, were extremely popular, and Dodin did

123

other figure-subjects. Morin specialized in shipping scenes, and Taillander, Tandart, Cornaille and others in the favourite flowers. Paintings of exotic birds by Evans and Aloncle were frequently copied on to English porcelain.

Although the factory did not make services in large numbers they produced handsomely decorated small cups and saucers, which were the origin of the cabinet cups and saucers made towards the end of the eighteenth century in England, by Derby especially. They also made services to special order for the King and the Court, and as gifts to foreign princes and ambassadors. After the removal to Sèvres production was diversified, even to the point of producing spittoons, chamber-pots, and *bidets*, but manufacture of such domestic objects was not on a large scale until after 1770, when the factory acquired a formula for making porcelain in the Chinese manner which was less expensive to produce and less fragile in use.

The manufacture of plaques for the decoration of furniture may have been suggested in the first place either by Machault or Mme de Pompadour, but their introduction is usually attributed to the dealer, Simon Poirier. Dominique Daguerre and his partner, Lignereux, were also dealers who bought plaques for this purpose, selling both to the French Court and to wealthy Englishmen. Leleu and Carlin were the two *ébénistes* who most frequently employed this kind of decoration, principally for *guéridons* and similar pieces of small furniture. Plaques were also employed to decorate such gilt-bronze objects as clock-cases, and the use of porcelain in the making of clock-cases is discussed on page 105.★

Among the many small objects of *vertu* must be included boxes and inkstands made from plaques mounted in a framework of gilt-bronze, or sometimes of gold. Some boxes were made in one piece, with the hinge of the lid in gold. Small plaques were adapted to the manufacture of jewellery and *étuis*, and among the many small objects a seed-box for a canary may, perhaps, be selected as the epitome of luxury.

The introduction of the true porcelain body soon after 1770 demanded considerable changes in technique, but the factory soon mastered the difficulties, and by 1783 they could make a vase five feet in height, now in the Louvre, which cost 70,000 *livres*. In keeping with the prevailing spirit of neo-classicism we find the so-called 'Etruscan' friezes used as decoration, beginning about 1783, and scrolls and arabesques probably date from the same time or a little earlier. Medallion portraits and friezes painted *en grisaille* are to be seen from the beginning of the reign of Louis Seize.

The fashion for rusticity brought orders to Sèvres for churns, milk-jugs, and butter-dishes for Marie-Antoinette's *hameau* at Versailles and her farm at Rambouillet, and a new departure, and hardly a commendable

124 ★ Le Beaupré, a more than usually expensive courtesan, had a coach with plaques of Sèvres porcelain, and the use of such plaques in the decoration of sedan chairs was not unknown.

one, was the imitation of relatively large oil-paintings enamelled on porcelain plaques and hung on the wall, of which hunting-scenes by Asselin after Oudry are fairly typical. One measured two feet square.

Among the earliest *biscuit* figures we may observe those from Vincennes in the manner of Oudry, of which a '*Chien poursuivant un cygne dans les roseaux*', modelled by Blondeau, is typical.* These were speedily followed by children after Boucher, a series of eight figures being issued in 1754. The famous 'Flute Lesson' of Boucher was a Vincennes favourite, later copied at Chelsea and Frankenthal, while Falconet's '*Baigneuse*' and its companion piece were so popular that almost every major porcelain factory in Europe produced a copy based on one or other of them. The stage provided subjects for the modeller, Fernex doing a portrait of the actress, Mme Favart, in 1753, and a milkmaid – '*La Laitière*' – by the same modeller was a reduced version of a statue intended for Mme de Pompadour's dairy at Crécy. Falconet was responsible for '*L'Amitié*' made before he actually joined the factory, representing friendship, which was complemented at Bellevue by another called '*L'Amour*' by Pigalle. '*L'Amitié*' depicts Mme de Pompadour standing beside a short flower-bedecked column offering her heart to the King, and it secured for Falconet the position of Director of Sculpture at Sèvres.

The growing interest in antiquity which is evident by 1760 manifested itself in a number of models based on classical art and legend, such as the '*Pygmalion amoureux de sa Statue*' which was probably inspired by the ballet of *Pygmalion* presented in 1760. Towards the end of the decade a series of portraits of Great Men was started, modelled by Caffiéri, Pajou, Clodion, and Boizot, and in 1770 Pajou produced a bust of Mme du Barry which was followed by a portrait of the Dauphine, Marie-Antoinette, a year later. Pajou got himself into trouble in 1782 when he made the group commemorating the birth of the Dauphin in allegorical form. This (plate 78) depicted a semi-nude Venus seated on two dolphins, symbolic of the Dauphin, and carrying in her arms a naked Cupid representing the newly-born child. Not only did the features of Venus resemble those of Marie-Antoinette to a marked degree, but Pajou emphasized the likeness by ornamenting what little drapery he provided with the fleur-de-lys. He was ordered to change the features and remove the fleur-de-lys, and Sèvres then issued the model in 1781. The plaster original is at Versailles, and a terracotta version was sold in New York at the Parke-Bernet Galleries in 1961. It is noteworthy that when the duc de Normandie's birth was to be celebrated in 1785 the commission went to Boizot. Pajou's son-in-law Clodion, a modeller with a taste for the erotic, also worked for Sèvres, providing the factory with characteristic models of nymphs and fauns.

Boizot became director of the modelling studios in 1772; his work was

125

competent and in a pronounced neo-classical style. The sentimentality of the period is to be seen in his model of 1774 called '*La Nourrice*', which depicts a young mother to whom a servant is presenting her newly-born baby. Boizot also designed an immense table-service for Catherine the Great, and a table-decoration in *biscuit* porcelain comprising about forty figures. The total cost of both was 322,000 *livres*, for which Catherine refused to pay, and the Foreign Ministers of France and Russia were involved in the quarrel over payment, while the unfortunate Boizot became bankrupt.

Throughout the period discussed edicts of one kind or another intended to strengthen the position of Sèvres and weaken that of its competitors continued to be promulgated. A porcelain factory started at Strasbourg by Hannong was pursued until he removed it across the border into the Palatinate to become the Frankenthal factory, and the others barely survived. After the death of Louis Quinze and the discovery of the secret of making porcelain in the Chinese manner, however, new factories were started under very august patronage. One in the rue Thiroux in Paris had the protection of Marie-Antoinette, and its products were known as *porcelaine de la reine*. Here porcelain was produced for the Queen's dairies, and much of the decoration was of her favourite corn-flower sprigs. The Fabrique de Clignancourt, also in Paris, enjoyed the patronage of the comte de Provence, the King's brother, where the work of Sèvres, and sometimes the mark, was copied. There is record that three thousand illegally marked pieces were seized by the police in 1779. A factory in the rue de Bondy owed its continued existence to the interest of the duc d'Angoulême, the eldest son of the comte d'Artois. With so many factories enjoying the protection of other members of the royal family it is hardly surprising that the powerful position of Sèvres became harder to maintain, and several privately owned factories sprang up, chiefly in Paris, some imitating Sèvres, including the *biscuit* figures, and others imitating Wedgwood's jasper stoneware. Most of them devoted the greatest attention to service-ware, of which many specimens survive.

Sèvres is now a French national enterprise, maintaining an excellent museum not only of its own work but of pottery and porcelain generally. It is a few minutes' walk from the Porte de Sèvres station on the Paris métro, and is well worth a visit.

The eighteenth-century porcelain collections of France have long since been dispersed, and it is therefore instructive to glance briefly at some of the porcelain once in the possession of Louis Quinze's Minister and Comptroller-General, Machault, whose interest and protection, added to that of Mme de Pompadour, contributed so much to the early success of the Sèvres factory while it was still housed at Vincennes. Some of the pieces described below were given to him by the factory as a token of gratitude, and may therefore be regarded as among their most valued work at the time, and quite probably representing newly-perfected processes. They descended by inheritance to the comte de Chavagnac who, with the marquis de Grollier, wrote a *History of French Porcelain Manufacture* which has been an invaluable source-book for later studies. The Chavagnac collection was sold at the Hôtel Drouot in Paris in 1911.

The prevailing fashion for *biscuit* figures was represented by two fine paperweights from Vincennes which Machault kept on his desk. These, given on the 31 December 1754, were a souvenir of Machault's former position as Treasurer to the Navy, and they are groups of two *putti*, each with emblems of the sea and fishing – anchors, coils of rope, shells, and so forth. They were mounted on gilt-bronze bases in a restrained and symmetrical version of the Louis Quinze style.

A lobed *sucrier* and cover, with a stand of the same porcelain, was decorated with flowering branches, and a cream-jug with a turquoise blue ground (the *bleu céleste* first introduced about 1752), had little naked *amorini* surrounded by flowering branches and gilding. Somewhat larger was a ewer, also with a turquoise ground, with flying birds in gilt silhouette in reserves framed by gilt-flowers.

Two four-lobed bowls – a shape directly derived from Japanese porcelain – with a wheatsheaf *motif* (the so-called 'banded hedge' pattern), flowers in colours, and gilding were in the Japanese style, the flowers being of the variety called at Meissen '*indianische Blumen*'. These bowls were copies of Arita porcelain of the Kakiemon type, but one was made at Meissen, and the other – reproduced from the Meissen version – came from Vincennes. This is an interesting example of Meissen influence on early Vincennes manufacture. The second bowl bore the fleur-de-lys in addition to the monogram of Louis Quinze, testifying to the King's interest in the factory.

Two large *cache-pots* (ten inches in height) were decorated in colours with flowers and birds, bordered at the top and bottom with blue and gold, and provided with rococo handles. A pair of tulip vases with *amorini* in reserves on a turquoise blue ground recall the love of flowers which was so much a feature of the time, and many vessels for containing them came from Vincennes-Sèvres. A *jardinière* decorated with birds by Taillandier and mounted in gilt-bronze had the very rare yellow ground, the *jaune jonquil* first produced in 1753, and another, fifteen inches long, had flying birds and garlands outside surrounded by an elaborately imbricated ground pattern, the interior with flowers.

A *rafraîchissoir* decorated in the *rose camaïeu*, which was a noticeable feature of early Vincennes painting, had children watering plants on one side and a landscape on the other, with rococo handles embellished with gilding. The *rafraîchissoir* was a vessel with a scalloped edge for cooling the bowls of wine-glasses, which were suspended from the edge by the foot and held by the scallops. It was, in fact, a form of the English monteith.

Three examples of the combination of porcelain with other materials are worth describing. The first is a pair of candlesticks with two lights

127

in the form of a bush made of gilt-bronze with added porcelain flowers of Meissen and Vincennes manufacture, and at the foot, a Chinese covered bowl in the form of a peach. The second is a chandelier for suspension with three lights in the form of a gilt-bronze swing-shaped arbour richly decorated with porcelain flowers. In the centre, as though it were on a perch, is a Meissen bird on a high base of the kind modelled by Kändler about 1745. The last is a cylindrical vase of Fukien porcelain (the so-called *blanc-de-Chine*) with two handles in the form of newt-like dragons. This was mounted on a gilt-bronze base ornamented with rococo scrolls, with bulrushes of the same material, and, on either side, two Meissen swans of the kind included with the 'Swan' service made for von Brühl.

No doubt the Chavagnac *heritage* was incomplete, and only some of the more interesting specimens have been mentioned here, but these represent the kind of porcelain which decorated the Machault mansion. Other such items, especially porcelain with bronze mounts, are mentioned in Lazare Duvaux's account books, from which extracts are given in Appendix II.

IV

When we recall the predominant position of France in the decorative arts generally it is astonishing that so little progress was made in the art of ornamental glass-making. Glass was a fairly well established craft in the days of the Romans, and an industry making domestic glass had survived in Lorraine from very early times. But the principal centres of European glass-making during the reign of Louis Quatorze were to be found in Venice and Germany, and for most of the seventeenth century Venice was the only source of supply for mirror-glass. The difficulty was largely one of making flat sheets, a problem only partly solved by the Romans, whose window-glass was small in size and extremely thick. Until the eighteenth century window-panes were small, the surface irregular, and the glass was set in numerous glazing bars. Large panes did not become common until the eighteenth century was fairly well advanced. For this reason bookcases often had solid doors, or doors of brass trellisage backed with silk.

Until about 1760 French table-glass was also of relatively poor quality, and the best was imported, although much better work was done by a few Italians who had settled in France. The very high cost of mirror-glass induced Colbert to set up the Manufacture Royale des Glaces de Miroirs in 1665, situated in the Faubourg Saint-Antoine in Paris. Here some Venetians were employed, but Colbert had forgotten the well-established Venetian custom of assassinating workmen who took their manufacturing secrets elsewhere. His Venetians died, probably poisoned, and after four years the project had to be abandoned. The mirrors for the Galerie des Glaces came from Venice, and the enormous cost of such work may be judged from the fact that, when Colbert died, an inventory was made of his possessions in which a Venetian mirror was valued at twice the amount of a painting by Raphael.

The factory situated at the gate of Saint-Antoine was opened towards the end of the seventeenth century after Bernard Perrot had discovered a process for casting glass into sheets. Hitherto sheet glass had been made by blowing a large bubble which was rolled into a cylinder on an iron table and then slit lengthwise and opened out flat, the ends being trimmed off with shears. Sheets of this kind have surface irregularities and blemishes which make them comparatively easy to recognize, and the size was strictly limited. When Martin Lister visited the Saint-Antoine works in 1698 he recorded that he saw 'a Looking-glass foiled and finished, 88 inches long by 48 inches broad, and yet but a quarter of an inch thick'. He found this astonishing, as indeed it was. 'This', he wrote, 'could never have been effected by the Blast of any Man; but I suppose to be run on Sand as Lead is.'

He found that six hundred men were employed, a number which the factory hoped to increase to a thousand. The glass was first polished with sandstone and then finished with something which Lister calls 'powdered Haematites' – apparently a kind of jeweller's rouge. 'The grinding of the edges and borders [i.e. bevelling]', he records, 'is very . . . odious for the horrid grating noise it makes. . . . [It] has made glass for Coaches very cheap and common.'

A factory had also been opened in Normandy in 1688 to exploit Perrot's invention and this was removed to Saint-Gobain in Picardy in 1693. Called the *Manufacture Royale des Grandes Glaces*, it was amalgamated with the Saint-Antoine factory in 1695, and Saint-Gobain remains the national manufacture of mirrors and plate-glass to this day, like the porcelain factory at Sèvres inherited by the Republic from the Kings of Versailles.

Despite the size of the sheets noticed by Lister it is doubtful whether any were used without being cut at this time, since most large mirrors continued to be made in sections, the old inventories frequently referring to this division. The practice of setting the various sheets in carved wood frames, which formed a more or less permanent part of the *boiserie*, made the sectional nature of the mirror-glass less noticeable. As in England, mirrors of all kinds continued to be extremely expensive throughout the first half of the eighteenth century.

The manufacture of crystal table glass was started in Lorraine in the 1730s, but the standard was low and most good table-glass, as well as lustres for *girandoles* and chandeliers, continued to be imported from Bohemia. Table-glass also came from England. The Baccarat factory (near Lunéville) was founded in 1765, and another Lorraine factory (that of Saint-Louis) in 1767. By 1784 Saint-Louis was making crystal glass equal in quality to English and German manufacture. A number of other factories were started towards the end of the eighteenth century with varying success, but it was not until the nineteenth century that the industry in France began to assume its present importance.

7

Tapisserie

It commonly happens that our view of the past is partial and inaccurate for the lack of some essential key which no longer exists. Just as we are inclined to think of Greece and Rome as a white world, inhabited by marble statues, because the paint and gilding of the marbles has yielded to the wind and rain, so we often overlook the part played, in the seventeenth century especially, by rich stuffs and superb embroideries. Today some notion of former glories can only be gained from a few drawings and paintings, contemporary descriptions, and tattered remnants of the materials themselves, but these alone are insufficient to recreate the scene. In England, the Stuart furniture at Knole still preserves its original coverings sadly worn and decayed, but such instances are very rare.

The textiles which furnished the seventeenth-century interior, and on which it depended for much of its magnificence, are difficult to imagine today in all their luxury and splendour. There were, for instance, the many hangings woven with gold and silver thread, sometimes enhanced with pearls of great value, resembling the techniques which had earlier been employed in the making of the finest tapestries. These have all perished. Then there were the *meubles brodés* at Versailles, which were embroidered panels in high relief reaching almost from floor to ceiling. A surviving drawing shows one such panel flanked by Corinthian pilasters, the figures with faces and hands of silver. Pillars were ornamented with embroidery, recalling the pillar carpets of ancient Rome and China. Embroidered statuary (such as supporting caryatids), was executed over a model carved by a sculptor. Cabinets on rich stands were also thus decorated. Embroideries and hangings adorned with the precious metals survived the economic difficulties of the 1680s only to be consigned to the flames in 1743, when gold and silver valued at more than fifty thousand *livres* (about £25,000) was recovered.

At the beginning of the seventeenth century France was importing her richest textiles – silks, satins, and velvets – from Italy and Flanders. The manufacture of luxury materials did not exist in France, apart from the silk of Lyon and Tours, and even this was often passed off as being of foreign make. Mazarin had a passion for fine stuffs of all kinds. Colbert, a draper's son to whom textiles were no mystery, was Mazarin's secretary. When his master at one stage in his career as Minister of State prudently removed himself from France to his native Italy, it was Colbert who made an inventory of the Cardinal's possessions – the crimson velvets of Venice, the damasks from Lucca, the flowered satins called 'chinois', the gold *passementeries* (decorative borders) and fringes, the gold cords and tassels for curtains and bed-drapes, and the laces of Marseille and Valenciennes. The situation in which the richest materials were imported was to change only slowly during the remainder of the century, but in the eighteenth century France was at last able to depend on stuffs produced inside her own borders, no longer sumptuously woven of gold and silver, but of superb quality nonetheless.

We can conveniently classify textiles employed for interior decoration into four categories. First, the imported materials from Flanders, Italy, and the Orient, and those produced in France itself, used for upholstery, bed-drapes, curtains, and *portières*. Second, tapestries from the looms of Gobelins, Beauvais, and Aubusson, as well as those imported from Flanders. Third, embroideries such as those already described, needle-run tapestries (which are not strictly tapestries at all – see page 135), and the less ambitious *gros point* and *petit point* work. Fourth, the pile carpets of Savonnerie, and the pileless carpets of the tapestry looms, both rare from the period discussed. These carpet materials were also adapted to the upholstery of seat-furniture, principally tapestries and very rarely the products of the Savonnerie factory. Since this chapter discusses wall-hangings as well as upholstery it will be a convenient point to mention also wall-papers and the use of leather for this purpose.

Velvet – the '*holoserica velosa*' of Pancirollus – was the principal luxury material, and at the beginning of the reign of Louis Quatorze the most splendid came from Genoa and Milan. Mazarin possessed a hanging of

crimson Milanese velvet with *grotesques* after Raphael, embroidered with gold, silver, and silk in *petit point*, comprising nine pieces, the middle of each with a great medallion representing scenes from the life of François Premier, and at the top of each piece the Arms of His Eminence.

The manufacture of velvet in France began in the seventeenth century with the establishment of a factory at Saint-Maur, near Paris, by a *Lyonnais*, Marcelin Charlier, where the quality rivalled if not surpassed that of imported velvets, some of which were sold for a thousand *livres* an *aune*.* Some, according to a contemporary source, 'were made to designs by the sieur Bérain, well known for this kind of work . . . . The little that has been made of this velvet has been used for *portières* in the apartments of Versailles.'

Velvets were almost infinite in their variety. Stripes of alternate long and short pile, cut-velvet, stencilled patterns, flowered velvet, and many others. The future Regent had two beds at Versailles, one of flame-coloured velvet ornamented with bands of gold and silver brocade, and the other of red flowered velvet lined with gold mohair, ornamented with fringes and valances. Crimson velvet was the most popular, a preference which perhaps began with Richelieu and was certainly continued by Mazarin, and by Louis Quatorze who regarded it as a royal colour in

* An *aune* (often translated by 'ell') was a little more than a yard.

conjunction with gold borders or galoons – '*le rouge pour le Roi, le vert pour Monseigneur, le bleu et l'aurore pour Monsieur et Madame*'.★

Satin is a silk fabric woven so that the surface is smooth and softly lustrous, the reverse being dull. This appealed especially to Mazarin, and it appears frequently in his inventory – green, flesh-coloured, dove-coloured, crimson, and pearl-grey (the colour Anne of Austria wore as a widow) with floral ornament, but it was under Louis Quatorze that the finest satins were produced in great variety. The Royal Inventories of the period refer to '*satin de la Chine blanc*' – white satin of China – decorated with a variety of ornament such as scrolls, flowers, foliage and birds, often in gold but sometimes '*au naturel*', with embroidered gold and silver borders, some of which also came from Saint-Maur. Painted satins certainly existed before the opening of the last quarter of the seventeenth century.

Damask (*damas*), so called from the rich figured silk of Damascus, at first came from Italy, but was being woven in France before the end of the seventeenth century. Mazarin's inventory refers to 'crimson damask of Naples with large flowers and urns'. Fouquet had a bed of Flemish damask, and the King possessed many pieces of red damask, some from Saint-Maur. *Lampas* is a variety of damask.

Brocade (*brocart*) was the name given to an especially rich fabric with a slightly raised pattern, often woven with gold and silver thread. The making of brocade began in Italy and Spain as early as the thirteenth century with a background of silk into which was woven a floral pattern, as often as not Islamic in origin. Until 1667, when Colbert introduced the industry into France, brocades had come from Lucca, Genoa, Florence, and Venice, but two or three years afterwards the manufacture was fairly well established at Lyon and Saint-Maur. Mazarin possessed hangings of 'gold brocade with figures of hunters, animals, birds, rivers, and fountains raised in gold on silks of various colours, nineteen pieces', as well as eighteen 'columns' of gold brocade with large flowers of gold and silver, apparently analogous to the pillar carpets mentioned earlier. Even more splendid brocades were later to be found at Versailles. Havard estimated that between 1665 and 1672 the King spent 207,734 *livres* on these exotic stuffs, including the brocades of Lyon, Paris, Tours, Venice, Florence, and '*des Indes*', which perhaps indicates an origin in either Persia or India. This sum, however, was far exceeded by the cost of embroidery. The King's State bed, for instance, was reputed to have cost 600,000 *livres*. One example from the Royal Inventories will suffice for a glimpse of the splendour of the time – 'the furnishing of the [King's] *cabinet*, consisting of four *fauteuils* and six *pliants* [folding stools] of embroidery ornamented with pictures enriched with gold and silver, representing the Elements, Seasons, and other subjects by figures of children, with borders round and oval, the embroidery of raised gold and silver, the

★ 'Red for the King, green for the Dauphin, blue and the gold of dawn for the King's brother and his wife.'

133

remainder of the said chairs filled with embroidered *motifs* on blue satin enhanced with gold in the manner of [Chinese] porcelain, on a ground of cloth of gold thread'.

Taffeta, a plain silk (the term derived from the Persian *tâfta*), came originally from the Orient. The import of Chinese silk especially has a long history in Europe, going back at least to the third century B.C., and it was an exceedingly fashionable material both in Rome and Byzantium. The Byzantines bought so much that they were driven by financial stringency to make their own silk, the cost threatening to bankrupt the city. Silk from the Orient was imported into France throughout the seventeenth century and especially during the eighteenth, although it met increasing competition from such factories as those established in Lyon and Tours, and to a lesser extent from Montpellier and Paris. Voltaire wrote:

Fine silk manufactures produced more than fifty millions in the currency of the day, and not only were the profits greater than the outlay, but the growing of mulberry trees enabled manufacturers to dispense with foreign silk for the weaving of their material.

Mazarin helped to make Chinese silk fashionable, although Chinese velvet was imported only rarely. Taffetas were nearly always expensive and hard to come by, but they were in vogue in the 1670s.

The name 'taffeta' later came to mean a mixture of silk and wool, or silk and cotton, less expensive than the silk taffetas, and these probably existed before the end of the century. A linen and cotton mixture, the *siamoise* of the eighteenth century, can be precisely dated to 1694, when M. de la Rüe first attempted to interweave silk and cotton at Rouen and, meeting with difficulty, he substituted linen for silk.

Of the commoner materials, such as the serges, we need take no account here, although serge was commonly employed for lesser apartments and for country houses. Voltaire wrote of the manufacture at Abbeville, where the sieur Van Robais, a Dutchman, established his factory in 1665 with the aid of fifty Dutch weavers: 'Fine stuffs which had hitherto come from Holland and England now come from Abbeville.' Colbert had invited Van Robais to make Dutch cloth for the King to defend France against English exports, and the King advanced 2000 *livres* for each loom set to work, in addition to grants on a considerable scale. In the year 1669 there were 44,000 wool-looms at work in France. Abbeville became especially noted for the quality of its dyeing.

This is a suitable point at which to mention hangings of embossed, painted, gilded, and silvered leather. Spanish leather of this kind was called 'Cordoban', and it was also employed for slung seats and backs to chairs, held in position by ornamental nails with large heads in the Spanish style. The antechamber of the duchesse d'Orléans in 1708 was furnished with a hanging of 'gilded leather with a white ground, decorated with festoons of fruit and garlands of flowers in gold, green, and red, with figures of Bacchus, goddesses, harpies, children with arrows, and birds in gold'.

Tapestries proper were the favourite form of wall-hanging in the seventeenth century, and those of French manufacture are separately discussed, but many wall-hangings of this kind were imported from Flanders during the first half of the seventeenth century. Mazarin had an especially noteworthy collection of Flemish tapestries. Another form of wall-hanging is the so-called needlerun tapestry, which is actually an embroidery. These were fashionable throughout the seventeenth century especially, Mazarin's collection containing many examples. Their making was a favourite occupation with the ladies of the Court, and they were employed both as wall-hangings and as covering for seat-furniture.

Today it is almost impossible to find seventeenth- or eighteenth-century seat-furniture with the original covering. A few examples, too fragile for use, survive in museums and one or two of the great houses, and fragments of the materials survive, some of which are illustrated here.

Eighteenth-century fabrics are today a little more common than those of the seventeenth century. They were no longer so richly patterned as they had been in the golden years of the reign of Louis Quatorze, and embroidery with the precious metals was exceptional. The most popular material was probably damask, the finest from Genoa, and it cost between 40 and 50 *livres* to cover an ordinary *fauteuil* with it. During the first half of the century crimson was the predominant colour, and a favourite with Louis Quinze, although green was also fashionable. Blue was employed comparatively rarely, while yellow occurs in conjunction with silvering rather than gilding. A superb instance of this colour combination survives in the recently restored Amalienburg pavilion in the grounds of the Schloss Nymphenburg at Munich, where yellow panels are contrasted with silver rococo mouldings even more extravagant in their curves than those ordinarily to be found in France. Damasks woven in as many as three colours were sometimes made, but these were extremely expensive.

Silk taffeta is represented by the *gros de Tours* which was popular, and the flourishing silk industry of Lyon continued to provide the Court with materials for chair-coverings and wall-hangings. *Pékin* was a silk decorated with painted flowers and a favourite with Mme de Pompadour. Satin, glossy on one side and dull on the other, which was fashionable in the seventeenth century, was to be had plain, with stripes, and sometimes brocaded. *Satinade* was a cheap variety made in Bruges, often striped in green and crimson, crimson and yellow, or blue and yellow. *Moire* was a kind of coarse silk, and *brocatelle*, resembling *moire*, a mixture of silk and a more common fibre, the glossy surface patterned with flowers.

The finest velvets still came from Genoa which had been, perhaps, the first weaving centre in Europe to make it. Silk velvet was extremely expensive, and the cost of covering a *fauteuil* with it was about a 100

135

livres. Velvet was principally employed to cover *bergères, fauteuils à la reine,* and *duchesses,* and it existed also in a ribbed variety. Cut velvets were rare. Utrecht velvet, with a goat's-hair pile, came into use after the middle of the eighteenth century, and was especially valued for its hard-wearing qualities.

Moquette, a coarse imitation of velvet, had a pile of wool instead of silk. It served numerous purposes – table-covers, wall-hangings in minor rooms, coverings for seats subjected to more than the usual degree of wear-and-tear, and even for carpets. This also existed in a cut variety.

The linen and wool mixture known as *siamoise* continued to be popular throughout the eighteenth century, principally for lesser rooms and private apartments.

The same materials were fashionable throughout the reign of Louis Seize, although colours and the manner of use underwent some modifications. The combination of silk with floral patterns was not suited to the severity of the neo-Greek style and the general reversion to classical models. The romantic classicism of this period was, despite some superficial resemblances, far removed in spirit from that of Louis Quatorze, and the decoration of the last half of the century is much more feminine than that of the seventeenth century, despite a luxury which was almost comparable.

For wall-hangings the more conservative among the rich and noble still preferred crimson damask secured to the walls with mouldings of gilt-wood, but occasionally yellow damask with silver mouldings, like those of the Amalienburg. The *fermiers-généraux* were more adventurous. Many adopted the new style from the start, and they turned to lighter colours in stripes of blue, green, and pink, with the occasional use of pearl-grey. Striped materials were especially fashionable during the last thirty years or so before the Revolution, to be seen also in dresses of the period, and the same care to match wall-hangings and chair-coverings may be observed as we have already noticed during the rococo period.

Throughout the eighteenth century the materials employed in interior decoration were in a descending scale of luxury, the richest to be found in the principal bedrooms, the *salon,* and the *salle de compagnie* (drawing-room) where silks, damasks, velvets, tapestries and embroideries were the rule. In minor rooms, and in the servants' rooms, were found *siamoise, moquette,* cotton, serges, and the printed linens of Oberkampf – *toile de Jouy* – as well as muslin for half-curtains.

Cotton cloth, unknown in Europe until the early years of the seventeenth century, was imported in increasing quantities by the various East India Companies from Indian *entrepôts,* most of it being made in that country. Decorated with gaily coloured designs these cottons were termed 'chints', or chintz, in England (perhaps from the Persian town of Chiniz), and under the general name of *toile peinte* (painted linen)* in

* The term *toile peinte* is used to include both painted and printed cottons and linens.

France. They were also known as *'indiennes'* and *'perses'* in the old inventories and records. It was not until the end of the seventeenth century that the first attempts were made to imitate hand-coloured oriental fabrics in Europe by means of block-printing, but by the early decades of the eighteenth century manufacture was fairly well established. A prohibitory edict of 1686, which remained in force until 1759, forbade the wearing of either the oriental fabrics or their European imitations. This was intended to protect the silk manufacturers of Lyon and Tours, but the edict was honoured almost as much in the breach as in the observance, and Mme de Pompadour furnished one of her *boudoirs* with oriental cottons under the name of *'perses'*.★

The printed *toile de Jouy* (linen of Jouy), today a fashionable revival in France, began with the establishment of a factory for its manufacture at Jouy, near Versailles, by Christophe Philippe Oberkampf, a Bavarian, in 1759, although a factory of this kind had been started in the border province of Alsace, at Mulhouse, in 1746.

Oberkampf managed to secure the services of some of the best designers of the period, notably Jean-Baptiste Huet, who took charge of the design department at the factory, and Jean Pillement, whose *chinoiserie* designs were not only popular as a textile decoration but also for many other ornamental purposes. An example of Oberkampf's *toile* appears on plate 109. The technique was widely used elsewhere after 1759, notably at Rouen, Nantes, Montpellier, Orléans, and Beautiron. Before 1770 monochrome printing was done with wood-blocks, but printing from copper plates began about this time, the wood-block technique being retained for a few years for polychrome printing. Before the Revolution, however, a method of printing in several colours using engraved copper rollers had been devised, greatly increasing the quantity produced.

II

Although the first record of an actual use of wallpaper goes back, in England, to the beginning of the sixteenth century, not much is known about it before the seventeenth. The first reference in France to marbled papers, one of the earliest varieties, occurs in 1609, and although flock-papers are usually regarded as an English invention, and a patent for making them was registered in England by Lanyer in 1634, Entwistle, the bibliographer of wallpaper, notes that flock hangings were perhaps being made in Rouen in 1630, and it is pertinent to note that Lanyer refers to his patent as *'tonture de laine'* (wool-hangings), which suggests that the invention may originally have been French. A Guild of *Dominotiers, Tapissiers,* and *Imagiers* was founded as early as 1586, a *Dominotier* being one who made marbled papers and those printed with various

★ Similar restrictions were introduced in England with the object of protecting the wool manufacturers.

devices. The same authority refers to Evelyn's entry for 13 July 1699, which mentions 'hangings' of Chinese papers in the collection of Queen Mary at Hampton Court, and another reference in 1699 to Chinese 'Paper . . . so printed as to be pasted on walls to serve instead of Hangings' is clear enough. Yet another English writer refers to Colen Campbell's Palladian Wanstead House, and says that the walls were 'freely adorned with Chinese paper, the figures of Men, women, birds and flowers, the liveliest [I] ever saw to come from that Country'. Before mid century English wallpapers were well known abroad and were being made in large quantities. They had even made their début in St Petersburg.

By 1751 printed, raised, and embossed papers for wall-hangings had been considerably developed in France, and were widely popular, the embossed papers often imitating plaster and *stucco* mouldings and ornament. The latter apparently passed from France to England in 1756, and were a kind of *papier mâché*. A couple of years later we find a *marchand-papetier* advertising in the *Mercure*: 'an assortment of paper-hangings from China of different sizes for walls, overdoors, firescreens, and folding-screens . . .' and a contemporary letter refers to a closet lined with the painted paper of Pekin.

English wallpapers were freely exported to France. Mme de Pompadour had a *garde-robe* and a passage hung with English paper in 1754, and in 1760 Mme de Genlis, referring to the spread of English fashions, says, '[The ladies] even relegate to storage their magnificent Gobelins tapestries to put English blue paper in their place.'

By 1765 the fashion for wallpaper in France had reached even the peasant classes, the stencilled and wood-block printed papers of Rouen decorating the walls of farm-houses, especially above the chimney-piece. In the year following J. B. M. Papillon published his *Historical Treatise of Engraving on Wood* in which he describes his father's techniques of decorating wallpaper. Réveillon was a noted manufacturer of the second half of the century who produced papers on a large scale, and who was associated with the aeronaut, Montgolfier. The elaborate pictorial papers of Dufour and Leroy belong to the early decades of the nineteenth century, and so do not concern us here, but pictorial papers existed in the eighteenth century, although in simpler form. Most eighteenth-century patterns were floral and closely repetitive, but the best were colourful and well printed.

Diderot's *Encyclopédie* illustrates the technique of paper-hanging, including ceiling-paper, from which it would seem that there has been little change, but the finest papers, especially the hand-painted varieties, were first pasted to a canvas stretched on a frame, the frames being nailed to the wall and the joints covered with mouldings. In England it appears sometimes to have been the custom to tack printed papers into position down one side, the edge of the next piece being pasted over the tacks to conceal them.

In 1790 Eckhardt and Company of Chelsea, who had been established four years earlier, were offering as wall-hangings not only paper, but varnished linen and silk oil cloth, painted silks and satins, paintings on cloth, leather, and other materials, and a patterned silver damask on varnished linen or paper. Apart from the last, which was new, all these may safely be assumed to have been available in France.

III

The word *tapissier*, apart from referring to a tapestry-worker, also means someone who is generally concerned with the soft-furnishings of the house, analogous to the English 'upholsterer' in its strictest sense. Soft-furnishings generally are termed *tapisserie*.

The term 'tapestry' is so often used loosely that it would be as well to start by defining it. A tapestry is a textile in which the pattern is formed by coloured weft threads when they are woven into the warp. This necessarily leaves a vertical slit along the margins of the various patterns where a particular colour ends, and these are drawn together by stitching. The forming of a pattern on a textile base by needlework is properly classified as embroidery.

The art of tapestry has a very long history, beginning in ancient Egypt. Tapestries decorated Roman interiors, and they were especially widely used during the Middle Ages both as wall-decoration and as baldachins. They hung on the walls of every house with any pretension to importance during the seventeenth century and a greater part of the eighteenth, although their place was increasingly taken by patterned fabrics and by wall-papers. Carpets were made on this principle, and tapestry carpets also came from the Middle East, notably the Soumak.

Tapestries were woven from cartoons prepared by artists and designers which were either placed under the warp-threads (low-warp weaving), or the outlines transferred directly to the warp (high-warp weaving). In the early period cartoons were usually freely interpreted by the weavers, but when Oudry became director of the Gobelins and Beauvais looms in the eighteenth century he demanded far more exact copies of the original designs than had been customary in the past. This was achieved largely by employing a much finer weave, increasing the number of threads to the square inch. The detailed reproduction of oil-paintings followed, even to the representation of the frames, and in some cases to their suspensory cords.

French interiors of the eighteenth century were especially notable for the harmony sought between all the decorative fabrics, and these, in turn, were required to blend with the rest of the decoration in other materials. Tapestries in the form of wall-hangings, with matching *portières* and *entre-fenêtres*, were sometimes accompanied by coverings for the seat-furniture woven *en suite*, and even carpets were designed for the same purpose. Tapestry carpets, however, belong principally to the nineteenth century. Most eighteenth-century carpets were of the Savonnerie type, with a pile in imitation of Turkish and Persian weaves, and a small number of pile carpets were made towards the end of the eighteenth century in the workshops of Beauvais and Aubusson, as well as being imported from England where the manufacture of carpets of this kind was well-established soon after the middle of the century at Axminster, Kidderminster, and in London, where Mr Moore of Chiswell Street, Moorfields, was making carpets to the designs of the Adam Brothers.

The Savonnerie carpet was not only the rarest but the most highly valued, being made only for the royal *châteaux* and for a few of the King's favourites, which caused it to be a much sought mark of distinction. The floor of the Galerie des Glaces was at one time covered with Savonnerie pile-carpets of exceptional size, and the same piled material was very occasionally employed for upholstering seat-furniture.

At the beginning of the reign of Louis Quatorze the manufacture of tapestry had been established in France with varying fortunes for many centuries. The old-established workshops of the Gobelins family were removed in 1662 by Colbert to a building bought especially for the purpose, and here he grouped together a number of scattered Paris looms, including some from the Louvre.

The enterprise came under the general direction of Le Brun who had earlier directed a similar enterprise at Maincy started by Fouquet, Colbert's predecessor. The notable part played by tapestry in the development of the French Court style dates from Colbert's organization of the Gobelins undertaking which, in fact, formed the basis for the establishment of the *Manufacture royale*. The decree of 1667 which instituted it refers to 'painters, high-warp tapestry weavers, gem-cutters and jewellers, metal founders, engravers, *ébénistes* and *menuisiers* in wood and ebony, dyers, and other workmen in all manner of arts and crafts'. The tapestry workshops were protected by decree from foreign competition, and although primarily founded to supply royal *châteaux*, they were given the right to take orders from private persons, native or foreign. About two hundred and fifty men were employed, and this figure, taken with that quoted by Lister for the employees of the glass-house in the Faubourg Saint-Antoine, help to prove the scale on which these royal manufactories were established.

Until Colbert's death in 1683 Le Brun remained in sole charge. Mignard, however, was appointed director of the tapestry workshops by Colbert's successor, Louvois, and in 1694 shortage of money compelled the undertaking to close for five years. It reopened in 1699.

From this point it came under the direction of a number of architects. The most prominent was Robert de Cotte, brother-in-law to Hardouin-Mansart and architect to the King, who assumed responsibility for its art-direction in 1699, remaining until his death in 1735. He was followed by the painter, Jean-Baptiste Oudry, and then by Boucher. A later director, of Scottish descent, was Jacques Neilson (from 1751 to 1788), and an example of this period from the Neilson workshop is illustrated in the frontispiece.

During the early period Gobelins was much influenced by the paintings of Raphael, but subjects soon became more varied, including a series of fourteen depicting the history of the King's reign, of which the 'Visit of the King to the Gobelins Workshop' at Versailles is well known. Another series depicted the twelve royal *châteaux*. These subjects apart, mythological and biblical scenes were commonly employed, usually made in sets and based on a central theme. Among the earliest, for instance, was a 'Story of Meleager' woven in eight pieces, and a 'Story of Alexander' in eleven pieces and an *entre-fenêtre*. The seventeenth-century love of symbolism and allegory, which persisted throughout most of the eighteenth century, is to be found in such sets as the 'Elements' (Earth, Fire, Air, and Water), and the 'Seasons', perennially popular, which the designers of the period loved to proliferate for their patrons. The twelve royal *châteaux*, just mentioned, also symbolized the months.

After the reopening in 1699 the grand manner of Le Brun began slowly to give place to a style more purely French, and less dependent for inspiration on Italian and Flemish sources. More direct imitation of oil-painting also became the rule, especially under Oudry, whose favourite hunting subjects may be observed in the 'Royal Hunting Parties of Louis Quinze', woven in eight pieces in a style reminiscent of the old Flemish *verdures*. Oudry was to a great extent responsible for the increasing influence of painting, and the 'Hunting Party' series was given a border imitating the carved gilt picture-frame. But a serious difficulty on practical grounds was the multiplication of colours necessary to an attempt to render the subtleties of oil-paint in a woven medium, and this led to a great increase in the number of dyes required (some of which were of doubtful stability), and to a fragmentation of design. These defects Neilson later strove to overcome by limiting the number of dyes permitted to the workpeople, but without much success.

Among the earliest productions of the reopened factory were a set of *portières*, 'The Gods', woven to designs supplied by Claude III Audran, which symbolized the 'Elements' and the 'Seasons', and reflected the beginning of changes in style which were to become much more apparent during the Regency. Audran who was Keeper of the Luxembourg was for a time the master of the young Watteau, and his work owed more than a little to that of Jean I Bérain. He designed his ornament for mural and ceiling decoration with spaces reserved for figure and other subjects which were filled in by artists working in his studio. 'The Gods', designed against a background of typical Bérain *motifs*, has the elements of the ornament more or less similarly disposed and treated, but it lacks the air of fantasy which is rarely absent from Bérain's own work.

141

This new style was an immediate success, causing Audran to follow the first series with another of twelve pieces representing 'The Months'. The story of Don Quixote after Coypel was extremely popular at the time, and continued to attract designers throughout the century. This is an instance of the early use of a new scheme in which the pictorial subject was placed in the middle of a panel, and surrounded by an ornamental framework, the remainder of the field being filled with such devices as trophies, flowers, allegorical *motifs*, and so forth, sometimes on a simulated damask ground. These *motifs* were termed *alentours* (which means, literally, 'round about'), and they were usually the work of someone other than the designer of the central panel.

Oudry died in 1755, and Boucher, who was already taking an influential part in the Beauvais undertaking, was appointed by the intervention of Marigny to be the superintendent of the Gobelins workshops. He was given a thousand *livres* in recognition of his previous services, with an annual salary of two thousand *livres*. To revive the manufacture, which had begun to fall on difficult times, the King commissioned Boucher to produce a new series of designs, and the painter finally fixed on a subject congenial to them both, the 'Loves of the Gods', although he contributed only three cartoons to the series, the remainder coming from Natoire, Carl Van Loo, Pierre, and Vien. These he followed with some of his favourite pastorals.

In the early years of the eighteenth century the taste for the exotic was becoming even stronger, especially for oriental things of all kinds. The art-dealer Gersaint, whose sign was, it will be remembered, painted by Watteau, called his shop *à la pagode*, referring to the fact that he sold Chinese *objets d'art*. Martin Lister mentions a Siamese embassy which had visited Paris only a short time before his own arrival, and the later visit of a Turkish embassy to the capital was commemorated in a set of tapestries woven at Gobelins between 1731 and 1734. Chinese and Japanese porcelain, as we have already seen, was avidly sought; lacquer was widely imitated when it was not to be had or was too expensive; and, a little later, gardens in the Anglo-Chinese taste were being laid out. The New World also, with aborigines in feathered headdresses, was often represented, and themes from this source were sometimes incongruously mingled with those of the Orient. All these themes were reflected in the design of tapestries, the 'New Indies' being produced in eight pieces in 1735, although earlier versions of the same subject date from 1692.

After 1770 tapestries were no longer so popular as a form of wall-decoration among the fashionable. Competition from wallpapers, especially painted papers from China imported in large quantities, and printed papers from France, was becoming increasingly severe. In tapestry the influence of Boucher lingered for longer perhaps than it did in other spheres because, although his style was no longer popular, tapestries took more time to weave, and there was always a greater time-lag in the adoption of new fashions in the tapestry workshops than in the other crafts.

The tendency to copy oil-paintings remained strong at a time when their reproduction on plaques of Sèvres porcelain was a popular feature of decoration at that factory. Like porcelain, tapestry did not fit easily into the new classical scheme of decoration, and both began to suffer a gradual eclipse.

The tapestry-looms of Beauvais were also Colbert's creation, but, unlike Gobelins, the enterprise never became royal property, although it received both protection and subventions. The director, Louis Hinard, supplied tapestries to the royal *châteaux*, usually of landscape subjects, but he became bankrupt in 1684. According to Voltaire: 'The first manufacturer in the town employed six hundred workmen, and the King made him a present of sixty thousand *livres*.' He adds: 'Sixteen hundred girls were employed in making lace; thirty of the best operatives from Venice were employed, and two hundred from Flanders, and they were presented with thirty-six thousand *livres* to encourage them', which is some indication of the importance of the town in the seventeenth century.

After Hinard's bankruptcy the workshops were taken over by Philippe Behagle, who remained until 1705, meeting with a considerable measure of success. An important series of this period was the 'Conquests of Louis Quatorze', started about 1690. Another popular series was designed by Jean I Bérain in association with the flower-painter, J.-B. Monnoyer. Started about 1690, these continued to be made throughout the first quarter of the eighteenth century.

The brothers Filleul assumed responsibility for the future of Beauvais in 1711, but they abandoned it in 1722 to M. de Mérou, and some *chinoiserie* subjects apparently date from this time. The difficulties in which the factory found itself at the death of Behagle in 1704 were not finally resolved until the appointment of Oudry as designer in 1726 at a salary of 3,500 *livres*, and in 1734 he took over the enterprise in partnership with Nicolas Besnier. Oudry's own designs include his favourite hunting and pastoral scenes, and Natoire provided cartoons for a series illustrating 'Don Quixote'. Boucher began his career as a designer for tapestry at Beauvais in 1736 with a series of fourteen pieces entitled 'Village Festivals', and his interest in Chinese art, which inspired a notable but perhaps less well-known aspect of his work as a painter, influenced designs for tapestries also, and these, which represent a high point of the rococo style, remained popular through the years.

The factory passed to A.-C. Charron in 1754, and at this time the practice of matching *suites* of wall-hangings with coverings for seat-furniture and beds, which were often presented to ambassadors and foreign rulers, became the vogue.

Like Gobelins, the Beauvais looms began to decline after 1760 with the onset of the new classical style, but belonging to this period are the

143

notable '*Jeux Russiens*' of 1769 by Le Prince, with a matching set of chair-covers, some 'Pastorals' by J.-B. Huet, and similar subjects illustrating the popular fashion for the simple life which caused fine ladies to play the milk-maid and the shepherdess, and a set of 'Military Convoys', by François Casanova.

Long before the period under review there were workshops at Aubusson in the South. Colbert granted them assistance in 1665, with the provision that each tapestry should be woven with a blue galloon border, and that each should bear the word 'Aubusson', which was sometimes abbreviated to MRD (*Manufacture Royale Daubusson*) and sometimes omitted altogether.

The Aubusson workshops suffered severely from the Revocation of the Edict of Nantes, losing some of the few skilled workers they possessed, and they constantly had recourse to makeshift expedients, copying the work of other factories, and turning to the making of pile-carpets in the oriental manner for a brief period. Further State assistance in the 1730s brought a time of relative prosperity, but designs were still borrowed, some from Oudry. Those taken from Boucher include Chinese scenes, and others of the same sort were derived from the designs of Jean Pillement whose *chinoiseries* are in a late rococo style. Pastorals and landscapes were also a popular subject with the Aubusson workshops. Not only wall-hangings, but coverings for seat-furniture, were produced in large quantities as well as smooth-faced or tapestry carpets which are a relatively common survival, although few specimens are earlier than the nineteenth century.

Aubusson tapestries are generally poorer in quality than those from the other two principal centres mentioned. Of the other workshops in Paris and the provinces, all were small and their products are difficult to identify.

IV

The pile carpet had its origin in the East, the earliest surviving specimens being referable to the fifth century B.C. although the technique is un-doubtedly much older. The tufts are formed by looping fibres, usually wool, through a coarse textile foundation woven in the usual way. They were known in France in the days of the Crusades as exotic imports from the Near and Middle East, and were not uncommon in the sixteenth century, especially from Turkey, as table and bed coverings, although they were only laid on the floor in the most luxurious houses.

Although oriental carpets were much valued in Europe they were not imitated in a comparable fashion until the beginning of the seventeenth century when Pierre Dupont was installed in the Louvre by Henri Quatre.* The enterprise was, in part, transferred to an old soap-factory on

---

* Earlier Spanish carpets exist, but the craft in Spain was Moorish in origin.

the Quai de Chaillot, on the opposite side of the river from the Garde-Meuble and the Quai d'Orsay, in 1627. Here it was under the direction of Dupont's associate, Simon Lourdet. In 1662 it came under the same management as the Gobelins, and its workshops were removed to the avenue des Gobelins in 1826. Carpets continued to be made at the Louvre after the establishment of the new factory, and the two were not completely merged until 1672.

Especially large pile carpets were made in the Savonnerie workshops for the Louvre and for Versailles, and until the end of the reign of Louis Quinze its products were almost entirely reserved for royal *châteaux*, as gifts to important princes, and for the King's especial favourites. The possession of a Savonnerie carpet became one of the most prized status symbols of the time. After about 1770 private persons were permitted to buy a Savonnerie carpet since royal orders could no longer absorb the whole of the output, but the price was so high that few could afford one.

Rarely, sets of coverings for seat-furniture were also made. The King had a number of specimens, and of a total of one thousand two hundred and twenty-three stools at Versailles, ninety-three were thus upholstered. Mazarin had such a *suite*, with carpet to match.

Technically the Savonnerie carpet was knotted in the Turkish manner, but the knotting was much coarser than the average contemporary Near-Eastern work. Knotted carpets were also made for a few years at Beauvais during the reign of Louis Seize, and at Aubusson and nearby Felletin during the eighteenth century. Those from the two last workshops are inferior in quality to carpets from either Beauvais or the Savonnerie. Elaborate floral patterns in keeping with the style of the period are usual whatever the source.

About thirty Savonnerie carpets of the seventeenth and eighteenth centuries are known to survive, most of which are in two or three collections, notably those of Paul Getty and the Rothschild family at Waddesdon.

Aubusson made a good many tapestry or smooth-faced carpets, technically somewhat in the manner of the Near-Eastern Ghilims and Soumaks, which are virtually indistinguishable from wall-tapestries, but, as might be expected, they are both heavier and stronger. Carpets of this kind, but of better quality, came in small numbers from Beauvais and the Gobelins, but apparently only to special order. Most surviving Aubusson tapestry carpets belong to the nineteenth century, eighteenth-century examples having worn out long ago.

Oriental carpets, predominantly Turkish and less often Persian, were popular throughout the seventeenth and eighteenth centuries. The earlier European practice of copying oriental patterns in a coarse embroidery stitch on a canvas foundation survived into the seventeenth century, and better quality, brilliantly coloured needlework carpets with European patterns were to be found in eighteenth-century interiors, placed where traffic was not unduly heavy.

Moquette of a coarse variety also served as carpeting in minor rooms and smaller houses. Commonly it came from Abbeville, where production started in 1667, but it was made also at Tournai and Utrecht. English carpets were imported from Axminster, Kidderminster, and Wilton during the second half of the eighteenth century, sometimes being specially commissioned from these looms. Verlet★ records three designs painted by Belanger for the duchesse de Mazarin, one to be made by the Savonnerie, one for Beauvais, and one 'to be executed in England'.

V

The rich fabrics of the seventeenth and eighteenth centuries, the stock-in-trade of the *tapissier*, were principally employed to drape beds and their canopies, for covering seat-furniture and walls, and for curtains, *portières*, and *entre-fenêtres*.

Patterned fabrics were usually ornamented with large stylized floral *motifs* in the seventeenth century. These had come by way of Italy from the Near East, brought to Europe originally by Saracenic weavers many of whom settled in Sicily and on the Italian mainland. Embroideries and *appliqué* work, however, while conforming to the general style of the period, usually differed at least to some extent from woven fabrics.

As we have seen, the most luxurious drapes were those which decorated the bed, and the status accorded to this piece of furniture both in the seventeenth and the eighteenth centuries was a product of custom and usage which went back for many centuries. The bed was the symbol of royalty, and the *lit de parade* – the *lit d'apparat* or State bed – had always been the focus of the greatest luxury. In earlier times it had been called the *lit de justice*, the King literally dispensing justice from his bed, which provoked the remark that it was so called because it was here that justice slept.

The *lit de parade* with its elaborate canopy and curtains was where the King was surrounded by his Court, and it was where he died in state when his reign drew to a close. In the Queen's bed her children were born in conditions which almost amounted to a public display, a custom which was, in the first place, designed to prevent substitution of one child for another. Members of the Court who attended on the King's person slept on portable beds or palliasses, usually in an antechamber.

Apart from his State bed the King possessed many others. Louis Quatorze had more than four hundred in a descending scale of pomp, and this multiplicity of beds developed into a large number of different types, the variations being principally marked by the presence or absence of head boards and pillars, or by differences in the drapes and canopies. The main varieties have already been discussed, but there were many others, some differing in little but the subject of the tapestries which draped them, which often gave the name to the bed.

146

★ *French Furniture and Interior Decoration of the Eighteenth Century*, London, 1967.

The luxurious nature of the bed, its drapes and carvings, its cords and tassels, its galloons and *passementeries*, extended to the bed-chamber itself, which increasingly became the province of the *tapissier*. The *ruelle*, the area between the bed and the side-wall, furnished for entertaining intimate friends and even for the transaction of business, was curtained off to provide a measure of privacy, and here, too, a *chaise percée* was sometimes to be found. The *ruelle* eventually became the *alcôve* – a deep recess at one side of the chamber, usually flanked with pilasters on either side of the opening and closed by drapes. The alcove diminished in size with the passing years until it was eventually large enough only to contain a bed or a *canapé*. In the eighteenth century a few private *alcôves*, notably those belonging to the *grandes horizontales* of the period, were lined with mirrors, including ceiling mirrors. This decrease in size was the natural product of the fashion for smaller rooms and the relaxation of that strict etiquette which had been so much a part of the Court of Louis Quatorze.

Throughout the whole period the bed-drapes were the most sumptuous of all the soft-furnishings of the apartment. The fabrics of the early decades of the seventeenth century were luxurious, but the manner of draping exhibited a certain severity. The frame of the canopy was rectangular, following the line of the bed beneath, and the overhead valances had a straight edge at the bottom, with, at most, slightly scalloped borders, or one of fringes or *passementerie*. The curtains were held back when required by tasselled cords. More pronounced scalloping made an appearance before the accession of Louis Quatorze, and the valances soon began to assume the outlines familiar from the *lambrequin* ornament of *faïence*. The *duchesse* bed, which lacked the front pillars, was closed with voluminous curtains looped back during the daytime, and this canopy, like several others, attained its greatest degree of complexity with the designs of Daniel Marot who specialized in drapes of all kinds.

With the Regency, bed-drapes tended to become simpler and less elaborate, especially the canopies, and lighter colours, pink and sky-blue, replaced the older crimson and purple, with patterns of natural flowers instead of the earlier stylized varieties. The asymmetry of the rococo style is not evident in bed-canopies, but its characteristics are to be sought rather in the fabrics employed and in their patterns. Flowers occur in profusion and in great variety, and *chinoiseries*, *turqueries*, *japonaiseries*, and other exotic *motifs* are novel and much livelier. The range of colours available to the *tapissier* continued to increase.

New forms of bed-canopy began to appear before mid century, such as the voluminous drapes of the bed *à la polonaise* and those of the bed *à la turque* (that, except for its several mattresses, resembled a *sopha*, with two end-boards terminating in crozier-like scrolls and a back which was placed against a wall), which were arranged in styles that were new, but which were to become increasingly popular. With the onset of the neo-classical style the canopy and its drapes were, perhaps, more severely arranged, but

147

they yielded nothing to earlier varieties in complexity which seems to have increased rather than diminished. Particularly is this the case with the canopies termed *à l'impériale* and *à la couronne*. Canopies of the popular dome-shape were often surmounted by vast plumes of feathers centrally placed instead of at the corners. Lalonde designed a number of such canopies, and from Delafosse came a design for a Turkish bed with a canopy of architectural form, and almost architectural proportions, surmounted by an enormous trophy of arms, although there is no evidence that it ever left the drawing-board, and it may have been a *jeu d'esprit* of the designer. The exact nature of the bed *à la romaine*, which Verlet suggests may have been inspired by the King's brother, the comte d'Artois, was, if one design thus called is to be accepted as typical, a forerunner of the Empire style, with the short pillars at the foot in the form of fasces with the lictor's axe, and with looped draperies suspended from the dome-shaped canopy commonly employed for the more sumptuous beds at the time. Similar, but even more elaborate, was a bed termed *à la Fédération*, which was designed just before the Terror. This, in addition to drapes of the same kind, was intended to be made with four short pillars in the form of fasces, either of gilded bronze or brass, proving that however severe the decoration of contemporary furniture, the bed was still regarded as an object of luxury. The fashion, in fact, did not end even with the Empire. Under Napoleon I beds became fantastically elaborate, with a high canopy *en couronne* and vast draped curtains, and they persisted until the Second Empire, then being represented by the designs of Liénard.

To be noted is a short-lived vogue for draped furniture from about 1785 to the Revolution. The *bergère* and the *lit de repos*, for instance, received the addition of tasselled drapes around the backs and from the horizontal rails joining the legs.

Curtains and *portières*, and their pelmets, usually repeated the drapes of the canopies in bed-chambers, and elsewhere they were on a recognizably similar plan. Pelmets were partly of carved gilt-wood with surmounting ostrich plumes, and cords and tassels for the curtains. Like the bed-drapes, curtains were bordered with *passementeries* which matched the fabrics for quality. Daniel Marot, who made many noteworthy designs for beds, also designed curtains, *portières*, and wall-hangings with multiple loops, scallops, and fringes with dependent tassels, which are reminiscent of the *faïence lambrequins*, especially those which the Rouen factory made a speciality at the beginning of the eighteenth century.

Analogous to curtains in its purpose was the *marquise* blind which was made of thin, light-transmitting material. This served as a screen from the sun during the heat of summer, and it completely covered the window when undrawn. Its place was sometimes taken by half-curtains of muslin which served much the same purpose.

Pelmets, and their attendant curtains, were employed for windows, doors, and the larger recesses termed alcoves, and also to disguise the tops of wall-hangings draping decorative panels which were part of the *boiserie*, and not only were great pains taken to harmonize the materials with those used for the seat-furniture and the bed itself, but the curves of the pelmets were designed to repeat curves elsewhere present in the room, either as part of the *boiserie*, or for example, the top rails of the chair-backs.

The lines of pelmets of the early years of the Louis Seize style were a reversion to the straight lines of the early part of the seventeenth century, but a return to loops and scallops is evident before 1780, while some were draped in swags on either side of a central oval medallion in characteristic neo-classic style.

8

The Decoration of the Interior

I

Since every interior is the product, ultimately, of an exterior, it is desirable to describe briefly the course of architecture in France from the beginning of the seventeenth century. Henri Quatre began a period of expansion, especially in Paris, and his completion of the Grand Gallery of the Louvre as a lodging for artists and craftsmen has already been mentioned. He also started the replanning and rebuilding of Paris, widening the streets and pulling down houses with an overhanging storey, a reform which, essential for sanitary reasons, had to wait in London for the Great Fire of 1666.

During the early decades of the seventeenth century many of the important *places* and squares of Paris were planned and laid out, and some notable buildings were started, particularly the palace of the Luxembourg for Marie de' Medici. Under Louis Treize a number of important *hôtels* were completed on the Isle Saint-Louis. François Mansart, uncle of Jules Hardouin-Mansart, undertook the rebuilding of the famous *château* at Blois, and was responsible for the *château* of Maisons which is regarded as one of the finest examples of French domestic architecture.

But the great period of building in France was between 1660 and 1690, and if Mazarin, whose tastes were centred on interior decoration rather than on architecture, did little to foster the love of building in the young Louis Quatorze, Fouquet at Vaux-le-Vicomte (which was designed by Louis Le Vau and cost 18 million *livres* to build) set an example that, with Colbert's ready assistance, the King was not slow to follow.

Colbert became Surintendant des Bâtiments in 1664 at a salary of 15,000 *livres* annually, which, twenty years later, had quadrupled. The Academy of Architecture, established in 1671, grew out of several advisory bodies set up by him. The Academy was charged with the duty of formulating the rules of architectural practice, which had a limiting and probably salutary effect on design, and of providing for the training of students.

It is, perhaps, surprising when we consider the whole picture that one of the principal architectural achievements of the time was not the work of a professional architect at all, but a commission achieved despite competition from some of the most widely known practitioners of the art. That Bernini's designs for the completion of the Louvre were eventually rejected was probably at Colbert's instigation, and something which he had intended from the first. The commission was given to a doctor, by name Claude Perrault, who was brother to Colbert's secretary. Perrault's own designs provoked a great deal of contemporary criticism, although the work was hailed half a century later as 'a masterpiece of the art'. But his designs remained incomplete, and Perrault himself returned to doctoring.

The most successful of the *architectes du Roi* was undoubtedly Jules Hardouin-Mansart (1646–1708), associated in the work at Versailles with the great garden designer, André Le Nôtre, who had laid out the grounds of Vaux-le-Vicomte between 1656 and 1660 on a grand and costly scale. Le Nôtre was also an architect, skilled in the design of elaborate garden pavilions, and he was elected a member of the Academy of Architecture, although he found the meetings tedious and attended only one. He specialized in water-gardens made regardless of expense, but he was personally a man of great simplicity of character and was extremely popular, particularly with the King.

Hardouin-Mansart on the contrary was an opportunist who secured the King's favour to a point where he was entrusted with virtually every official project of any importance. He appears to have headed a practice which included a number of young architects of great ability, of whom his relative by marriage, Robert de Cotte (1656–1735), was one. These men worked out the details from Hardouin-Mansart's rough sketches. That he was rather a designer than a competent architect seems proved by the collapse of bridges for which he was responsible. Bridge-designing is usually an excellent test of skill.

Hardouin-Mansart died in 1708, but his influence persisted in the subsequent work of his staff, of whom Robert de Cotte, who succeeded him as *premier architecte du Roi*, is the most widely known, notably for his interior designs. De Cotte did a certain amount of work outside France, especially in the Rhineland where French styles were popular, and where French was the Court language. Germain Boffrand (1667–1754) studied with Hardouin-Mansart, and was responsible for the *hôtel* de Soubise which he enlarged and decorated in an early rococo style, often cited as among the finest examples of rococo designing still surviving.

Two important eighteenth-century names are Jacques-Jules Gabriel (1667–1742) and his son, Ange-Jacques Gabriel (1698–1782). The first became *premier architecte du Roi* in succession to Robert de Cotte in 1734, a position which fell to his son in 1742. The younger Gabriel worked for Mme de Pompadour as well as for Mme du Barry, while the elder helped to take the influence of Paris to Bordeaux where he worked in association with Jacques Verberckt. Among the major works of Ange-Jacques Gabriel may be numbered the Place de la Concorde, much altered since his day, and the Petit Trianon at Versailles.

After Gabriel's retirement in 1775 the tradition of classical architecture in France was largely replaced by the taste for the pseudo-antique of de Caylus and Winckelmann, but Jacques-François Blondel (1705–70) was a sound traditionalist, better known perhaps as a writer on architecture and as a teacher. Of his major works, *L'Architecture française* was published in 1752 and his *Cours d'architecture*, completed by Pierre Patte, in 1777.

Patte (*fl.* 1772–1812) was a conservative designer whose work was in the same spirit as that of Blondel. Of his several published works, the *Monuments à la gloire de Louis XV* of 1765 is the most important. Jacques-Germain Soufflot (1713–80), the architect of the Panthéon who had accompanied Marigny and Cochin on their journey to Italy, was a follower of de Caylus and Winckelmann whose ideas were received but slowly by the architects of the time.

The principal influences in the closing decades of the eighteenth century were Claude-Nicolas Ledoux (1736–1806), who designed the Pavillon de Louveciennes for Mme du Barry and later became a notable exponent of Romantic classicism much influenced by Piranesi's engravings, and Étienne-Louis Boullée (1728–99) who is perhaps more remarkable for his teaching than for his actual work.

It was not until the end of the century that architecture fell into the pompous and pedantic style developed from the neo-classical concept of classical architecture of which the Empire style was the interior counterpart.

II

Great changes took place in the house and its decoration during the seventeenth century. The house was no longer fortified. Cannon were by now so efficient that any defences which could be incorporated into its construction, no matter what the size, were useless. The idea of the house as a strongpoint was abandoned, and attention was increasingly directed to the cultivation of the more civilized arts of decoration and display. Rooms became larger and more airy, windows – no longer embrasures – increased in size and admitted more light, and interiors were furnished in a more luxurious and comfortable style.

At the beginning of the century the bed-chamber was still the focus of the activities of the entire household. It was the place where visitors assembled and business was transacted, and both men and women received visitors while in bed. The more intimate friends joined the master or mistress of the house in the space between the bedside and the wall called the *ruelle* – hence the old expression *courir des ruelles*, to frequent ladies' chambers. The *ruelle* varied in size, and most could be closed off from the remaining part of the chamber by curtains which extended from the bed to the adjoining flank wall. The *ruelle* was, in fact, a small *salon*, and it was also the convenient scene of gallantries. The *alcôve* which developed from it was Spanish in origin, and it can be traced back to the Near East. It first arrived in France in the middle of the seventeenth century, and in 1652 there is record of changing chimneys and doors to make an *alcôve*. The folding draught-screen, introduced a few years earlier, played its part in the furnishing of the *ruelle*.

The *cabinet*, the *petite pièce* or closet, was not an invention of the seventeenth century. It already existed as a study, a place in which secret business was transacted, an office, a dressing-room, a water-closet (*cabinet d'aisance*), or a room in which a collection of trifles and small works of art was housed. The latter sense was common in England in the eighteenth century. Horace Walpole's *cabinet* at Strawberry Hill was used for this purpose. An *homme de cabinet* was a studious man, and it was here that books were often kept. The ladies of the household, especially in winter when the larger and more formal rooms were too cold to use, favoured living in small rooms which adjoined the great ones, and here small circles foregathered for conversation or gambling.

The usual seventeenth-century arrangement was an antechamber, a bed-chamber, and several *cabinets*. These were not specialized in the way in which they were later to become. Meals were taken not in a dining-room, but in whichever room was most convenient. The antechamber was a general purpose room, often of considerable size, where company assembled and such events as were impossible in a bed-chamber, such as musical recitals, took place. Members of the Court often slept in the ante-chambers on portable beds.

Heating arrangements at the beginning of the seventeenth century were fairly primitive, but more numerous fireplaces became the custom quite early in the reign of Louis Quatorze, and the massive stone chimney-pieces of earlier times less fashionable. They were replaced by those of carved wood and marble, the former profusely ornamented with *stucco* reliefs, and both sometimes with gilt-bronze. Bas-reliefs and paintings decorated the space above.

The chimney-piece became increasingly the focal point of every room of consequence, at first high, but lower towards the end of the century, with a mantelshelf. The fashion for the chimney-piece mirror followed and the mantelshelf became the place for ornaments, either the formal, *garniture de cheminée*, or an informal selection of small trifles.

The chimney-piece varied in its position according to structural requirements, sometimes facing the windows, sometimes to one side, and more rarely set across the corners. The latter arrangement was usually necessitated by the presence of a central circular Salon, an example in England by the Palladian, Colen Campbell, being the chimney-pieces of the rooms surrounding the rotunda at Mereworth Castle.

It seems that the chimney-piece design was executed first, the remainder of the decoration of the room being designed to match it. The panelling elaborately ornamented with carved work and mouldings of a kind rarely to be seen in England justifies the retention of the term *boiserie* to describe it, and this repeated the theme set by the chimney-piece, which was, in turn, extended to door and window-cases, the former embellished more or less elaborately with a cresting known as the *dessus de porte* or overdoor.

The marbles which became so popular for interior decoration in the eighteenth century were of great variety. The kind termed *le grand*

154

antique was black with white veining and striations; *portor* was also black, veined with grey and white, with golden-yellow markings from which it derived its name; the French marble called 'Sainte-Anne' was veined in grey and black, and the Flanders marble of the same name was similarly coloured, but marbled in white on a black ground. The prized Sarancolin (also called *marbre d'Antin*) was streaked with yellow, red, grey, and violet; *brèche d'Alep* was a brecciated stone predominantly yellow, with greys, browns and black; *brèche violette* was also brecciated, in grey, white, and dark red, with well-marked violet passages; Italian *griotte* was red, with a marbling of black and small spots of white; Flanders *griotte* was a dark red with light grey marbling; *brocatelle violette* was a wine-dark red with many small spots of yellow, greyish yellow, and crystalline white; *vert Campan* was a light green stone marbled with dark green with streaks of grey; while *Campan mélange* had a rose-pink ground veined with red and a network of green. The marble of the Languedoc, where the quarries were worked in Roman times, was a light pinkish shade veined with grey and white; the *bleu turquin* of Italy was greyish blue with black and white striations, and the *bleu fleuri*, greyish blue veined with black. Onyx marble was so-called from its resemblance to the hardstone.

Coloured marbles, at least until the onset of the Louis Seize style, were especially prized for the tops of *console* tables, and the reign of Louis Quatorze saw limited use of marble mosaic for this purpose, geometrically patterned instead of the natural patterning of brecciated stones which yielded a somewhat similar effect. The use of marble as the tops of case-furniture, for the tops of small tables, and for the shelves of bedside tables, came later. Chimney-pieces were usually of white marble in the eighteenth century, and less often of black. These interfered least with changing colour-schemes. Coloured marbles were employed in a variety of places in conjunction with gilt-bronze mounts, and the two materials blended admirably. Marbles, both black and white, were used for bath-rooms, especially for the floors and wall-tiling, as well as for the bath itself.

Flooring with marble was fairly common for important rooms in the form of alternating black and white slabs laid in a lozenge pattern. Earthenware tiles and stone slabs were frequently employed for the less important rooms, although parquetry of wood blocks became increasingly fashionable, often laid in elaborate geometrical patterns. Carpets woven at La Savonnerie were very occasionally laid over these floors in the finest interiors, and more commonly, piled carpets and rugs from the Near and Middle East, although carpets did not become at all usual as a floor-covering until after the middle of the seventeenth century. Old-fashioned plank flooring was still to be found in the less important rooms and in the minor corridors, sometimes covered with carpets of *moquette*, or with rugs and carpets which had become too shabby to use in the public rooms.

We cannot leave the chimney-piece without referring to the furniture, the *chenets* and the fire-irons often of handsomely chiselled gilt-bronze, which emphasized its importance. It lost some of its point during the summer, however, and then, during the reign of Louis Quinze, it became fashionable to place a *trompe l'œil* painting in front of the hearth in place of the winter fire-screen. This was usually mounted on a frame of wood which more or less fitted into the hearth aperture. A variety of subjects were employed. One exists of a table with a cat on a footstool beneath it. Oudry painted one of a dog with a bowl of Chinese porcelain filled with water which is now in the Louvre. Usually these paintings were of furniture, books, and animals. Few have survived, but there are quite a number of contemporary references to them, of which we may select one referring to the house of Edmé Bouchardon, the sculptor, taken from his inventory – 'a picture for the front of the chimney-piece painted on canvas representing a dog'.

The mirror in the eighteenth century was an integral part of both the chimney-piece and the *boiserie*. Mirrors as interior decoration may date back to Roman times. Pliny refers to mirrors from the glass-houses of Sidon, but of their nature nothing is certainly known. A passage in the life of Horace by Suetonius refers to the poet's bed-chamber as being lined with mirrors and lascivious pictures which were multiplied by the reflection, but this may be an old interpolation, although it foreshadows the ceiling-mirrors of some Paris *alcôves* of the eighteenth century. The large wall-mirror, however, does not occur before the seventeenth century. The difficulty was always in the making of large sheets, which was technically impossible until Perrot devised his method of casting glass. The seventeen arched mirrors of the Galerie des Glaces actually comprise over three hundred and fifty separate sheets, twenty-one to each arch, and the making of mirrors in several sheets within a single frame was common at least throughout the first half of the eighteenth century. All the royal palaces of France, apart from Versailles, were extensively decorated with mirrors, and even a grotto at La Ménagerie was thus embellished.

Inspired by the Galerie des Glaces, advantage was taken of Perrot's discovery to enlarge mirrors for the purpose of multiplying interior reflections, making the rooms seem larger and lighter, and giving a new air of spaciousness to smaller rooms. The effect was enhanced at night by wall-sconces and by multi-branched candleholders attached to the frame of the mirror itself, as well as by numerous candlesticks and candelabra. The suspended *chandelier* glittered in the candlelight with many prismatically-cut drops, either of rock-crystal (especially in the days of Louis Quatorze), or of crystal glass from Bohemia, which was much more satisfactory for the purpose than Venetian glass. Candelabra with dependent drops, termed *girandoles*, were placed on *commodes, console* tables, and mural *consoles* or wall-brackets.

The piers between the windows, above either *console* tables or *commodes,* were adorned with pier-glasses (*trumeaux*), which often faced the chimney-piece mirror giving rise to multiple vistas, and in some cases virtual mirror-rooms were created, the walls, and even the leaves of the doors, being lined with mirrors. One designed by Robert de Cotte followed the luxurious fashion perhaps first set by Marie de' Medici at the beginning of the seventeenth century. She had a room with over a hundred Venetian mirrors set in the panelling. Fouquet had such a room at Vaux-le-Vicomte, and the Grand Dauphin's room at Versailles was provided with ceiling-mirrors. The Regent had a room of this kind, and Marie-Antoinette's bathroom, which has long since disappeared, was lined with mirrors. The surface of the mirror was sometimes covered with ornament of carved gilt wood, the mirror-surface providing a background.

Mirrors sliding back into the walls were devised to cover windows at night, being housed in the piers during the day,★ and similar mirrors sometimes hid the fireplace during the summer months.

The ornamental mirror often approached the ceiling in height, and the top sometimes framed a painting or a piece of tapestry, while mirrors were often framed as overdoors.

During most of the seventeenth century pieces of furniture were few in number, although in the finest houses their luxurious nature was compensation. The multiplication of furniture began in the eighteenth century, when many new varieties were devised. This tendency reached its height after 1750, when the general relaxation of etiquette became extremely marked. Tables and seat-furniture of all kinds for specialized purposes appeared in considerable variety, many such pieces, such as the tip-up breakfast-table, being for occasional use and therefore movable rather than fixed in position.

The differences between fixed and movable furnishings have been discussed at length by Pierre Verlet (op. cit.), but briefly the fixed furniture was an integral part of the decorative scheme of the room for which it was made, and in its carved ornament it usually repeated the decoration of the room itself, including the *boiseries*, or, in the case of seat-furniture, the wall-drapery and the curtains in its coverings. Some furniture was fixed in its position by its very nature – the *console* table attached to the wall, the *armoire* built in or too heavy to move, case-furniture which repeated in its outlines and decoration the curves of the *boiserie* against which it stood, or *secrétaires* and *chiffonniers* made for a special position; but certain seat-furniture was also fixed in its position, not only by its carving and covering but also by etiquette. I have already commented on the development of the kind of table termed '*ambulante*' in France and 'occasional' in England, where the Pembroke table is an excellent example of an increasingly common type. The equivalent in chairs were those '*en cabriolet*', which could be moved at will without transgressing established custom,

157

★ An English example is to be seen at Apsley House, in London.

and the many comfortable chairs that developed such as the *bergère* and its derivatives, which also had no truly fixed position.

The custom which demanded that furniture should be a fixed and integral part of a room was undoubtedly Italian in origin, and was partly a product of the costly nature of sixteenth- and early seventeenth-century interiors. Renaissance interiors were conceived as a whole, not as a series of parts, and marble panelling and elaborate *stucco* ornament could not easily be changed to give a room a fresh appearance. The problem became less difficult to solve with the greater use of textile hangings, which was strictly a reversion to an earlier fashion, and the development of smaller rooms (less specialized in design if more specialized in purpose) made a fixed scheme less necessary. Thus we find, as the eighteenth century progressed, that furniture increasingly tended to fall into two principal categories – show-pieces such as the *bureau de roi* which were intended for a particular place, and lighter, more mobile, less expensive furniture which was much more adaptable. The provision of carrying-handles, especially on bedroom furniture, is evidence of this mobility.

Much of the lighter furniture was introduced by dealers. Although dealers existed in the seventeenth century, they did not become really influential until the eighteenth century was well advanced. There is a good deal of difference between the stock-in-trade noticed by Evelyn in Noah's Ark, probably a fashionable establishment of the period, and that of Gersaint almost a century later as noted on his trade card. The business of Lazare Duvaux at mid century much more nearly approached that of the twentieth-century art-dealer and interior decorator, and the eighteenth century marked the rise of the professional decorator, part architect, part art-dealer, and part *tapissier*. In Appendix II some extracts from Duvaux's account books have been reprinted, from which may be deduced the nature of his business. That he suggested new ideas to the craftsmen of his time cannot be doubted, and in this he was followed by others, such as Poirier, Daguerre, and many more.

Paris dealers of the period also made hiring a part of their business. Crystal chandeliers were hired out for festive occasions, as well as dinner-services. One of the reasons why dealers preferred Chinese or Meissen services to those from the royal factory of Sèvres was that the former, being of true porcelain, withstood the wear-and-tear of dinner-parties rather better than the expensive products of the French factory. This factor, also, must have been one of the reasons why Sèvres so vigorously prosecuted the search for the materials and formulae which would enable them to reproduce this kind of porcelain. Its introduction in the 1770s had a bad effect on the artistic character of the royal factory's wares, but this was a secondary consideration. It made those things intended for use a much more practical alternative to the wares of its competitors.

Throughout the second half of the eighteenth century dealers multiplied in number and in influence, and it can, perhaps, fairly be said that the

158

Louis Seize style was largely their work, inspired by the demands of a handful of influential patrons for novelty. It was also a period during which the influence of Versailles weakened and that of the financiers increased.

The financiers had begun to exert a noticeable influence with the Regency. Typical of them we may perhaps take Samuel Bernard – millionaire, banker, and patron of the arts, with a collection worth more than a million *livres*. Of a *fête* given by Bernard a contemporary wrote: 'Even royal marriages were not more splendid.' By his first wife Bernard had three children, and by his second, one. All did well and rose in the social hierarchy. His son, Samuel Jacques Bernard, became President of the *Parlement* of Paris and comte de Rieux. The influence of the financiers was greatly strengthened by Mme de Pompadour, who came from this class, and they continued to gain in power and influence until the Revolution.

The financiers (a word which is intended to include the *fermiers-généraux*) who knew well how insecure was the value of the *livre* during the period after Law's inflation, invested heavily in the interior decoration of their houses, but their motives were mixed, being for the most part a blend of a love of display and a desire for an investment independent of an unsound currency. Consequently their inclinations increasingly turned towards objects which were not only movable, but negotiable apart from the interior of which they formed a part.

The changing of textile decorations to mark the progression of the seasons from winter to summer was already an established custom in the seventeenth century in the great houses. It became far more fashionable in the eighteenth century, when the upholstery of some kinds of seat-furniture was even mounted on detachable frames which could be changed at the same time as the curtains and wall-hangings. In this way the whole character of a room could be altered while retaining the same woodwork.

The introduction of occasional furniture meant that this, too, could be changed more frequently, not with the seasons but in response to changes in fashion. The dealers of the last half of the eighteenth century were beginning to grasp the advantages of planned obsolescence. The old custom of matching furniture to the fixed decoration of the room meant that people had little incentive to renew old furniture, except in response to a major change in style such as occurred with the development of *rococo*, but the dealers of the reign of Louis Seize assiduously promoted new fashions for no other purpose than to ensure the relegation of outmoded furniture to the attic. They also devised new ways of decorating walls, such as the greater use of wallpaper and fabrics, which did not impose the same difficulties of matching as the older tapestries and carved *boiseries*.

The end of the reign of Louis Seize also marked the close of a brilliant period in European art and decoration which had begun with the Renaissance in Italy. Henceforward the decorative arts in Europe were to be

159

a sterile exercise in the old styles which formerly had meant so much and were soon to mean nothing. The nineteenth century ushered in a period of dependence on the art of earlier times, often mechanically imitated by newly-invented machines. The greatness of European art, which began in Greece five centuries or more before the present era, ended 'not,' in the words of T. S. Eliot, 'with a bang, but a whimper'.

Appendix I

The Directory and the Empire

The style which immediately followed the fall of the monarchy is termed the *Directoire*, although a good deal of the furniture in this style was probably made before the Directory, and some even before the Revolution. Little furniture of this kind has survived, partly because the whole period was one of turbulence and few people thought of buying or commissioning new furniture, and partly because it did not outlive the onset of the following Empire style.

The Guilds were suppressed by the Revolutionaries, with an effect which was so obviously disastrous that even Marat was forced to notice the slipshod workmanship and lack of interest in their tasks among the workpeople, whose labours were inadequately rewarded. 'I should not be surprised', wrote Marat, 'if in twenty years time it will prove impossible to find a single workman in Paris who knows how to make a pair of shoes or a hat.' This seems to be characteristic of revolutions; it was certainly the case in Russia many years afterwards, and when shoes appeared at all they were inclined all to be for one foot, or of one size. In France skill among the *ébénistes* and *menuisiers*, the *tapissiers*, the metal-workers, and the porcelain-makers was at a disastrously low ebb.

During the Directory an even more rigid insistence on the copying of classical models was the rule. The lines of furniture in particular were simple and severe, and the bronze mounts sparse. Plain mahogany was the vogue, relieved by stringing of brass and slight inlays.

The change in the direction of what was to become the Empire style began with the appointment of Napoleon Bonaparte as First Consul, when the *parvenus* who had been astute enough to make money from the Revolution thought it safe to spend. Napoleon realized the value of France's leadership in the making of works of art, and he began to foster the tradition of luxury and refinement. The two most noted designers of the Empire period were Percier and Fontaine, who were employed to decorate Malmaison in 1798, and these two men were henceforward overwhelmed with the Emperor's commissions. With David, sometimes thought of as the new Le Brun, whose revolutionary fervour was forgotten, they became the architects of the Empire style in more senses than the most obvious. This was deliberately contrived as an expression of the new France, and not only Malmaison, but the old royal *châteaux* of Compiègne, Saint-Cloud, and Fontainebleau, were transformed at the hands of Percier and Fontaine. In 1803 they were ordered to complete the Louvre, and they added the parts overlooking the rue de Rivoli and the Seine. Their Arc de Triomphe of 1806 is based on the Arches of Septimus Severus and Constantine.

But the style was not confined to France. In England, where its designs were avidly copied, it appears as the Regency style, and it furnished the palaces of St Petersburg. It is to be found alike in Italy, Sweden, and Spain, and it lingered well into the nineteenth century.

The period of the Empire was also an era of counterfeit. Just as today the appearance of rare woods, marbles, and so forth are simulated in plastics, so plaster, *stucco*, *papier mâché*, cardboard, and glass were substituted for the exotic materials of the days of Versailles, although *papier mâché* imitations of plaster-work had been an established custom in France by 1760. Veneering everywhere took the place of solid wood, joints were glued instead of being dowelled and dovetailed, paint was a common finish for woodwork, and instead of Sèvres plaques the jasper medallions of Wedgwood became so fashionable that the Sèvres factory imitated them in the prized *biscuit* porcelain. The magnificent *bureau du Roi* had its Sèvres plaques, painted with the monogram of Louis Quinze, removed and Wedgwood jasper substituted. Matt gilding, the invention of Gouthière, became the rule, sometimes burnished in parts. Everywhere anything which could possibly remind the beholder of the *ancien régime* was either destroyed or sold, and the wealthy changed their furniture and interior decoration, down to the last item.

The *motifs* of the style were predominantly classical, taken from a number of sources, principally from vase-paintings, but they differed from those which had attracted the earlier designers. Many of the mythological beasts of antiquity, such as the griffin with a cruelly hooked beak, were employed as mounts. Caryatids were common, as were lion-paw feet, lion masks, and urns. The Egyptian campaign inspired the employment of sphinxes, scarabs, and zoömorphic gods.

The new fashions completely ousted the old. The furniture of Louis Seize, and especially that of Louis Quinze, could hardly find a buyer, even for *assignats*, the latest excursion into paper currency which was discredited even more swiftly than that of Law.

The furniture and decoration of the Directory to some extent harked back to the early days of neo-classicism, to the simplicity of the neo-Greek phase, before Marie-Antoinette brought her influence to bear on its development. It was plain and austere. The Empire style which developed from it was as luxurious in its own way as the later phases of the Louis Seize style, but the *motifs* were different. It was more consciously ostentatious and more contrived.

The nineteenth century was a period of derivations and repetitions. A degenerate Empire style marks the period of Louis XVIII, followed by a revival first of the Renaissance, then rococo, and finally a minor Gothic revival, called the Troubadour style, which was on a much slighter scale than in England. The great days of French decorative art ended when

Louis Seize and Marie-Antoinette left Versailles for the last time. Indeed, it might perhaps be more nearly accurate to say that they ended in 1764 with the death of Mme de Pompadour. What followed the Revolution was an anti-climax, variations on a theme which, however great when it was first stated, became increasingly banal and vulgar by repetition, a judgement equally applicable to art elsewhere in nineteenth-century Europe.

Appendix II

Extracts from the *Livre-Journal* of Lazare Duvaux
(*L = livres: s = sols: d = deniers*)

September 1748

(1) 17th   M. Boulogne owes: two *encoignures* in satinwood inlaid with flowers, decorated with ornamental feet, *chûtes* and so on, with a cartouche of gilded bronze on each door, the whole surmounted by a top of Serancolin marble with moulding. 450*L*. Carriage 4*L*.

(5) 23rd   Received from the heirs of M. le Marq. de Bissy the sum of 324*L* on account against the invoice of 424*L*. Set against a loss of about one-tenth, 44*L*.

(7) 26th   Received from Her Majesty the Queen through M. Mosaque, the sum of 228 *Livres* against my invoice of 1224*L* for three pairs of sconces; tip to his son, 4*L*.

November 1748

(41)   Mme la Duchesse de Lauraguais: a candelabrum of Bohemian crystal, mounted as a lyre with six branches, 300*L*. A table support, carved and gilt with yellow gold, and a marble top of *brèche d'Alep.* $3\frac{1}{2}$ feet long. 180*L*.

(47) 23rd   His Majesty the King. For the apartments of Mesdames: four pairs of double-branched Meissen candelabra with Vincennes flowers on the base, and branches of gilded bronze; two pairs with figures, two with birds – 12 Louis the pair – 1,152*L*. Carriage to Versailles, 5*L*.

December 1748

(82)   Mademoiselle: A pot-pourri vase in Chinese porcelain, square, in three tiers. 96*L* (returned).

(96)   Mme de Fulvy: Exchanged a paper-weight for a Meissen potpourri in the form of a grape-gatherer.

February 1749

(140) 16th   M. Boucher, painter. A service of six cups and saucers, sugar-bowl and teapot. Celadon with figures, and the tray, 240*L*. Received on account 144*L* – received 90*L*.

March 1749

(156)   Mme la Marq. de Courcillon: a *commode* four-and-a-half feet high, with deer's feet, in red polished lacquer,

decorated with *chûtes*, feet, handles, and knobs of gilt bronze, with its top of Flanders marble, 220L – two *encoignures* with deer's feet, in red polished lacquer with Flanders marble tops, 130L – two *gradins* to match, same lacquer, 42L – carriage, 3L – repairing a Chinese figure (*pagod*), supplying an arm, 6L.

May 1749

(226) Mme la Dauphine: To placing above the chimney-piece of her room at Versailles a pair of three-branched sconces comprising realistically lacquered branches with Vincennes flowers, each one different; the top branch being composed of lilies, tulips, jonquils, narcissus, and blue hyacinths; the middle one of roses; the outer branch of anemones; the central one of red and purple gilly-flowers; the junction decorated with different flowers, the base with gold knobs and bear's ears [*oreilles d'ours*], the pans of the same porcelain, with gilded sconces. 1,200L – Another pair of the same size placed between the pillars opposite: the highest branch composed of three large double carnations, cornflowers, orange-flower branches, tulips, campanulas; the central arm of anemones; the outer one of Dutch four-eyed hyacinths; the inner one of double jonquils; the junction of the branches decorated with different flowers, the base with gilded knobs and large hyacinths with red eyes, the pans of porcelain and gilt sconces 1,200L – Journey and carriage to Versailles 24L.

January 1750

(420) M. Dangé, *fermier-général:* To cleaning and fixing the [porcelain] flowers and plants of a table-centre: replacing missing flowers etc. 24L.

(425) 14th Mgr le Duc de Villeroy: To supplying the case and packing, and customs duty, for the wall-lights and twelve bottles sent to Boulogne, 17L 4s.

February 1750

(440) Received of M. de Cury the sum of 416L, made up of 324 for the balance of his account and 92L for Mme la Marq. de Pompadour.

March 1750

166 (461) Mme la Vicomtesse de Rochechouart, Dowager: A screen of gilt-bronze mounted with a Meissen figure and Vincennes flowers, 156L.

May 1750

(497) 4th Mme Geoffrin: Two teapots of Chinaware at 18L each, 36L; four birds 7L – a fan 1L, 4s.

(514) Mme la Marq. de Pompadour: Two Japanese monkeys with movable heads, 960L – A commode with drawers of old lacquer, mounted in gilt bronze with a top of Antin marble, 864L – Three small tables in aventurine lacquer, the tops of Oriental lacquer, 60L each, 180L – to making silver dice-boxes, and lining the drawers with silk 30L.

December 1750

(677) 17th Mgr le Duc de Rohan: a *secrétaire* veneered with amaranth, chamfered edges, and gilt bronze mounts, 240L – Carriage 1L.

(682) 20th His Majesty the King owes for a lacquer box with four tobacco compartments, gold ground, enamel, 60 Louis, 1,440L.

January 1751

(724) 26th Mme la Marq. de Pompadour: a pair of *chenets* in gilt bronze in the form of a hen and pigeons, the finials gilded, with tongs and shovel, for the bathroom, 726L – A similar pair representing Amor and Psyche, the finials gilded (for the King's bed-chamber) 970L – A fire-screen with child-huntsmen and gilt finials (King's study) 530L – Another pair of *chenets* with a shepherd and shepherdess with their attributes of dogs and sheep, the finials gilt, with tongs and shovel, for the mezzanine, 562L – Carriage to Bellevue, 15L – A perfume-burner, vase and silver lamp, the base gilded and a piece of old porcelain, 210L – A garniture of two celadon porcelain bottles with gilded mounts 55L.

February 1751

(728) 4th Mme le Marq. de Pompadour: Bought a cedar cabinet at the Louvre, 51L – Carriage to Bellevue, 15L – Twelve feather plumes, 12L.

March 1751

(748) M. de Cury: To removing the handle from a Meissen cup, 6L.

(751) Mme la Marq. de Pompadour: To garnishing and lining a pierced vase of old, crackled porcelain with gilt bronze, 480L – To removing the mounts from a similar vase, replacing the bronze, and carriage to Versailles, 12L. (This is the last article on the latest invoice despatched, amounting to 53, 199L 11s 6d.)

(771) M. le Cte du Luc: A Meissen chamber-pot with flowers, 24L – A Chantilly ditto, 10L – Four Chinese chamber-pots in blue and white, 15L – Two crystal *carafes*.

(780) 19th Mme la Marq. de Pompadour: A veneered night-table which is not included on the invoice supplied, 22L – An *encoignure* in Coromandel lacquer for the *garde-robe* on the ground-floor, 48L – Carriage and hire of two men for a day to hang and clean the sconces, crystal candelabra, and *encoignures*, 10L – Two drawers made for the King's room, relacquered and mounted with gilt bronze, 48L.

(782) 21st Received of Mme la Marq. de Pompadour, on account, the sum of 12,000 *Livres*, in a written instruction to M. de Montmartel, a receipt for which has been supplied to M. Collin.

June 1751

(825) 2nd M. de Boulogne, Intendant of Finance: A writing-table in the form of a *bureau*, veneered with different Oriental woods and mounted with gilt bronze, 864L.

July 1751

(865) M. Roussel, *fermier-général*. To supplying a medium-sized fire-grate with gilt-bronze and chiselled mounts, tongs and shovel, 185L – A pair of sconces with one branch, blue and white, and decorated with flowers. 42L.

September 1751

(896) M. Gaignat: Two old celadon porcelain fish in the form of ewers with gilt-bronze mounts, 1,200L. To gilding the mounts of two birds of prey, 120L.

October 1751

(923) 15th Mme la Marq. de Pompadour: Packing and materials for three vases decorated with Vincennes flowers dispatched to England, 48L.

November 1751

(923) 29th M. le Cte de Choiseul: To repairing two large Coromandel *encoignures*, varnishing and refurbishing the bronze, 50L.

December 1751

(988) 24th M. Boucher: Two ewers of old turquoise blue porcelain with gilt-bronze mounts, and two vases of the same

porcelain mounted for potpourri with gilt-bronze and flower-garlands, 1,200L.

January 1752

(1006)   2nd   Mme la Duchesse de Fleury: a wooden screen, reddened and polished, covered with Oriental paper, 15L.

(1016)   Mme la Marq. de Pompadour: To dispatching a box of trees to London, paid, 6L.

February 1753

(1353)   M. de Jullienne: A gadrooned and moulded gilt-bronze base for a blue cat; to supplying and fitting two enamel eyes, 48L.

April 1753

(1388)   M. Dangé, *fermier-général*: To supplying a pair of double-branched candlesticks with varnished foliage and Vincennes flowers, 96L – Two trays for *encoignures*, round in polished lacquer, imitating veneering 72L – A walnut box with locks and internal compartments, lined with silver-bordered silk, a *nécessaire*, 65L.

December 1755

(2360)   Mme Lambert (for Milord Havré): Two square boxes in turquoise blue painted with birds, 720L – A [Vincennes] vase *à la Hollandaise*, turquoise blue painted with flowers, 384L – Two small [Vincennes] vases *à oreilles*, turquoise blue, painted with children, 264L – cases, package, and freight 9L.

September 1756

(2590)   Milord Bolingbroke: Delivered to the Widow Mme Lambert since August 20th last: a large dessert tray, bronze and gilt bronze mounts, with its glass on which stands an oval vase with masks of Vincennes porcelain, a new model, the rim gilded and decorated with branches after nature and each plant with beautifully matched flowers; eight small vases, turquoise blue with gold *cartouches*, decorated with twisted rims and matching porcelain flowers arranged round the large vase on the tray, 3,250L – Forty-eight chamfered plates in turquoise blue with different birds and flowers in reserves, 48L each, 2,304L – Four matching shell *compotiers* 480L – Four square turquoise blue *compotiers* 480L – Four others, the so-called cabbage-leaf pattern, 480L – Two cheese-covers and their trays, 480L –

169

Two triangular trays and six small cups, 192L, 384L – Two square boxes painted with birds, 432L – A mahogany cover for the basket and vase, which is raised by a screw, 38L – Four *pots-pourris*, urn-shaped, in *gros bleu*, painted with children *en camaïeu*, 720L – the rest of the white service: twenty-four plates of white porcelain painted with flowers, at 216L, 432L – Four square *compotiers*, at 27L, 108L – Two cabbage-leaf pattern at 30L, 60L – six large goblets without handles and saucers, 90L – A sugar-bowl and teapot 37L – A creamer, 27L – Twelve egg-cups at 12L, 144L – to supplying the cases, packing, transport, and customs costs, not including the costs of correspondence, total 272L.

Appendix III

Extracts from the sale catalogue of the property of the Duke of Hamilton, sold by Christie, Manson & Woods at their Great Rooms, 8 King Street, St James's, June 1882. (The Hamilton Palace Sale.)

To bring prices to the equivalent of the modern £, multiply by eight.

A pair of tall oviform vases of old *gros bleu* Sèvres porcelain mounted with or-molu with bird's-head handles and festoons of flowers and foliage, chased in high relief by Gouthière. 14 in. high. £1,680.

A Louis XVI clock by Kinable, with enamelled dial, in lyre-shaped case of old Sèvres *gros bleu* porcelain mounted with or-molu, with a mask of Apollo at the top, and wreaths and festoons of flowers and foliage chased in high relief, the pendulum formed as a circle of fine old pastes. 25 in. high. £462.

A Louis XIV chandelier by Buhl [Boulle] of or-molu, for sixteen lights, with a vase in the centre with arabesques in relief, boldly chased with scrolls and foliage. £220 10s.

A Louis XIV knee-hole writing-table by Buhl (*sic*) covered with ornaments in engraved white metal and brass upon tortoiseshell, the inside lined with marquetrie, with six drawers and eight legs, with stretchers. 3′ 9″ × 2′ 4″. £210.

A Louis XIV pedestal cabinet by Buhl, inlaid with fine designs in engraved brass and white metal on tortoiseshell, richly mounted with or-molu mouldings, masks, festoons of foliage, a circular medallion of Louis IV in the front, black marble slab. 2′ 8″ × 1′ 8″, 3′ 6″ high. £2,310.

An oblong Louis XVI cabinet of ebony inlaid with panels of japan lacquer, with buildings and trees in gold on black ground, mounted with or-molu, with terminal figures of bacchanalian boys at the angles, the friezes and mouldings of classical design, with Grecian honeysuckles, with slab of antique Egyptian granite. 4′ 6″ × 2′ 2″, 3′ 2″ high. £598 10s.

An Upright Secrétaire, en suite. 3′ × 1′ 5″, 4′ 8″ high. £630.

The D'Artois cabinet, a Louis XIV commode, of ebony inlaid with fine panels, by Buhl, of brass and white metal on tortoiseshell, mounted with massive handles and ornaments of or-molu, chased with bacchanalian and other masks in high relief, the monogram C.A. and the arms of France surrounded by boys with garlands of flowers forming the key-plates, and a steel key with openwork handle, surmounted by a fine slab of malachite. 5′ 4″ × 2′ 2″, branded with the monogram ME. £766 10s.

A Louis Seize secrétaire of pollard oak and amboyna wood by G. Benemann, with cylinder enclosing drawers, a glazed cabinet and three drawers above, with statuary marble slab and brass gallery mounted with or-molu. £320 5s.

A Louis Seize clock, by Robin, with enamelled dial showing the days of the month and phases of the moon – in case of chased or-molu, with figures of boys allegorical of Sculpture and Architecture, surmounted by a vase, with festoons of foliage. £661 10s.

A Louis Seize upright secrétaire made for Marie Antoinette by Riesener, with an oval chasing in the centre by Gouthière representing doves with a quiver of arrows and flowers in a shield-shaped panel of marquetrie, with wreaths of flowers in colours; an oblong panel of marquetrie beneath, with a basket of flowers and fruit and other ornaments, with borders of flowers and parquetrie trellis pattern, mounted elaborate chasings of flowers and mouldings of or-molu, white marble slab, and or-molu gallery. Signed *Riesener fe. 1790*. Branded with the cypher of Marie Antoinette and Garde Meuble de la Reine on the back. 4′ 9″ high by 3′ 6″ wide. £4,620.

A commode, en suite. Signed *Riesener fe 1791*. £4,305.

An oblong writing-table, en suite, with drawer fitted with inkstand, writing-slide, and shelf beneath, an oval medallion of a trophy and flowers on the top, and trophies with four medallions round the sides. Stamped J. Riesener, and branded underneath with the cypher of Marie Antoinette and the Garde Meuble de la Reine. £6,000.

[The last three were exhibited at the South Kensington Loan Exhibition of 1862 in what is now the Victoria and Albert Museum. The catalogue says: 'In both the wood and metal work, the utmost perfection of design and execution is displayed at the culminating period of French decorative art, and in all probability this suite of furniture, as a whole, is the most important and beautiful work of its kind produced in the age of Louis XVI.' The total for the three pieces of £15,000 in gold is equivalent to £120,000 in today's paper pounds.]

A jug with handle carved out of a solid mass of aventurine jasper, beautifully variegated with red, green, and other colours, plain surface, with a raised belt round the neck, it is mounted in gold in bold scrolls of the time of Louis XV, which pass over the neck and round the foot and cover, surmounted by a cupid, and on the top of the handle is a goat. The mounting bears the Paris hall-mark of the letter S crowned and a boar's head. The jasper ewer is of Byzantine origin, of the 8th or 9th century. H. 12¾″. (The hall-mark is of 1734, H. Louvet, controller.) £2,467 10s.

172

An oval-shaped plateau [of Sèvres porcelain], painted with a subject from the life of Ulysses in a landscape in *gros-bleu* border, enriched with festoons and medallions in imitation of moss agate, gold chasing, and jewels. $11\frac{1}{2}'' \times 6\frac{1}{2}''$. £430 10s.

An old Sèvres vase and cover, turquoise ground, with white and gold bands with gilt festoons of foliage, beautifully painted with a female peasant and two children with a cat in a large oval medallion, a medallion of flowers on the reverse. $13\frac{1}{2}''$ high. £1,585 10s.

A Louis XVI upright secrétaire of marquetrie with a figure of Silence in a medallion suspended by festoons of foliage on the door, and vases of flowers on the lower doors, richly mounted with or-molu, with female terminal busts at the angles, and frieze with a head of Hercules, terminal figures, and scroll foliage, statuary marble slab and or-molu gallery; with chased key, partly gilt, made by Louis XVI. 3' 8" × 1' 5", 4' 9" high. £1,575.

A pair of Louis XVI candelabra of or-molu, with branches for five lights each, chased with foliage and surmounted by flames – on stands formed of tall vases of or-molu, partly enamelled deep blue, with festoons of fruit and sprays of foliage on the fluted necks, the handles formed as mermaids of bronze. 4' 6" high. £2,362 10s.

A Louis XIV clock with enamelled dial, chased with medallions of the king and crown, in case of red buhl, surmounted by a figure of Fame, with Apollo in his car and other figures in or-molu, and feet formed of horses on red buhl plinth. £367 10s.

A grand Louis XIV armoire by Buhl, from the design of Le Brun, the frame of ebony inlaid with brass, with panels of tortoiseshell elaborately inlaid with trophies, and a variety of ornaments of engraved brass divided into compartments, of fine design, with male and female figures, cupids, and masks in or-molu chased in high relief, and with rich mouldings of the same. 9' 6" high. Formerly in the Louvre. From the collection of the Duc D'Aumont and Fonthill Abbey [William Beckford's collection]. With the companion armoire, £12,075 [or about £100,000 in today's currency].

A rock-crystal chandelier for eight lights, formed of numerous large finely cut pendants of rock-crystal, and with festoons of beads and drops, with very large centre pendant, on frame partly mounted with chased silver. £441.

The Duc de Choiseul's writing-table and cartonnière; an oblong Louis XV writing-table of parquetrie, with six drawers, mounted with vases and festoons of foliage of or-molu, the top covered with green leather with fine old gilt tooling; the cartonnière of pedestal form, with cupboards and drawers at the ends, and open shelves above, surmounted by a clock by Alard, in finely chased or-molu case, surmounted by a group of allegorical boys with a cock. £5,565.

A Louis XIV sarcophagus-shaped commode [*en tombeau*] of black buhl with two drawers, with terminal winged figures at the angles in relief, and massive mountings of or-molu, surmounted by a slab of Verona marble. £1,081 10s.

The Seasons, a set of four emblematic busts of the size of life, of old Rouen faience, by Vavasseur, the celebrated potter, on terminal pedestals, enamelled with flowers and ornaments in brilliant colours. Busts 32" high; pedestals, 54" high. £2,646.

A Louis XVI circular hanging lantern of or-molu chased with female figures at the sides, and cupids, birds, and festoons round the upper part, the border of foliage underneath, with glass panels – fitted for gas. £84.

A pair of ebony commodes each with eight drawers, inlaid at the angles with engraved brass and white metal, and with chased or-molu foliage capitals, the fronts of the drawers and ends formed of plaques of old black and gold lacquer, and mounted with borders, feet, and key-plates of chased or-molu, surmounted by slabs of giallo marble. 3' 1½" × 2' 9". Stamped E. Levasseur. £3,150.

A Louis XVI Sofa of unusual dimensions, with settees at the ends, the frame elaborately carved with trophies of arrows and flowers in high relief, and richly gilt, covered with fine old Gobelins tapestry of flowers in colours, on pink ground. From Versailles. £1,176.

A set of six Louis XVI carved and gilt fauteuils en suite, £441.

A Louis XVI bedstead richly carved and gilt, with a vase of flowers at the head, the back stuffed and covered with a panel of Gobelins tapestry, with lofty canopy lined with tapestry, and with double valances and back of the same, with garlands and wreaths of flowers and foliage, and tapestry bolster covers; and a pair of yellow silk curtains. £1,155.

An oblong piece of Gobelins tapestry, with a subject from Tasso's 'Jerusalem Delivered' in border, with caryatid figures, masks, flowers, and fruits by Nouzou, in carved gilt frame. 12' × 20' 10". Signed and dated 1735. £488 5s.

Two pairs of rich satin brocade window-curtains, the flowers in colours on a crimson ground, lined with yellow silk, and trimmed with gimp. £52 10s.

Four square pieces of tapestry for overdoors, with groups of flowers – in carved and gilt frames. 4' square. £57 15s.

Note: Not all the attributions would be accepted today.

Appendix IV

Extracts from the sale-catalogue of works of art removed from the Hermitage, the Palais Michailoff, and the Gatschina, sold at Rudolph Lepke's sale-room, Berlin, in November 1928, by order of the Soviet Government. Prices in Reichsmarks.

A small commode on four feet with slightly swelling panels and edges. Three drawers in front, with a compartment and sliding door between. Top of grey marble. Rich marquetry, also on the back, in a pattern of flowers on a ground of rosewood. The edges inlaid with rosewood wood. Stamped: DAV, perhaps by Davaux or Devaux, d. 1757 (cf. Salverte [*Les Ébénistes*] p. 101).   H. 75 cm. W. 49 cm. Paris, about 1755. 11,700 R.M.

Toilet-table of mahogany, curving shape on four slightly splayed legs with bronze mounted toes. Rich coloured marquetry of flowers on the sides and on the top divided into three compartments on a ground of rosewood and tulipwood veneer. Under the top, a rising mirror and stand. H. 78 cm. W. 82 cm. France, about 1765. 9,600 R.M.

Small writing-table (*bonheur du jour*) of dark mahogany with gilt-bronze mounts, rectangular, the four square legs supported by a stretcher. On the drawer, and on each side, an ornament in bronze of wave design. The upper part with a fretted gallery, the centre section open and flanked by two doors with a *pietra dura* plaque to each, on the left showing a woman, and on the right a man, against a black marble ground. Paris, *c.* 1780. H. 102 cm. W. 71 cm. 4,000 R.M.

Chimney-stool, low, the frame carved with traces of gilding, and upholstered in the style of a *bergère*, without cover, legs fluted, rams' heads on the arm-rests, and acanthus foliage and garlands in high relief. Unsigned, but the deep carving is in the style of Louis Delanois (Paris, *maître* 1761, d. 1792). cf. Salverte, p. 88. H. 72 cm. W. 60 cm. Paris, perhaps by Delanois, *c.* 1770. 3, 900 R.M.

Long-case clock of figured wood with gilt-bronze mounts, the face with the inscription *Roentgen & Kinzing a Neuwied*, the circular dial set in a gilt-bronze plaque and framed with chiselled garlands of flowers and fruit, and supported by a kneeling Saturn. Above is a bronze pediment with a triglyph frieze and masks. In the pediment a relief of two *putti* holding a lyre. Above, a bronze balustrade with four corner urns, and, crowning all, a group of Apollo with the lyre, his right hand raised, and seated on a rock (Roentgen used this [Apollo] group several times—on a writing-desk belonging to King Friedrich Wilhelm I in Berlin, cf. Feulner, *Kunstgeschichte des Möbels*, pl. 465, and Salverte, *Les Ébénistes*, pl. 56). On the central part of the lower section, an applied trophy with doves, &c. after a model used by Riesener (Feulner. pl. 392). H. 217 cm. W. 61 cm. Neuwied, *c.* 1785, by David Roentgen. From the Castle of Pawlowsk (cf. D. Roche, *Le mobilier français en Russie,* pl. 2, page 77). 24,000 R.M.

Cylinder-top writing-desk in oak, with marquetry in light-coloured wood, and gilt-bronze mounts. Below the writing-surface four drawers with an inlaid lozenge-pattern. The cylinder top with two bronze handles and an inlaid pattern representing a globe, a palette, busts, and large rosettes on either side. Three drawers above with a wave-pattern, and on the sides a vase with a trellis pattern. W. 170 cm. H.125. France, about 1770, probably by Jean-Francois Hache of Grenoble (b. 1730, *maître* until 1784. cf. Salverte, *Les Ébénistes,* pl. 28). 27,000 R.M.

Secrétaire with fall-front of mahogany with gilt-bronze mounts. The lower part with two drawers decorated with pearl stringing, and two drawers with bronze handles inside. On the rectangular flap, a round bronze medallion with the profile of a bearded man turning to the right hanging from a ribbon-tie and surrounded by a laurel wreath [after a Paris model]. The central panel surrounded by a ribbed bronze strip and pearl stringing. Inside, a set of drawers of pale figured wood, and roll closure of the upper central section. The flap is covered with green hand-tooled leather. A small bronze gallery above. H. 135 cm. W. 98 cm. Neuwied, about 1785, work of David Roentgen. 9,900 R.M.

Serving-table, mahogany, with richly gilded bronze mounts and a grey marble top. Six pillars with bronze capitals are joined below by a wooden shelf and carry the frieze comprising two drawers in front, and two triangular swivelling drawers at the sides. Chiselled gilt-bronze ornament in the form of a leaf pattern with large flowers runs above the drawers between bands of twisted gilt-bronze ropes and ribbons [the ornament similar to the mounts on Schwerdfeger's toilet-table made for Marie-Antoinette in the Louvre]. Similar plaited and twisted ornament surrounds the lower shelf and the three panels at the back. In the middle section, four bronze lion-masks. The drawers are of solid mahogany, and on the left-hand drawer in black letters is the signature *FERDINAND SCHWERDFEGER ME EBENISTE A PARIS 1788.* H. 86 cm. W. 140 cm. D. 47 cm. By Schwerdfeger (*maître* after 1786, cf. Salverte, p. 317). Illustrated by Roche, pl. 85. (An exactly similar table with the same signature and date is in the Louvre. Illustrated by Feulner, *Kunstgeschichte des Möbels,* pl. 396.)

Commode-bureau with companion clock, mahogany with gilt-bronze mounts. In the lower half, two long drawers with pearl stringing, each with two handles. The corner pilasters fluted. On the flap, an *appliqué* after a Paris model with doves, quiver, *flambeau,* and flower-baskets (as on the clock). Inside, green hand-tooled leather. Above, a pedestal base and a rectangular clock with the inscription [*sic*], *Roentgen & Kinzing a Neuwied*, surrounded by a laurel wreath hanging from a ribbon-tie. On the bronze balustrade four, and on the clock eight, small urns. The back also veneered with mahogany. H. 182 cm. W. 132 cm. D. 45 cm. Neuwied, about 1785, by David Roentgen. 12,000 R.M.

Chandelier of gilt-bronze, richly decorated cut and hanging lustres, a red vase in the centre, and matching cover above. Three two-branched sockets, glass lustres between. Three bronze chains. From a vase above spring curved stalks with hanging lustres. 80 cm. Late eighteenth century. 9,200 R.M.

Mantel-clock of bronze and white marble. At the rounded ends of the base are two *amoretti* beside the clock carriage which is faced with applied bronze ornament. They hold the cornice, itself supporting two goats reaching up to a basket of fruit on the centre of the clock. The clock inscribed *Guy damour a Paris*. Paris, *c.* 1790. H. 45 cm. W. 34 cm. 9,200 R.M.

Wall-hanging designed as a triptych in three scenes, a landscape in the large centre portion which has a peasant's house with trees above, in the mid-ground cattle by a river, a shepherd standing by a bull, and in the right foreground a pair of lovers. On the left, two women with water-pots and sheep outside a village. On the right, in the foreground, a reclining shepherd playing a flute in a river landscape, with the village church and trees in the background. The border and division of the three fields imitating a picture-frame. H. 280 cm. W. 340 cm. Aubusson, eighteenth century.

Wall-hanging woven of wool and silk with a mythological scene in a landscape. A king wearing his crown, with two companions, is in the act of killing two people with his sword. Behind, a castle with trees to the side. The border, flower garlands woven with acanthus leaves. Above, a French Ducal coat of arms. H. 310 cm. W. 260 cm. Aubusson, seventeenth century.

Gobelins tapestry woven of silk and wool from the series *Esther*, made at the Manufacture royale des Gobelins in Paris. Esther's supper-table in the open before a pillared hall. Seated at the table, Ahasuerus and Esther; to the left, Mordecai surrounded by servants and spectators. On the right, Esther's women. The border simulating a gold frame with shellwork and flower garlands. Signed on the right: *Fait par de Troy a Rome 1733, et exécuté par Cozette, 1760*. H. 450 cm. W. 510 cm. Paris, Manufacture royale des Gobelins, after de Troy's cartoon of 1733, made in Cozette's workshop, 1760.

Jean-Antoine Houdon. Portrait bust of a lady, the head slightly turned to the right. She wears a ribbon with roses in her hair. The right shoulder

177

bare. Her dress decorated with rose-buds and leaves. Marble base. Terra-cotta with original matt brownish tone. Height, including base, 78 cm. About 1775.

(We were informed just before going to press by M. Paul Vitry, Conservateur at the Louvre, that this bust might also be attributed to Pajou.) 24,000 R.M.

Jean-Baptiste Lemoyne (1704–1778). Portrait bust of the Queen Marie-Antoinette, the head looking slightly to the right. She wears an ermine cloak leaving her left breast uncovered, and fastened by a clasp below the left shoulder. She wears flowers in her hair. The base carved and rectangular. White marble, height including base, 89 cm. The features, although freely handled, seem to be characteristic, especially the mouth and chin, and it is probably a portrait of Marie-Antoinette. Between 1770 and 1778. 90,000 R.M.

Three silver dishes with curving edges, polished, engraved with a coat of arms and a princely crown. Paris mark *X* with a crown (1761), *A* with crown (1756–1762), *fermier* Eloy Brichard, and the master-stamp F.T.G. Average dia. 25 cm. Weight, 182⁰ grammes. Paris, 1761. By François-Thomas Germain, *maître* from 1745. 1700 R.M.

Bibliography

Alfassa and Guerin, *Porcelaines Françaises*. Paris, 1932.
Argenson, Marquis d', *Memoirs*. Paris, 1825.

Bazin, Germain, *Baroque and Rococco*. London and New York, 1964.
Beurdeley, Michel, *Porcelain of the East India Companies*. London, 1962.
Blomfield, Sir R., *A History of French Architecture, 1661–1774*.
    London, 1921.
Boulanger, G., *L'Art de Reconnaître des Meubles Régionaux*. Paris, 1966.
Bourgeoise, E., *Le Biscuit de Sèvres au XVIIIe Siècle*. Paris, 1909.

Christie, Manson & Woods, The Hamilton Palace sale-catalogue of 1882.
    London.
Clergue, Helen, *The Salon*. New York, 1907.
Colombier, Pierre du, *Le Style Henri IV – Louis XIII*. Paris, 1941.
Cordey, J., *Inventaire des Biens de Mme de Pompadour Rédigé après son Décès*.
    Paris, 1939.

Dacier, E., *La Gravure en France au XVIIIe Siècle*. Paris, 1925.
Dennis, F., *Three Centuries of French Domestic Silver*. New York, 1960.
Diderot, D. and D'Alembert, J. le R., *Encyclopédie, ou Dictionnaire Raisonné
    des Sciences, des Arts, et des Métiers*. 1751–77.

Fremy, E., *Histoire de la Manufacture Royale des Glaces de France*. Paris, 1909.

Giacomotti, Jeanne, *French Faience*. London, 1963.

Jones Collection, The (South Kensington Museum Art Handbook).
    London, 1884.

Kimball, Fiske, *Creation of Rococo*. Philadelphia, 1943.

Lane, Arthur, *French Faience*. London.
Lejard, Andre (ed.), *French Tapestry*. London, 1946.

Marie, Alfred, *Jardins Français Classiques des XVIIe et XVIIIe Siècles*.
    Paris, 1949.
Mitford, Nancy, *The Sun King*. London and New York, 1966.

Nolhac, Pierre, *Versailles and the Trianons*. London, 1906; *Versailles et la Cour
    de France*. Paris, 1925.

Percier, Charles and Fontaine, P. E. L., *Recueil de Décoration Intérieure*.
    Paris, 1812.

Reitlinger, Gerald, *Economics of Taste, Vols 1 and 2*. London, 1961 and 1963.

Saint-Simon, duc de, *Memoirs* (various editions).
Savage, G., *17th and 18th Century French Porcelain*. London, 1960.
Strange, T. A., *An Historical Guide to French Interiors* (reprinted).
    London, 1950.

Tapié, Victor, *The Age of Grandeur*. London, 1960; rev. ed., New York, 1966.

Verlet, Pierre, *Sèvres, Le XVIIIe Siècle*. Paris, 1952; *Royal French Furniture*. London, 1963; *French Furniture and Interior Decoration of the 18th Century*. London, 1967.

Voltaire, *The Age of Louis XIV* (various editions).

Wallace Collection, Catalogue of Furniture. F. J. B. Watson, 1956; Catalogue of Sculpture. J. G. Mann, 1931.

Walpole, Horace, *Letters* (various editions).

Watson, F. J. B., *Louis Seize Furniture*. London, 1960.

Weigert, R.-A., *French Tapestry*. London, 1962.

Zweig, Stefan, *Marie-Antoinette*. London, 1933.

1 Regency *commode* attributed to Charles Cressent, perhaps after a design by Nicholas Pineau. The superb mounts are still symmetrical. *c.* 1725.

2 *Commode* by A. R. Gaudreau with mounts by Jacques Caffiéri. The design was probably adapted from the brothers Slodtz. The mounts are markedly asymmetrical. *c.* 1740.

3 Versailles. The marriage of Louis,
Dauphin of France, to Maria Theresa,
Infanta of Spain, 24 February 1745.
Print by C. N. Cochin the Younger.

4 *Buffet à deux corps*. Walnut cupboard in
two parts, the lower with two drawers
at the top. Architectural in style and
handsomely carved. Late sixteenth century.

5 Water was a popular theme among rococo
designers. This porcelain tureen is from the
Swan service made at Meissen in 1737,
although the inspiration was French.

6 A sheet from the design-book of Jean I Bérain illustrating the characteristic grotesques which are a feature of his work.

7 Most of the elements of the rococo style are present in this gold-mounted mother-of-pearl sewing-box – the asymmetrical scrollwork, the floral *motifs*, and the elegant pastoral figures. Mid-eighteenth century.

8 Design for two chimney-pieces juxtaposed, from Jean I Bérain. Similar designs for *cartouches* may have suggested the asymmetrical scrollwork of the rococo style.

9 Interior of the shop of the art-dealer Gersaint. Painted by his friend, Watteau. The lacquer mirror (right) is not unlike the one shown in plate 10 which is about the same date.

10 Toilet-mirror in the manner of
A.-C. Boulle.

11 Reverse of plate 10 showing a
marquetry of brass and tortoiseshell in the
manner of Bérain, probably executed for
the daughter of the Duc de Saint-Simon.

12 *Gaine* or pedestal in the manner of
A.-C. Boulle. Late Louis Quatorze period.

13 *Commode* with floral marquetry of
dark- and light-coloured woods and ivory
formerly in the *château* of Montargis
(Orléanois). Period of Louis Quatorze.

14 and 15 Writing-table in a marquetry of
tortoiseshell and brass, probably by A.-C.
Boulle and decorated in the manner of
Bérain. *c.* 1700.

16 A carved walnut *fauteuil* with caned
seat. *c.* 1670.

17 A carved walnut chair upholstered
in crimson velvet. *c.* 1690.

18 Corner-table, one of a pair, the top of
tortoiseshell, copper, and white metal with
gilt-bronze mounts. Late Louis Quatorze
period.

19 A *table de milieu* (centre-table) inlaid with
mother-of-pearl. It well shows the curve
and counter curve of the period. *c.* 1690.

20 A *commode* of the Louis Quinze period decorated with trellisage and flowers in *vernis Martin* (page 64), with a pattern like those appearing on Sèvres porcelain.

21 A small Louis Quinze marquetry *secrétaire à abbatant* with rich gilt-bronze mounts. Its curving lines may be compared with the straight lines of the Louis Seize example in plate 22.

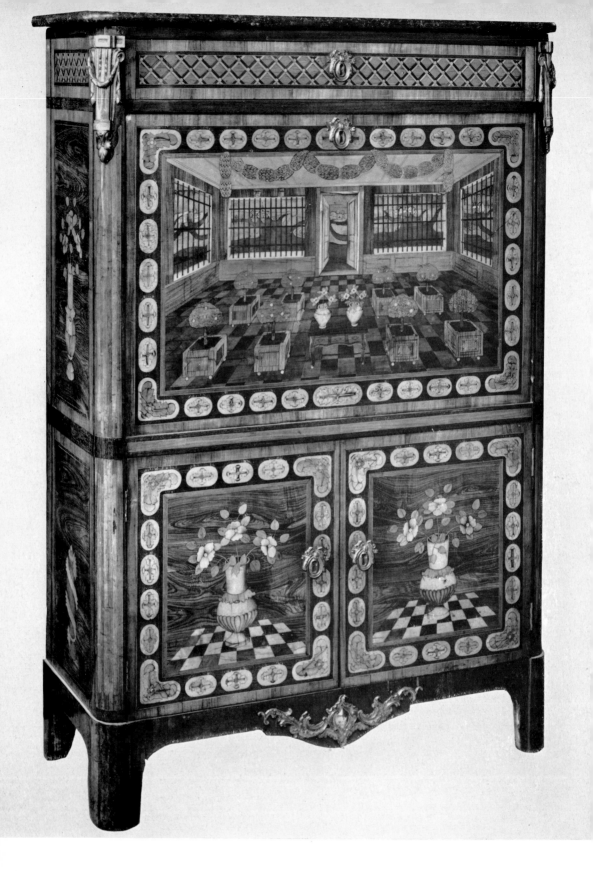

22 A Louis Seize fall-front *secrétaire*, the top
marquetry panel showing the interior of
an orangery. The lines are characteristic of
the period.

23 *Secrétaire* made for Marie-Antoinette by
Riesener about 1783, superbly decorated
with gilt-bronze. The oval panel
represents a sacrifice to Love.

24 The richness of the late Louis Seize
style appears in this *secrétaire-commode* from
Marie-Antoinette's *cabinet-intérieur* at
Saint-Cloud. Of black and gold lacquer
panels, the *ébénisterie* is by Riesener about
1787.

25 *Encoignure* by J. H. Riesener *en suite* with plate 23. According to the Journal du Garde Meuble it was delivered to Marie-Antoinette on 12 February 1783.

26 *Bureau-plat* of the period of Louis Quinze in kingwood and tulipwood marquetry mounted in gilt-bronze. Stamped by the *ébéniste*, Durand.

27 *Cartonnier* (*serre-papiers*) on a pedestal
cabinet. These usually stood at one end of
the *bureau-plat*. Mid-eighteenth century.
Cartonnier by Bernard van Risenburgh.

28 The top of the writing-table in plate 29 which illustrates its curving contours, and shows the quality of Oeben's marquetry.

29 A superb Louis Quinze marquetry writing-table by the German *ébéniste*, J. F. Oeben.

30 An *espagnolette* decorating the corners of a superb Regency *commode* in the manner of Cressent.

31 *Bureau à cylindre* (the *bureau du Roi Stanislas*) which resembles the famous *bureau du Roi Louis Quinze*. Made for the King's father-in-law by Riesener, it was completed in 1769.

32 *Armoire* decorated with *contre-partie*
brass and tortoiseshell marquetry. Although
the technique is that of A.-C. Boulle it may
be as late as the middle of the eighteenth
century.

33 *Console* table for attachment to a wall on a *gradin* or base. The latter has rarely survived. Perhaps from the Boulle workshop.

34 Copy of a granite chimney-piece of *c.* 1750 made for the Cabinet du Grand Dauphin at Versailles. The mounts are partly gilt. The original mounts were by Jacques Caffiéri.

35 *Console* table (side-table) in the Louis
Seize style on a richly-carved gilt
menuiserie support, the stretcher with
a 'nut' in the form of an urn.

36 One of a pair of low *armoires* in the style of
Boulle, the top of brecciated marble. By
J. L. F. Delorme (1763–80).

37 One of a pair of *guéridons* in the late Louis
Quatorze style decorated with marquetry
in the manner of Boulle.

38 *Guéridon* table decorated with marquetry,
fitted with a small cupboard and shelves
and surmounted by a candleholder. Period
of Louis Seize.

39 Small Louis Quinze *table à ouvrage* or work table; an *ambulante* or occasional table by Bernard van Risenburgh.

40 A rare small Louis Quinze dual-purpose table – a *secrétaire-poudreuse* – with original porcelain and glass fittings. Signed by Roger Vandercruse, called Lacroix (RVLC).

41 Candelabrum, one of a pair, of carved
gilt wood on scroll-shaped supports. Period
of Louis Quatorze.

42 Revolving tray-top table in mahogany signed by J. P. Letellier. English influence. *c.* 1775.

43 Work-table by Martin Carlin, *c.* 1785. It once belonged to Marie-Antoinette, who gave it to Mrs Eden, wife of the Rt. Hon. William Eden, Minister-Plenipotentiary to France in 1786.

44 *Escritoire à toilette* attributed to C. C. Saunier and decorated with a marquetry of tulipwood, harewood, and other exotic woods. *c.* 1760.

45 Back of *escritoire* shown in plate 44.

46 The Sèvres porcelain top of table shown
in plate 47, dated 1759.

47 Tray-top table by Garnier and Ledoux
with a marquetry of ebony and mahogany.
Period of Louis Quinze.

48 Small *bureau à pente* (*secrétaire en tombeau*)
of black lacquer in the Louis Quinze style.
By Jacques Dubois.

49 *Bonheur du jour* in the Louis Quinze style
decorated with marquetry panels by
C. Wolff.

50 A fire-screen (*écran*) of Beauvais tapestry
in a gilt wood frame. Period of Louis Seize.

51 Folding-screen (*paravent*) painted in oils
with garden scenes and pastoral subjects in
the manner of Lancret. *c.* 1740.

52 Although the silver tables of Louis Quatorze have long since disappeared, this one, from Knole in Kent, helps to recreate their appearance.

53 Painted and gilded chair from the Sené
workshop originally made for Marie-
Antoinette's apartment at Saint-Cloud.

54 *Sopha* of carved gilt wood made by
Tilliard for Mme de Pompadour and
bearing her Arms. Mid eighteenth century.

55 *Fauteuil-bergère* covered with blue and white damask in the Louis Seize style.

56 *Canapé* in walnut covered with Beauvais tapestry with animal subjects. By Georges Jacob in the Louis Seize style.

57 *Causeuse* or small *canapé*. A 'conversation'
settee for two people in the Louis Seize
style. The covering is of Beauvais tapestry.
Part of a *suite*.

LA SOLLICITATION AMOUREUSE

58 *La Solicitation Amoureuse*. An engraving
by P. A. Le Beau after J. B. P. Le Brun
(1748–1813). Beds are rare survivals but
are known from prints and paintings.

59 Part of the *boudoir* of Mme de Sérilly
acquired by the Victoria and Albert
Museum in 1860. The chimney-piece is
turquoise-blue marble; the bronze mounts
are perhaps by Gouthière. The *arabesques*
are typical of the Louis Seize style.

60 Harpsichord lacquered in the Chinese
style. By Pascal Taskin à Paris. 1786.
Superbly decorated musical instruments
were a feature of concerts given in
fashionable *salons*.

61 Soup-tureen from the Berkeley
Castle service.

62 The Berkeley Castle dinner-service by
Jacques Roettiers, Paris, 1735–8. One of the
few services of the period to escape being
sent to the Mint.

63 Silver *écuelle*; a two-handled covered
bowl. Bordeaux. *c.* 1720–22. Provincial
French silver has more commonly survived.

64 Pair of octagonal silver candlesticks
by Martin Brunot, Dijon, *c.* 1718.

65 Pair of table-candlesticks in the style of
J.-A. Meissonnier (1693–1750). The cupids
are silver, the remainder bronze. About 1745.

66 Candelabrum in the manner of Gouthière,
perhaps after a design by Boizot. Period of
Louis Seize.

67 A page from the design-book of J.-A.
Meissonnier showing silver tureens of a
pronounced asymmetrical character.

68 Pair of chamber candlesticks of
gilt-bronze with Meissen porcelain figures
and Vincennes porcelain flowers. *c.* 1750.

69 *Baigneuse*. A bronze reduction of the
original marble statue by E.-M. Falconet.
First exhibited in the Salon of 1757, it is
one of the most reproduced of
all eighteenth-century works.

70 Bust of Louis Quatorze by Coysevox. A bronze
repetition of a marble bust now in Dijon,
and a remarkably fine portrait of about
1680.

71 One of a pair of bronze garden vases,
reduced from marble vases made by
Girardon for Colbert, now in the Louvre.

72 and 73 *Les chevaux de Marly*, by or after
Guillaume Coustou the Elder. Originally
of marble, executed for the Riding School
at Marly, they have been the subject of
innumerable bronze reductions.

74 *Cupid vanquishing Pan*, originally a
terracotta by Jean-Jacques Caffiéri who
became chief modeller to the Sèvres
porcelain factory.

75 Portrait bust of Mme de Sérilly (see plate 59) signed by J.-A. Houdon and dated 1782. Portrait busts were fashionable throughout the century.

76 *Cupid and Psyche*, a terracotta by Claude Michel, called Clodion, and characteristic of the mildly erotic nature of much of his work.

77 A reclining *Bacchante* (a favourite subject
of the time) in marble by Louis-Simon
Boizot, chief modeller to the Sèvres factory.

78 An allegorical terracotta group entitled
La Naissance du Dauphin by Augustin Pajou.
1781. It is an undisguised portrait of
Marie-Antoinette (see page 102).

79 An exceptional pair of *chenets* in the form of a lion's and a boar's head partly enclosed by scrolling acanthus. Attributed to Jean-Jacques Caffiéri. *c.* 1750.

80 Pair of *chenets* of gilt bronze attributed to Philippe Caffiéri, about 1765. The transitional nature of the style is easily apparent.

81 Cartel clock in the rococo style, the
subject being the familiar one of Love
Triumphing over Time. The case was
made by Cressent about 1747.

82 A typical chimney-piece *garniture* of
mounted porcelain. The style of the mounts
suggests Gouthière, and the *garniture* is in
the Louis Seize style of the early 1780s.

83 The Avignon clock designed by L. S.
Boizot and executed by Gouthière.

84 A *régulateur* clock by Ferdinand
Berthoud F.R.S., Paris, in the style of
Louis Seize. The case is richly mounted
in gilt-bronze.

85 A rococo mantel clock in the form
of an elephant, the top surmounted by
a monkey. By Jean-Baptiste Bartheu.

86 Wall-light, one of a set of four, in gilt-
bronze formed from acanthus scrolls.
Eighteenth-century examples in carved gilt
wood may, in some cases, have been models
for bronze sconces.

87 Among the notable examples of mid-
eighteenth-century wrought ironwork may
be included this handrail from Mme de
Pompadour's *château* at Bellevue.

88 A rare plaque of Chinese porcelain
copied from a contemporary engraving and
painted in Canton. The bed is in the Louis
Seize style and surmounted by a canopy called
an *impériale*.

89 A porcelain watch-holder on the rococo theme of water, made at Vincennes about 1755. The tip of the foliage above the watch is turned to one side.

90 Chinese porcelain. *Blanc-de-Chine* from Fukien Province mounted in gilt-bronze. A similar example was in the former collection of the Minister Machault. 1755.

91 A pair of powder-blue Chinese vases
mounted in gilt-bronze in the manner of
J. C. Duplessis *père*, of the kind referred to
in the *livre-journal* of Lazare Duvaux. Mid
eighteenth century.

92 Vase from Prince de Condé's factory at
Chantilly painted in the manner of Sakaida
Kakiemon (Arita, Japan) known as *première
qualité du japon. c.* 1740.

93 A superb *faience* ewer of about 1670 from
Nevers in a baroque metalwork style. An
example of the finest French *faience*.

94 A rococo tureen of Marseille *faïence*
painted with birds amid floral scrolls by
Gaspard-Robert. *c.* 1765.

95 A Rouen plate brilliantly decorated
in colours with the cornucopia pattern.
c. 1750.

96 One of a pair of perfume vases with
pierced necks and covers painted with
harbour scenes by Morin, the reverse
with floral trophies. Dated 1768. Sèvres.

97 *Diana* of glazed white porcelain, probably
modelled by Louis Fournier. Vincennes.
c. 1750.

98 *Cupid*, a model in *biscuit* porcelain
by Falconet. Sèvres. 1758.

99 Designed by Duplessis, this *vaisseau
à mât* is one of the most impressive of
Vincennes productions. The Banner of
France is suspended from the mast and bears
the fleur-de-lys. 1755.

100 Plaque in *biscuit* porcelain in
Wedgwood style depicting the rape of
Helen, probably intended as a furniture
mount. Sèvres. 1790.

101 Tapestry: *Zephyr and Psyche*. Louvre. 1650–60.

102 Tapestry: *Acrobats*, early eighteenth century, after Bérain. Beauvais.

103 Tapestry: *Capture of Lille*. After
Le Brun. Gobelins. 1728.

104 French brocaded satin. First quarter of the eighteenth century.

105 Silk brocade in the style of Jean Revel (1684–1751). Early eighteenth century.

106 Red velvet cushion cover.
Regency period.

107 Brocaded yellow *gros de Tours*. Mid-
eighteenth century.

108 Brocaded silk tissue. Seventeenth
century.

109 Printed cotton (copper-plate). *Toile de Jouy* after Pillement.

110 Royal Savonnerie carpet. Period of Louis Quatorze.

111 Two fragments of wall-paper printed at Réveillon's factory in the rue de l'Arbre Sec, Paris.

112 (far right) French wall-paper from Vaison. Late eighteenth century. Printed in colour with wood-blocks.

113 One of a rare series of engravings,
satirizing the *neo-grec* fashion. The costumes
of this and the other figures in the series
are made up from architectural *motifs*.

Index